Generating Plans from Proofs

The Interpolation-based Approach to Query Reformulation

Synthesis Lectures on Data Management

Editor
Z. Meral Özsoyoğlu, *Case Western Reserve University*

Synthesis Lectures on Data Management is edited by Meral Özsoyoğlu of Case Western Reserve University. The series publishes 80- to 150-page publications on topics pertaining to data management. Topics include query languages, database system architectures, transaction management, data warehousing, XML and databases, data stream systems, wide scale data distribution, multimedia data management, data mining, and related subjects.

Generating Plans from Proofs: The Interpolation-based Approach to Query Reformulation
Michael Benedikt, Julien Leblay, Balder ten Cate, and Efthymia Tsamoura
2015

Veracity of Data: From Truth Discovery Computation Algorithms to Models of Misinformation Dynamics
Laure Berti-Équille and Javier Borge-Holthoefer
2015

Datalog and Logic Databases
Sergio Greco and Cristina Molinaro
2015

Big Data Integration
Xin Luna Dong and Divesh Srivastava
2015

Instant Recovery with Write-Ahead Logging: Page Repair, System Restart, and Media Restore
Goetz Graefe, Wey Guy, and Caetano Sauer
2014

Similarity Joins in Relational Database Systems
Nikolaus Augsten and Michael H. Böhlen
2013

Information and Influence Propagation in Social Networks
Wei Chen, Laks V.S. Lakshmanan, and Carlos Castillo
2013

Data Cleaning: A Practical Perspective
Venkatesh Ganti and Anish Das Sarma
2013

Data Processing on FPGAs
Jens Teubner and Louis Woods
2013

Perspectives on Business Intelligence
Raymond T. Ng, Patricia C. Arocena, Denilson Barbosa, Giuseppe Carenini, Luiz Gomes, Jr., Stephan Jou, Rock Anthony Leung, Evangelos Milios, Renée J. Miller, John Mylopoulos, Rachel A. Pottinger, Frank Tompa, and Eric Yu
2013

Semantics Empowered Web 3.0: Managing Enterprise, Social, Sensor, and Cloud-based Data and Services for Advanced Applications
Amit Sheth and Krishnaprasad Thirunarayan
2012

Data Management in the Cloud: Challenges and Opportunities
Divyakant Agrawal, Sudipto Das, and Amr El Abbadi
2012

Query Processing over Uncertain Databases
Lei Chen and Xiang Lian
2012

Foundations of Data Quality Management
Wenfei Fan and Floris Geerts
2012

Incomplete Data and Data Dependencies in Relational Databases
Sergio Greco, Cristian Molinaro, and Francesca Spezzano
2012

Business Processes: A Database Perspective
Daniel Deutch and Tova Milo
2012

Data Protection from Insider Threats
Elisa Bertino
2012

Deep Web Query Interface Understanding and Integration
Eduard C. Dragut, Weiyi Meng, and Clement T. Yu
2012

P2P Techniques for Decentralized Applications
Esther Pacitti, Reza Akbarinia, and Manal El-Dick
2012

Query Answer Authentication
HweeHwa Pang and Kian-Lee Tan
2012

Declarative Networking
Boon Thau Loo and Wenchao Zhou
2012

Full-Text (Substring) Indexes in External Memory
Marina Barsky, Ulrike Stege, and Alex Thomo
2011

Spatial Data Management
Nikos Mamoulis
2011

Database Repairing and Consistent Query Answering
Leopoldo Bertossi
2011

Managing Event Information: Modeling, Retrieval, and Applications
Amarnath Gupta and Ramesh Jain
2011

Fundamentals of Physical Design and Query Compilation
David Toman and Grant Weddell
2011

Methods for Mining and Summarizing Text Conversations
Giuseppe Carenini, Gabriel Murray, and Raymond Ng
2011

Probabilistic Databases
Dan Suciu, Dan Olteanu, Christopher Ré, and Christoph Koch
2011

Peer-to-Peer Data Management
Karl Aberer
2011

Probabilistic Ranking Techniques in Relational Databases
Ihab F. Ilyas and Mohamed A. Soliman
2011

Uncertain Schema Matching
Avigdor Gal
2011

Fundamentals of Object Databases: Object-Oriented and Object-Relational Design
Suzanne W. Dietrich and Susan D. Urban
2010

Advanced Metasearch Engine Technology
Weiyi Meng and Clement T. Yu
2010

Web Page Recommendation Models: Theory and Algorithms
Sule Gündüz-Ögüdücü
2010

Multidimensional Databases and Data Warehousing
Christian S. Jensen, Torben Bach Pedersen, and Christian Thomsen
2010

Database Replication
Bettina Kemme, Ricardo Jimenez-Peris, and Marta Patino-Martinez
2010

Relational and XML Data Exchange
Marcelo Arenas, Pablo Barcelo, Leonid Libkin, and Filip Murlak
2010

User-Centered Data Management
Tiziana Catarci, Alan Dix, Stephen Kimani, and Giuseppe Santucci
2010

Data Stream Management
Lukasz Golab and M. Tamer Özsu
2010

Access Control in Data Management Systems
Elena Ferrari
2010

An Introduction to Duplicate Detection
Felix Naumann and Melanie Herschel
2010

Generating Plans from Proofs: The Interpolation-based Approach to Query Reformulation

Michael Benedikt, Julien Leblay, Balder ten Cate, and Efthymia Tsamoura

ISBN: 978-3-031-00728-6 paperback
ISBN: 978-3-031-01856-5 ebook

DOI 10.1007/978-3-031-01856-5

A Publication in the Springer series
SYNTHESIS LECTURES ON DATA MANAGEMENT

Lecture #43
Series Editor: Z. Meral Özsoyoğlu, *Case Western Reserve University*
Founding Editor: M. Tamer Özsu, *University of Waterloo*
Series ISSN
Print 2153-5418 Electronic 2153-5426

Generating Plans from Proofs

The Interpolation-based Approach to Query Reformulation

Michael Benedikt
Oxford University

Julien Leblay
National Institute of Advanced Industrial Science and Technology (AIST), Tokyo

Balder ten Cate
Google, Inc.

Efthymia Tsamoura
Oxford University

SYNTHESIS LECTURES ON DATA MANAGEMENT #43

ABSTRACT

Query reformulation refers to a process of translating a source query—a request for information in some high-level logic-based language—into a target plan that abides by certain interface restrictions. Many practical problems in data management can be seen as instances of the reformulation problem. For example, the problem of translating an SQL query written over a set of base tables into another query written over a set of views; the problem of implementing a query via translating to a program calling a set of database APIs; the problem of implementing a query using a collection of web services.

In this book we approach query reformulation in a very general setting that encompasses all the problems above, by relating it to a line of research within mathematical logic. For many decades logicians have looked at the problem of converting "implicit definitions" into "explicit definitions," using an approach known as interpolation. We will review the theory of interpolation, and explain its close connection with query reformulation. We will give a detailed look at how the interpolation-based approach is used to generate translations between logic-based queries over different vocabularies, and also how it can be used to go from logic-based queries to programs.

KEYWORDS

data integration, query optimization, query reformulation, views, tableau, Craig interpolation, Beth definability

Contents

Preface

Query reformulation. Query reformulation refers to a process of translating a *declarative source query* into a *target plan* that abides by certain *interface restrictions*, restrictions that the source query may not satisfy. By a source query we mean some request for information in a high-level logic-based language. For example a query asking for the names of the advisors of a university student called "Smith" would be written in the standard database language SQL as

```
SELECT profname FROM Professor, Student
WHERE Student.advisorid = Professor.profid
AND Student.lname = "Smith"
```

and in first-order logic as:

$$\{\mathsf{profname} \mid \exists \mathsf{profid}\ \exists \mathsf{dname}\ \exists \mathsf{studid}\ \mathsf{Professor}(\mathsf{profid}, \mathsf{profname}, \mathsf{dname}) \wedge \mathsf{Student}(\mathsf{studid}, \text{“Smith”}, \mathsf{profid})\}$$

Here it is assumed that the user posing the query thinks of the information in terms of two tables, Student and Professor. Student contains the student id and last name of each student along with the id of their advisor, while Professor contains entries for the id, last name, and department of each professor.

What kind of translation might we perform on an expression like the one above? It might be that to answer the source query it is necessary to access information stored in a different format. The stored data may have a table Professor′ where the professor's id attribute is dropped, and a table Student′ where the advisor's id is replaced with an attribute advisorname giving the advisor's last name. In order to retrieve the information over these reformatted sources, the query should be transformed. It is easy to see that in this case the correct transformation is just to get the advisorname attribute of rows corresponding to "Smith" in Student′. In SQL the translation would be:

```
SELECT advisorname FROM Student′ WHERE Student′.lname = "Smith"
```

and in first-order logic it would be:

$$\{\mathsf{advisorname} \mid \exists \mathsf{studid}\ \mathsf{Student}'(\mathsf{studid}, \text{“Smith”}, \mathsf{advisorname})\}$$

In order to say that this represents a correct translation of the source query we need to know something about the semantics of the data. For us this will be captured by *integrity constraints*. In the above example, integrity constraints would describe the relationship between the accessible tables (Student′ and Professor′) and the tables mentioned in the source query (Student and Professor). Relative to those constraints, the SQL and logic translations above are correct.

Our notion of a target plan is very broad. We could be translating from one high-level query to another, as in the example above. We also consider translations from a high-level query to something operational, like a low-level program that makes calls to data access APIs. A basic function of a database management system is to translate a high-level language (e.g. first-order logic) to a low-level program. The goal there is to produce not just any equivalent program, but an efficient one. We will therefore look at the impact of efficiency considerations on reformulation. How to measure the efficiency of plans will not be our concern here—there is a rich research literature on the subject. We will instead be interested in algorithms that can return low-cost plans without specialized knowledge of the cost functions.

Reformulation via interpolation. Reformulating queries over restricted interfaces may sound very remote from concerns in mathematics. But it turns out that this problem is closely connected to a long line of research within mathematical logic. This book will provide an overview of the connection, explaining how ideas from logic can solve all of the reformulation problems above (and more). For each type of reformulation we will isolate a *semantic property* that any input query Q must have with respect to the target language and integrity constraints in order for the desired reformulation to exist. We then express this property as a *proof goal*: a statement that one logical formula follows from another. We will explain how to translate reformulation tasks into proof goals.

Reformulation proceeds by searching for a proof that witnesses the goal. From the proof we will then extract an *interpolant*, a logical formula that contains "only the necessary information" for the proof. We show that interpolants can be converted into reformulations through a very simple algorithm.

This "recipe" for reformulation dates back to work of the logician William Craig in the late 1950s. We show that it applies to a wide variety of reformulation scenarios. It is not a magic bullet that can always produce practical reformulation algorithms, but it often provides algorithms with optimal worst-case complexity, and it can be coupled with techniques for proof search and minimization of reformulations to become competitive with other reformulation techniques. We will explain the interpolation-based approach first for vocabulary-based restrictions, then for access-method based restrictions, and finally in the presence of cost information. We proceed in each case by explaining how the method is applied, then proving theorems stating that the resulting technique is complete—if a reformulation exists, the method will find it—and finally analyzing the worst-case complexity of the resulting algorithms.

About the book. This book has a number of objectives. It aims to explain formally what the interpolation-based method is, to exhibit the diverse ways in which it can be applied, and to explain the properties of the reformulations produced by the method. We also want to relate the interpolation-based approach to prior work on generating implementations from high-level queries.

This book has the most obvious interest to theoretically minded computer scientists. The focus throughout is on theorems: characterizations of reformulation (e.g., when does a source query have a reformulation of a certain kind?), expressiveness results (can a source query have a reformulation in one class, but no reformulation in another class?), and complexity bounds (what is the complexity of finding a reformulation in a certain class?). We connect our theorems to lines of research within a number of communities within theoretical computer science, particularly database theory, finite model theory, and knowledge representation. In a few cases, we state a theorem but omit the verification, pointing the reader to a paper where the full proofs appear. But the main results are proven in detail in order to present the theory in a self-contained manner. For many of the results, complete proofs have never appeared in print prior to this work.

A second audience for the book consists of researchers in logic. They will be very familiar with basic results about interpolation, along with the related topic of going from implicit definitions to explicit ones, but perhaps not with either the theory or the practice of databases. We aim to introduce logicians to the application of interpolation in data management. We hope that the results here give a new constructive perspective on the relationship between syntax and semantics, a major theme of research in both theoretical computer science and model theory. This book can be seen as working out more practical consequences of what are called "preservation theorems" in first-order model theory —theorems that characterize subclasses of first-order logic via semantic properties.

Finally, we hope that parts of the text will be of interest to researchers in databases, even those who do not work in theory. Chapter 4 and Chapter 5 are the most accessible parts of the text for researchers in data integration and query optimization with a more applied background. These two chapters deal with algorithms that can be understood without reference to interpolation, and without a background in first-order logic.

In trying to give a comprehensive picture of the theory of reformulation, we have completely omitted a host of issues that are critical in practice. For example:

- We deal only with set semantics for queries, not the bag semantics used in SQL.
- We consider only first-order queries, without considering aggregates like COUNT and SUM that play a crucial role in many database applications.
- Our model of data is "un-typed," assuming every column takes values from a fixed infinite set. We assume this infinite set has no structure that can be referenced in queries or constraints. Thus we do not allow queries and constraints that can mention integer inequality or arithmetic, string concatenation or substring comparisons, all of which appear in constraints and queries in practice.
- We do not cover all the integrity constraints that are important in practice. We present some general results about reformulation with arbitrary first-order logic constraints, which

are applicable to all common SQL schema constraints, including referential constraints and key constraints. We obtain decidability and complexity results for reformulation, for some limited constraint classes. But we omit an analysis of a few classes that are significant for database applications. For example, we do not give any special attention to equality-generating dependencies, which subsume the key constraints that play a fundamental role in SQL.

- We consider the problem of getting low-cost reformulations, but our theoretical results apply only to the case of very simplistic cost functions. We do not analyze realistic cost functions that are used in the database or the web data integration setting.

Many of these pragmatic issues are discussed in an earlier textbook [Toman and Weddell, 2011]. Others (like aggregation) represent difficult open problems for any theory of reformulation.

Although the book is focused on theory, we try to give a sense of how the interpolation-based framework is useful in practice. Thus throughout the book we present examples of the results in (simplified) application scenarios, and give pointers to further work concerning systems based on the theory.

Michael Benedikt, Julien Leblay, Balder ten Cate, and Efthymia Tsamoura
February 2016

Acknowledgments

The authors are very grateful to the following people for reviewing early copies of the manuscript and providing extensive comments: Antoine Amarilli, Cristian Riveros, Michael Vanden Boom, and James Worrell. We are also thankful to Carsten Lutz, Jan Van den Bussche, and Victor Vianu for their detailed feedback on the first official draft of the book. Benedikt's work was sponsored by the Engineering and Physical Sciences Research Council of the United Kingdom, grants EP/M005852/1 and EP/L012138/1.

Michael Benedikt, Julien Leblay, Balder ten Cate, and Efthymia Tsamoura
February 2016

CHAPTER 1
Introduction

This chapter starts by explaining the topics discussed in the book through examples. It then outlines the overall structure of the book, explaining how each chapter relates to the motivating examples. The remainder of the chapter reviews the basic definitions concerning the database models, constraint languages, and query languages used in the text. In the process we will go over some "fine print" concerning the relationship between the languages and semantics used in mathematical logic and those used in databases.

1.1 OVERVIEW

This book is about translating a *declarative source query* into a declarative query or procedural plan in a *target language* that abides by certain *interface restrictions*. By a declarative source query we always mean a request for information from a database specified using a formula of first-order logic, or its equivalent in the database query language SQL. We often focus on source queries given in the language of *conjunctive queries*, which correspond to a very simple subset of SQL. In logical terms these correspond to formulas built up using only conjunction and existential quantification. By a plan we may mean either another declarative query, or something more operational, such as a relational algebra expression, possibly using some restricted set of physical operators.

Translating from a declarative source query to a target in this broad sense captures a huge number of activities that take place within data management. One of the basic features of modern database systems is to decouple the vocabulary employed by users to ask questions about a dataset from the data structures that are used to implement data access: the "logical model" and the "physical model." In relational databases, the logical model might be a set of tables given an SQL schema: users interact with the data by sending SQL queries that mention these tables. The database manager performs a translation of the queries written over this high-level vocabulary into a program that interacts with the data using some set of data access functions.

In this "classical query evaluation" scenario, the relationship of the source vocabulary to the target vocabulary is very simple: every source relation corresponds to one or more "physical datasource" relations or functions. A more complicated example comes from data integration systems. The goal there is to mask a diverse set of datasources by providing a single unified schema. Suppose we have a multitude of "local databases" with information about different hotel chains. A data integration system would present to users a "global schema"—an easier-to-understand vocabulary that can model information in all of the sources. The system accepts queries written over the global schema and translates them into queries over the various local sources. The "global database" is virtual, implicitly defined by its relationship with local data.

In this book we will look at only a few flavors of interface restrictions that represent targets for a translation. The most basic kind of restriction we look at is a *vocabulary-based restriction*. There the target is another declarative query, but we limit the query's vocabulary: we begin with a query Q written using some relations $R_1 \ldots R_j$, and want to convert it to a query $Q_{\vec{V}}$ making use of a different set of relations $V_1 \ldots V_k$. If the queries Q and $Q_{\vec{V}}$ mention different relations, we cannot expect Q to give the same answers as $Q_{\vec{V}}$ on arbitrary instances. But our schema will come with *integrity constraints* which restrict the possible instances of interest. We will thus be considering equivalence only on instances satisfying the constraints.

An example of vocabulary-based restriction comes from *reformulating queries over views*. We have a collection of view relations $V_1 \ldots V_k$, and each V_i is associated with a query Q_i defined using some other set of relations $R_1 \ldots R_j$. Given a query Q defined over $R_1 \ldots R_j$, the goal is to find an equivalent query $Q_{\vec{V}}$ that mentions only $V_1 \ldots V_k$. Generally, additional restrictions will be put on $Q_{\vec{V}}$. For example, it should be a conjunctive query, or a union of conjunctive queries, or a relational algebra query. The view-based query reformulation problem can thus be seen as a special case of vocabulary-based restriction, where the integrity constraints are of the form:

$$\forall x_1 \ldots \forall x_n \; V_i(x_1 \ldots x_n) \leftrightarrow Q_i(x_1 \ldots x_n).$$

Example 1.1. A university database has a table Professor containing ids and last names of professors, along with the name of the professor's department. It also has a table Student listing the id and last name of each student, along with their advisor's id.

The database does not allow users to access the Professor and Student tables directly, but instead exposes a view Professor′ where the id attribute is dropped, and a table Student′ where the advisor's id is replaced with the advisor's last name.

That is, Professor′ is a view defined by the formula:

$$\{ \text{lname, dname} \mid \exists \text{ profid Professor(profid, lname, dname)} \}$$

or equivalently by the constraints:

$$\forall \text{profid} \, \forall \text{lname} \, \forall \text{dname Professor(profid, lname, dname)} \rightarrow \text{Professor}'\text{(lname, dname)}$$
$$\forall \text{lname} \, \forall \text{dname Professor}'\text{(lname, dname)} \rightarrow \exists \text{profid Professor(profid, lname, dname)}$$

Student′ is a view defined by the formula:

$$\{\text{studid, lname, profname} \mid \exists \text{profid} \, \exists \text{dname Student(studid, lname, profid)} \wedge \text{Professor(profid, profname, dname)}\}$$

or equivalently by constraints:

$$\forall \mathsf{studid}\ \forall \mathsf{lname}\ \forall \mathsf{dname}\ \forall \mathsf{profid}\ \forall \mathsf{profname}\ [\mathsf{Professor}(\mathsf{profid}, \mathsf{profname}, \mathsf{dname}) \wedge \mathsf{Student}(\mathsf{studid}, \mathsf{lname}, \mathsf{profid}) \rightarrow \mathsf{Student}'(\mathsf{studid}, \mathsf{lname}, \mathsf{profname})]$$

$$\forall \mathsf{studid}\ \forall \mathsf{lname}\ \forall \mathsf{profname}\ [\mathsf{Student}'(\mathsf{studid}, \mathsf{lname}, \mathsf{profname}) \rightarrow \exists \mathsf{profid}\ \exists \mathsf{dname}\ \mathsf{Professor}(\mathsf{profid}, \mathsf{profname}, \mathsf{dname}) \wedge \mathsf{Student}(\mathsf{studid}, \mathsf{lname}, \mathsf{profid})]$$

Consider the query asking for the names of the advisors of a given student. We can answer this by simply using the Student′ view, returning the profname attribute of a tuple in the view. But a query asking for the last names of all students that have an advisor in the history department can *not* be answered using the information in the views: knowing the advisor's name is not enough to identify the department. ◁

Integrity constraints need not be restricted to expressing view definitions. A natural use of constraints is to represent *relationships between sources*, such as overlap in the data. This overlap can be exploited to take a query specified over a source that *a priori* does not have sufficient data, and reformulate it over a source that provides the necessary data.

Example 1.2. We look at an example schema from [Onet, 2013]. It has a relation Employee containing the id, name, and department id of each employee, and also a relation Department, containing the department's id, name, as well as the id of the department's manager. The schema contains the constraints:

$$\forall \mathsf{deptid}\ \forall \mathsf{dname}\ \forall \mathsf{mgrid}\ [\mathsf{Department}(\mathsf{deptid}, \mathsf{dname}, \mathsf{mgrid}) \rightarrow \exists N\ \mathsf{Employee}(\mathsf{mgrid}, N, \mathsf{deptid})]$$
$$\forall \mathsf{eid}\ \forall \mathsf{ename}\ \forall \mathsf{deptid}\ \mathsf{Employee}(\mathsf{eid}, \mathsf{ename}, \mathsf{deptid}) \rightarrow \exists D \exists M\ \mathsf{Department}(\mathsf{deptid}, D, M)$$

That is, every manager of a department works in it, and every employee works in a department. Suppose further that only the relation Department is accessible to a certain class of users. Intuitively, it should still be possible to answer some questions that one could ask concerning the relation Employee, making use of the accessible relation Department. Suppose a user poses the query asking for all department ids of employees, writing it like this:

$$Q = \{\mathsf{deptid} \mid \exists \mathsf{eid}\ \exists \mathsf{ename}\ \mathsf{Employee}(\mathsf{eid}, \mathsf{ename}, \mathsf{deptid})\}$$

The query can be reformulated as:

$$Q_{\mathsf{Department}} = \{\mathsf{deptid} \mid \exists \mathsf{dname}\ \exists \mathsf{mgrid}\ \mathsf{Department}(\mathsf{deptid}, \mathsf{dname}, \mathsf{mgrid})\}$$

Intuitively, the constraints ensure that the set of department id values in the Department and Employee tables are the same. ◁

Access methods. A finer notion of interface than vocabulary-based restrictions is based on *access methods*, which state that a relation can only be accessed by lookups where certain arguments must be given. One example of a restricted interface based on access methods comes from web forms. Thinking of the form as exposing a virtual table, the mandatory fields must be filled in by the user, while submitting the form returns all tuples that match the entered values. Other examples include web services and legacy databases.

Example 1.3. Consider a Profinfo table available via a web form, containing information about faculty, including their last names, office number, and employee id, but with a restricted interface that requires giving an employee id as an input. The interface could be implemented as a web form that requires entering an employee's id and then pressing a submit button to get the matching records. The query Q asking for ids of faculty named "Smith" cannot be "completely answered" over this schema:[1] that is, there is no function over the available data in this schema which is equivalent to Q.

But suppose another web form provides access to a Udirectory table containing the employee id and last name of every university employee, with an interface that allows one to access the entire contents of the table. Then we can reason that Q is answerable using the information in this schema: a plan would pull tuples from the Udirectory form and check them within the Profinfo form to see if they correspond to a faculty member. ◁

In Example 1.3, reasoning about access considerations was straightforward, but in the presence of more complex schemas, we may have to chain several inferences, resulting in a plan that makes use of several auxiliary accesses.

Example 1.4. Suppose we have two directory data sources with overlapping information. One source exposes information from $\mathsf{Udirectory}_1(\mathsf{uname}, \mathsf{addr}, \mathsf{uid})$ via an access method requiring a uname and uid. There is also a "web table" Ids(uid) with no access restriction, that makes available the set of uids (hence we have a "referential integrity constraint" saying that every uid in $\mathsf{Udirectory}_1$ matches a uid in Ids). The other source exposes $\mathsf{Udirectory}_2(\mathsf{uname}, \mathsf{addr}, \mathsf{phone})$, requiring a uname and addr, and also a web table Names(uname) with no access restriction that reveals all unames in $\mathsf{Udirectory}_2$ (that is, a constraint that each uname in $\mathsf{Udirectory}_2$ appears in Names). There is also a constraint saying that each uname and addr in $\mathsf{Udirectory}_2$ appears in $\mathsf{Udirectory}_1$. The schema is shown in Figure 1.1, with the arrows indicating referential constraints and underlining indicating the input positions of each relation. A query asking for all phone numbers in the second directory could be written:

$$Q = \{\mathsf{phone} \mid \exists \mathsf{uname}\ \exists \mathsf{addr}\ \mathsf{Udirectory}_2(\mathsf{uname}, \mathsf{addr}, \mathsf{phone})\}.$$

There is a plan that implements this query: it gets all the uids from Ids and unames from Names first, puts them into the access on $\mathsf{Udirectory}_1$, then uses the uname and addr of the resulting tuples to get the phone numbers in $\mathsf{Udirectory}_2$. ◁

[1] We will formalize the notion of "completely answerable" in Chapter 3.

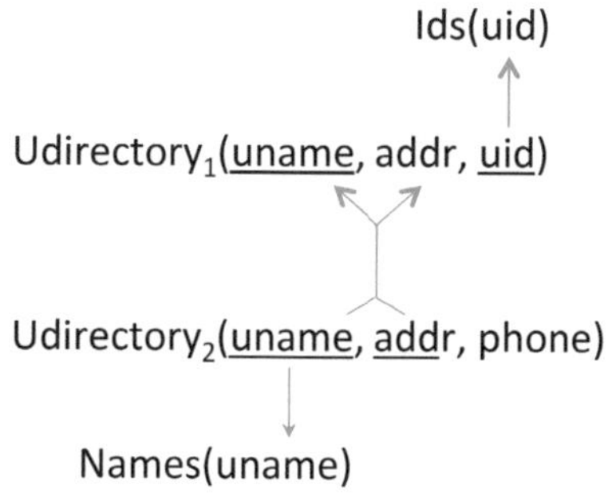

Figure 1.1: The schema for Example 1.4.

We emphasize that our goal in this work is getting plans which give *complete answers to queries.* This means that if we have a query asking for the office number of all professors with last name "Smith," the plan produced should return all tuples in the answer, even if access to the Professor relation is limited. This contrasts with a line of work in data integration that considers the broader question of how to answer any query "as much as possible given the available data:" how to get the *certain answers* or how to compute the *maximally contained query* [Lenzerini, 2002].

In the last part of the book, we look not just at getting any plan in the target language, but one with low cost. In doing this, we are moving closer to the traditional concerns of query optimization in database systems. Examples of access cost include the cost in money of accessing certain services and the cost in time of accessing data through either web service calls, iteratively inputting into web forms, or using particular indices.

Reformulation via interpolation. This text will provide an overview of a general approach that has emerged from the computational logic and database communities. The idca is to go from "semantics to syntax" by means of interpolation algorithms. The "meta-algorithm" for reformulation is as follows:

1. Isolate a *semantic property* that any input query Q must have with respect to the target $\mathcal{T}$ and constraints Σ in order to have a reformulation of the desired type.

2. Express this property as a *proof goal* (in the language we use later on, an *entailment*): a statement that a certain formula follows from another formula.

3. Search for a proof of the entailment within a given proof system. Here we focus on tableau proofs, a well-known proof system within computational logic.

4. From the proof, extract an *interpolant* using an interpolation algorithm. We will review some standard interpolation algorithms and also present new ones.

5. Convert the interpolant to a reformulation.

This approach is very general and can be applied to a variety of proof systems and restrictions on the target, with different target languages corresponding to different entailments. We prove theorems saying that the method is complete: there is a reformulation exactly when there is a proof of the semantic property. These completeness theorems give as a consequence a *definability or preservation theorem*: a query Q has a certain kind of reformulation if and only if it has a certain semantic property. Such theorems are well-known in model theory, and indeed our theorems can be seen as "database versions" of the preservation theorems that are known from classical model theory textbooks, e.g., [Chang and Keisler, 1990].

The fact that interpolation theorems can be used to prove preservation theorems is not new. As early as the 1950s, the logician William Craig used interpolation to prove a definability theorem, and all of our results can be seen as generalizations of Craig's technique. The connection between interpolation and preservation has been explored more recently by Otto [Otto, 2000]. It is also known that interpolation theorems can be adapted from the classical semantics of first-order logic to the setting used in databases, and can be used to characterize when a query can be reformulated over a certain target. This idea goes back to the work of Segoufin and Vianu [Segoufin and Vianu, 2005].

What is less well-known is that this connection between reformulation, interpolation, and preservation can be made effective: *interpolation algorithms yield reformulation algorithms*. We will show that the interpolation technique yields many of the algorithmic results about reformulation mentioned in the database setting. We will also demonstrate that it produces reformulation algorithms in new settings.

Thus our results will link: a semantic property of Q (with respect to $\mathcal{T}$ and Σ), a reformulation property of Q, and a proof goal and interpolation algorithm that achieves the reformulation.

Organization of the book. In the remainder of this chapter we give preliminaries on database schemas, query languages, and logics. Much of it can be found in database textbooks. But we also include some less standard material on the relationship of logic to databases, and present a particular proof system for first-order logic which will play a significant role in our approach.

Chapter 2 begins the exposition of the interpolation-based approach in the setting of vocabulary-based restrictions. It presents theorems concerning the ability to generate reformulations in a variant of first-order logic. It proceeds to refinements of the technique that guarantee that the reformulation will satisfy additional properties. The remainder of the chapter analyzes the decidability and complexity of the reformulation algorithms.

In Chapter 3 we extend interpolation-based reformulation to the setting in which the target is given by access methods. We apply the same approach as in the vocabulary-based case, providing an entailment that captures a property of the input query that is necessary for a reformulation to exist, and then applying interpolation to generate the reformulation from a proof witnessing the entailment. This requires a new interpolation theorem, generalizing one previously stated in [Otto, 2000]. The exposition parallels that in the previous chapter, starting with general theorems for first-order logic and then analyzing the complexity of reformulation for restricted classes of constraints.

The previous chapters show that one can use interpolation to perform reformulation in theory. But when can we make the reformulation process effective, and when can we make it efficient? We focus on more practical concerns in Chapter 4. We show that for a wide class of constraints used in databases, tuple-generating dependencies, interpolation-based reformulation reduces to a particularly simple algorithm. This setting will also allow us to connect the interpolation-based approach to the main method for reformulation discussed in the prior database literature, based on *the chase* (see Section 1.3).

In Chapter 5 we turn to getting reformulations that are efficient. In the setting of overlapping data sources, there can be many plans with different costs. The chapter presents a method for finding the lowest-cost plan. The main idea is to *explore the full space of proofs, but guiding the search by cost as well as proof structure.* Thus instead of generating a single proof and then sending the corresponding plan on for further optimization, we interleave exploration of proofs with calls to estimate cost (and perhaps further optimize) the corresponding plans.

1.2 FIRST-ORDER LOGIC AND DATABASES

This book applies techniques from mathematical logic to databases. We will thus need to discuss differences between the syntax and semantics of classical mathematical logic and the languages used in databases, and how we can nevertheless apply mathematical logic techniques in the database setting.

Schemas. In order to describe a querying scenario we will use a *basic schema*, which consists of:

- A finite collection of *relation names* (or simply *relations* henceforward), with each relation R associated with an *arity*, denoted $\mathsf{arity}(R)$. A *position* of a relation R is a number between 1 and $\mathsf{arity}(R)$. A relation will also be referred to as a *table.*

- A finite collection of *schema constants* ("Smith", 3, ...). Informally, these represent a fixed set of values that a user might use within accesses, in addition to values that emerge from the database. For example, if the user is performing a query involving the string "Smith," we would assume that "Smith" was a schema constant—but not arbitrary unrelated strings. Throughout this work, *we will assume that all constants used in queries or constraints are schema constants.* Several results, like Theorem 1.4, depend upon this.

- A collection of *integrity constraints*, which will be sentences in some logic.

Syntax of first-order logic. We use standard terminology to describe formulas in first-order logic without function symbols, including the notion of free variable, quantifiers, and connectives [Abiteboul et al., 1995].

First-order logic is built up from *atomic formulas*, which can be either:

- *relational atoms* of the form $R(\vec{t})$, where R is a relation name and each t_i in $\vec{t}$ is either a constant or a variable;
- *equality atoms* of the form $t_i = t_j$, with t_i, t_j either a constant or a variable.

Formulas include atomic formulas and are closed under boolean operations, with formation rules $\varphi_1 \wedge \varphi_2, \varphi_1 \vee \varphi_2$, and $\neg\varphi$. They are also closed under existential and universal quantifiers, allowing the inductive formation of formulas $\forall x\ \varphi$ and $\exists x\ \varphi$. A formula φ whose relations and constants all come from a given schema Sch is said to be a *formula over* Sch. A formula with no free variables is a *sentence*.

The *equality-free* first-order formulas are built up as above but without equality atoms. Note that the equality atom $x = x$ expresses the formula True that is always true, while the equality formula $\neg x = x$ expresses the formula False that is always false. In equality-free first-order logic, we still want to express these, so we allow the special atomic formulas False and True to be in equality-free first-order logic as well.

If φ is a formula whose free variables include $\vec{x}$, while $\vec{t}$ is a sequence of constants and variables whose length matches $\vec{x}$, then $\varphi[\vec{x} := \vec{t}]$ denotes the formula obtained by simultaneously substituting each x_i with t_i. When the mapping of the free variables x_i to constants or variables t_i is either clear from context or unimportant, we denote this as $\varphi(\vec{t})$. We often omit universal quantifiers from formulas, particularly for formulas where the only quantifiers are universal. For instance, we write $P(x, y) \rightarrow Q(x, y)$ as a shorthand for $\forall x\ \forall y\ [P(x, y) \rightarrow Q(x, y)]$.

We need to discuss the distinction between the data model and query languages used in databases and the syntax and semantics of first-order logic as used in mathematics. The differences involve at least five issues: 1. the range of universal and existential quantifiers; 2. the treatment of constants; 3. positional notation for tuples vs. named attribute notation; 4. the range of free variables; 5. and finite vs. arbitrary data domains. We will cover the first four issues in the course of introducing our semantic notions below. The discussion of the last issue (finite vs. infinite) will be deferred until later in the text (see, e.g., Section 2.8).

Structures, instances, and range of quantification. A database *instance* I for a schema Sch without constant symbols assigns to every relation R in Sch of arity n a collection of n-tuples $[\![R]\!]_I$, in such a way that all integrity constraints of Sch are satisfied. We call $[\![R]\!]_I$ the *interpretation* of R in I. An association of a database relation R with a tuple $\vec{c}$ of the proper arity will be referred to as a *fact*. A database instance can equivalently be seen as a collection of facts. An instance of a schema that has only a single relation R is a *relation instance*. The *active domain* of an instance I, denoted $\mathsf{adom}(I)$, is the union of the one-dimensional projections of all interpretations of relations: that is, all the elements that participate in some fact of I.

Example 1.5. Suppose our schema consists of only one unary relation UEmployee, containing the ids of university employees. One possible instance I interprets UEmployee by the singleton set $\{e_0\}$. We can alternatively define I by the set of facts $\{\mathsf{UEmployee}(e_0)\}$. In this case we have $\mathsf{adom}(I) = \{e_0\}$. ◁

Classical logic considers *structures* rather than *instances*. A structure consists of a set, the *domain* of the structure, interpretations for each relation as sets of tuples with values in the domain, and an interpretation for each constant as a single element of the domain.

Example 1.6. Returning to the schema in Example 1.5, one structure M that conforms to it consists of a two-element domain $\{e_0, f_0\}$, with UEmployee interpreted as $\{e_0\}$. ◁

In the *classical semantics* of first-order logic, quantifiers range over the domain of the structure. In databases, quantifiers are usually given the *active domain* semantics, in which the quantified variable ranges over the union of the values in the interpretations of relations. The active domain semantics can be used to give a meaning to a sentence in an instance, since the meaning only depends on the instance, not some domain in which the instance sits.

Example 1.7. Let φ be the sentence $\exists x\ \neg\mathsf{UEmployee}(x)$. In the instance I of Example 1.5, φ is intuitively false, since there is only one element mentioned in facts, and it lies inside UEmployee in the instance. The active domain semantics of first-order logic formalizes this intuition, and under it the sentence is false in I.

Now consider the structure M in Example 1.6 which interprets UEmployee as in I, but has a two-element domain $\{e_0, f_0\}$. Under the classical semantics of first-order logic, φ is true in M, since f_0 can be a witness for the existential quantifier. ◁

In order to avoid the confusion that could be caused by using two different semantics for the same syntax, we will not formally define the active domain semantics for a logical formula—the interested reader can refer to [Abiteboul et al., 1995]. Instead, we define a syntax in which quantification is explicitly restricted to data in a certain relation within the instance. Once we restrict to this syntax, *the same semantics for quantifiers can be used both over structures and over instances, there will be no ambiguity about the semantics of quantifiers, and the reader will not have to worry about what quantifiers range over.*

We will use *first-order logic with relativized quantifiers*, RQFO. RQFO is built up from equality and relational atoms via the boolean operators and the quantifications:

$$\exists \vec{x}\ R(\vec{s}, \vec{x}) \wedge \varphi(\vec{s}, \vec{x}, \vec{t})$$

and

$$\forall \vec{x}\ R(\vec{s}, \vec{x}) \rightarrow \varphi(\vec{s}, \vec{x}, \vec{t})$$

for R a relational symbol and φ an RQFO formula. Those familiar with active domain semantics will be able to see that it is subsumed by RQFO, in the sense that an active domain semantics formula can be converted to an equivalent RQFO formula under classical semantics: the active domain interpretation of the quantification $\exists x\ \varphi$ is a disjunction $\bigvee_i \exists \vec{x}\ R_i(\vec{x}) \wedge \varphi$, while a quantification $\forall x\ \varphi$ under active domain semantics translates into a conjunction of relativized universal quantifications.

We can similarly talk about equality-free RQFO formulas, by disallowing equality atoms. By convention, we allow the prefix of existential quantifiers $\exists x_1 \ldots \exists x_n$ to be empty, and similarly for universal quantifiers. In this way we can capture an atom $R(x_1 \dots x_n)$ and negated atoms $\neg R(x_1 \dots x_n)$ as specialized RQFO formulas $R(\vec{x}) \wedge$ True and $R(\vec{x}) \rightarrow$ False, respectively. Thus for equality-free formulas we can in fact assume that the only base formulas are True and False.

The truth value of an RQFO sentence without constants is well-defined over an instance, since from the instance we can determine the range of each relativized quantifier. Similarly the truth value for an RQFO formula without constants is well-defined given an instance and a mapping of the free variables to some values (a *variable binding* or just *binding* for short).

Treatment of constants. In classical first-order logic, constants are *uninterpreted.* They are just symbols used in logical formulas that always represent an individual element. A structure must provide an interpretation of each constant: a mapping of each constant to a value. Using this mapping we can determine, for example, whether $c = d$ holds in the structure. In this work we allow formulas to mention uninterpreted constants, as in classical first-order logic. This will be important in modeling formulas that are generated within first-order proof systems such as tableau, used in Chapters 2 and 3.

In databases, constants usually come with a fixed interpretation, independent of any instance: each constant symbol is associated with a unique value, with distinct constants having distinct values. Thus one can identify the constant with the value. Thus R(“Smith,”“Jones”) holds in an instance if the instance includes the fact R(“Smith,”“Jones”); no additional mapping is required. Our schema constants, which are the only constants allowed in queries and constraints, are always database-style interpreted constants.

Example 1.8. Returning to the setting of Example 1.5, suppose our schema also includes schema constants “Smith” and “Jones” and the relation Manager. Consider the instance I consisting of the facts {Manager(“Jones”), UEmployee(“Smith”)}. The sentence UEmployee(“Smith”) $\wedge$ Manager(“Jones”) is true in this instance.

Now consider the sentence UEmployee(c) where c is an uninterpreted constant. If bind is a mapping taking c to “Smith,” then the sentence holds in instance I with mapping bind. If bind′ is a binding taking c to “Jones,” then the sentence does not hold in instance I with mapping bind′. ◁

In this text we make use of both interpreted and uninterpreted constants. But for the most part those more comfortable with uninterpreted constants can ignore interpreted ones, as we now explain.

Interpreted constants can be modeled with uninterpreted constants plus additional axioms added to the integrity constraints stating any special properties of the constant symbols.[2] In our setting, it suffices to assume that the integrity constraints include explicit assertions of inequalities between distinct schema constants. With these additional integrity constraints, one can consider all constants to be uninterpreted throughout the text: interpreted constants are used as a kind of “shorthand” for uninterpreted constants supplemented with additional axioms.

[2] This is an idea that goes back to Reiter [1984].

Interpreted constants are a useful shorthand, since they allow us to drop the additional mapping of constants to values in evaluating a formula, and we will make use of them often. In most of the text it will be clear from context whether a constant we are speaking of is uninterpreted or interpreted. Thus we simply refer to something as a "constant" for brevity.

We emphasize the bottom line of this "fine print" discussion of interpreted vs. uninterpreted constants and of instances vs. structures:

> The semantics of our queries and constraints can be stated in terms of instances and interpreted constants, as is common in databases, rather than structures and uninterpreted constants used in classical logic. Since RQFO sentences are syntactically restricted so as to be independent of a surrounding domain, and interpreted constants can be seen as a shorthand for uninterpreted constants plus additional axioms, we are free to make use of results from logic in reasoning about our queries and constraints.

Fragments of relativized-quantifier first-order logic. RQFO formulas that are built up as above but disallowing $\neg$ or $\forall$ will be called *positive existential formulas*, or $\exists^+$ *formulas* for short. Formulas that are built up as above but disallowing $\forall$ and allowing $\neg$ to be applied to only atomic formulas will be called *existential formulas*, or $\exists$ *formulas*.

Although we have defined first-order logic and its variants as including equality, we will usually make explicit when equalities are allowed. The presence or absence of equality in one of our logics will revolve around the ability to express inequalities (e.g., two constants are distinct, there are four distinct elements that satisfy a property). Note that we do not have the inequality symbol $\neq$ as a primitive in our logics. In first-order logic with equality, we can express inequality, since $\neq$ can be seen as an abbreviation for $\neg(x = y)$. But in equality-free first-order logic, we cannot express $\neq$. We can extend the existential fragment to allow negation only in the form $\neg(x = y)$. We refer to such a formula as an *existential formula with inequalities*, or $\exists^{\neq}$ formula. Similarly we can extend the positive existential fragment to *positive existential formulas with inequalities*, or $\exists^{+,\neq}$ *formulas*.

Example 1.9. Consider a schema that includes the relation UEmployee containing ids of each university employee, along with relations Researcher containing the same information but only about researchers, and a relation Lecturer containing the same information about lecturers.

- An RQFO sentence stating that every researcher is a university employee could be written:

$$\forall x \ \mathsf{Researcher}(x) \rightarrow \mathsf{UEmployee}(x).$$

- The $\exists$ sentence below states that there is some university employee who is not a researcher:

$$\exists x \ \mathsf{UEmployee}(x) \wedge \neg\mathsf{Researcher}(x).$$

- This $\exists^+$ sentence states that there is either a researcher or a lecturer:

$$\exists x \ \mathsf{Researcher}(x) \vee \mathsf{Lecturer}(x).$$

The sentence above is not written explicitly in RQFO, but it can be converted to one, namely

$$(\exists x\ \mathsf{Researcher}(x) \wedge \mathsf{True}) \vee (\exists x\ \mathsf{Lecturer}(x) \wedge \mathsf{True}).$$

We have defined the $\exists^+$ formulas as a subclass of RQFO formulas, and similarly for $\exists, \exists^{\neq}, \exists^{+,\neq}$. Since it is often inconvenient to write out formulas in the syntax of RQFO, we will often abuse notation by referring to a formula as being in one of these subclasses when it has an "obvious conversion" into a formula in this subclass, as above.

- This $\exists^{\neq}$ sentence states that there are two university employees who are not researchers:

$$\exists x\ \exists x'\ x' \neq x \wedge \mathsf{UEmployee}(x) \wedge \mathsf{UEmployee}(x') \wedge \neg\mathsf{Researcher}(x) \wedge \neg\mathsf{Researcher}(x').$$

- The following $\exists^{+,\neq}$ sentence states that there are two entities that are either researchers or lecturers:

$$\exists x\ \exists x'\ x' \neq x \wedge (\mathsf{Researcher}(x) \vee \mathsf{Lecturer}(x)) \wedge (\mathsf{Researcher}(x') \vee \mathsf{Lecturer}(x')).$$

◁

Queries via relativized-quantifier first-order logic. Remember that two key inputs to our reformulation problems are a source query and some integrity constraints, while the desired output of reformulation is a declarative query or a plan. By a *query* we mean a mapping from instances of some schema to interpretations of some relation. A *boolean query* is a query where the output is a relation of arity 0. There are only two interpretations for a relation of arity 0, the empty set and the set consisting of the empty tuple. If we denote the former by False and the latter by True, a boolean query is thus a mapping where the output takes one of the values in $\{\mathsf{True}, \mathsf{False}\}$. A query where the output relation has non-zero arity is a *non-boolean query*. Given a query Q and instance I, $[\![Q]\!]_I$ denotes the output of Q on I. The definition of a query as a mapping is very general, but in this text the queries will be described in either a logic-based language or an algebraic language which is equivalent in expressiveness to a logical formula. We now explain how logical formulas define queries, and then give the algebraic formalism for expressing queries.

RQFO sentences clearly can be used to define boolean queries: the result of the query on an instance is True exactly when the sentence holds in the instance. RQFO formulas can similarly be used to define non-boolean queries. Given an RQFO formula with its free variables enumerated as $v_1 \dots v_n$, we can associate a non-boolean query whose output relation has arity n: the outputs will correspond to variable bindings which make the formula true. Recall that we evaluate RQFO formulas over an instance, not a structure. But we do not restrict the bindings to come from the instance. Instead we consider the free variables to take values within some fixed infinite "universal domain of values"—a set that will contain all elements in the domain of any instance that we consider. We take the result of a query given by an RQFO formula to be all bindings that take values within that domain and satisfy the formula.

Example 1.10. Consider the RQFO formula $R(x, y) \wedge S(x, y)$. This defines a query that takes as input an instance I consisting of interpretations of R and S, returning as output the relation instance consisting of all pairs in $[\![R]\!]_I \cap [\![S]\!]_I$. ◁

A query given by an RQFO formula will be called an RQFO-*query*. For our query language we often restrict further, to *conjunctive queries* (CQs), logical formulas of the form $Q(\vec{x}) = \exists \vec{y}\ (A_1 \wedge \cdots \wedge A_n)$, where A_i is an atom using a relation of the schema, with arguments that are either variables from $\vec{x}$ and $\vec{y}$ or schema constants. A normalization argument shows that any logical formula built up using $\wedge$ and $\exists$ can be expressed as a CQ. For a conjunctive query Q, a variable binding that witnesses that Q holds in an instance I will also be called a *homomorphism of Q in I*.

In Chapter 3, we also consider *unions of conjunctive queries* (UCQs), which are disjunctions of CQs in which every CQ has the same free variables. Another simple normalization argument, found in [Abiteboul et al., 1995], shows that any $\exists^+$ sentence can be converted to a UCQ.

Example 1.11. In Example 1.9, the $\exists^+$ sentence stating that there is either a researcher or a lecturer can be written as a UCQ: $(\exists x\ \text{Researcher}(x)) \vee (\exists x\ \text{Lecturer}(x))$.

A formula returning the researchers that are also lecturers can be expressed as a CQ:

$$\text{Researcher}(x) \wedge \text{Lecturer}(x)$$

◁

Throughout the text we will state properties of *an* RQFO *query*, *an* $\exists^+$ *query*, and so forth. The reader can freely substitute the word "formula" for "query" in these assertions, but keeping in mind that the formula will likely play the role of either the source or the target in a reformulation problem.

Named vs. positional notation and relational algebra. In our semantics of first-order logic, a relation was associated with an arity n and was interpreted by a set of n-tuples. This is what we refer to as *positional notation*. An alternative notation considers schemas where a relation R is associated not just with an arity n, but with a collection of n attribute names. An instance for such a schema interprets each such relation R by a collection of functions from the attributes of R. A query over such a schema is a function mapping instances of the schema to an interpretation of a relation. There is a correspondence between schemas/instances/queries in the "named attribute" perspective and schemas/instances/queries in the "positional" perspective.

Example 1.12. Recall the schema from Example 1.5, which contained a unary relation UEmployee. The example contained an instance of this schema which consisted of the fact $\{\text{UEmployee}(e_0)\}$. In named notation, we could state that UEmployee has a single attribute eid. Under this notation instance I would be represented by interpreting UEmployee as a single tuple with $\{\text{eid} = e_0\}$. ◁

Relational algebra (RA) is the main "database-style" language we will use for queries and constraints. Relational algebra expressions refer to relations using named attributes. That is, the inputs are schemas where each relation has named attributes, and the output is a relational instance with named attributes. An expression in relational algebra is a term built up from relations by composing the following families of operators:

- selection (denoted σ), which selects tuples satisfying some equality or inequality condition. For example, $\sigma_{\mathsf{lname}=\text{"Smith"}}\mathsf{Employee}$ is an expression that takes as input an instance of the relation Employee, returning the instance containing tuples whose lname attribute is "Smith";
- projection (denoted π) which selects a subset of the attributes in a relation. An example is the relational algebra expression $\pi_{\mathsf{lname}}\mathsf{Employee}$, which takes as input an instance of Employee and returns the projection of each tuple in the instance onto the attribute lname;
- renaming (ρ), which renames the attributes according to some mapping;
- difference ($-$), and union ($\cup$), which have their usual set-theoretic meaning; and
- join ($\bowtie$), which merges tuples from two input relations, where the pair of tuples must satisfy some equality or inequality condition. For example, $\mathsf{Employee} \bowtie_{\mathsf{dname}=\mathsf{dname}} \mathsf{Department}$ takes as input an instance of the Employee relation and an instance of the Department relation, and returns a relation instance that includes each employee tuple in Employee extended with the matching information about the employee's department.

In order to be able to handle constants that are not part of the data, we also include in relational algebra the *constant operators* for each schema constant c: these take no input and produce a single-attribute relation instance containing one row with the attributes value being c. The semantics of these operations is standard (e.g., [Abiteboul et al., 1995]).

Just as we talked about fragments of first-order logic and RQFO, we have corresponding fragments of relational algebra, each defined as compositions of a subset of the operators. The most restricted fragment, SPJ, only allows the constant, selection, projection, renaming, and join operators. We use the prefix "U" to allow the union operator, and the "$\neq$" symbol to allow inequalities in selection and join predicates. We append an "AD" suffix to allow "atomic difference": we can allow subexpressions $E - E'$ only when E' has the form $E \bowtie_\alpha R$ where R is a relation and α is a set of equality conditions that identifies each attribute of R with an attribute of E. We abbreviate this as $E -_\alpha R$. For example, $USPJAD^{\neq}$ supplements SPJ by allowing union, inequality selections, and atomic difference.

Each relational algebra expression has a set of *input relations* and a set of *output attributes*. For instance, the relational algebra expression $\pi_{a,b}(R \bowtie S)$ has input relations $\{R, S\}$ and $\{a, b\}$ as output attributes. A relation with no attributes has only two interpretations, just like a relation with arity 0 under the positional perspective. Thus relational algebra queries with no output attributes define boolean queries, while relational algebra queries with a non-empty set of output attributes define non-boolean queries. It is well-known that every boolean relational algebra query can be efficiently converted into an RQFO sentence and that every RQFO sentence using only interpreted constants can be converted to a boolean relational algebra query [Abiteboul et al., 1995]. Abiteboul et al. [1995] also presents correspondences between positive existential logical sentences and boolean $USPJ$ queries. These correspondences preserve the semantics of queries, up to the difference between positional and named notation. The argument given there extends in a straightforward way to show that existential sentences correspond to $USPJAD$ boolean queries, and similarly for the counterparts with inequalities (e.g., $\exists^{+,\neq}$ corresponds to $USPJ^{\neq}$). In particular, UCQ sentences, $\exists^{+}$ sentences, and $USPJ$ boolean queries have the same expressiveness. CQ sentences are equivalent in expressiveness to boolean queries defined in the SPJ fragment of relational algebra.

We next present some examples of the correspondence between relational algebra queries and RQFO formulas. Formally, these correspondences rely on a mapping between the positional and named perspectives. We will usually not spell out the mapping, moving back and forth between logic-based notation and relational algebra notation for queries. In the examples, we will omit the equality conditions in joins $E \bowtie F$ when they are the "obvious conditions": those that identify each output attribute of E with the output attribute having the same name in the output of F. This special kind of join is called a "natural join."

Example 1.13. Consider the assertions from Example 1.9. These are all sentences, so to model them in relational algebra, we need to look at queries that return an instance for the relation with no attributes, with the empty instance representing False and the non-empty instance denoting True. We can accomplish this by coming up with queries that return a non-empty output whenever the sentence is true and an empty output whenever the sentence is false, and then projecting those onto the empty set of tuples. We use this tactic in all the examples below.

- The RQFO sentence stating that every researcher is a university employee could be written in relational algebra as:

$$\mathsf{True} - \pi_{\emptyset}(\mathsf{Researcher} - \mathsf{UEmployee})$$

  where True is a query that always returns a non-empty instance with no attributes (such a query can be formed by applying a projection to a constant operator).

- The $\exists$ sentence stating that there is some university employee who is not a researcher could be expressed in $USPJAD$ as:

$$\pi_{\emptyset}[\mathsf{UEmployee} - \mathsf{Researcher}]$$

- The $\exists^{+}$ sentence stating there is either a researcher or a lecturer could be expressed in $USPJ$ as:

$$\pi_{\emptyset}[\mathsf{Researcher} \cup \mathsf{Lecturer}].$$

- The $\exists^{\neq}$ sentence stating that there are two university employees who are not researchers could be written as the $SPJAD^{\neq}$ query:

$$\pi_{\emptyset}[(\textsf{UEmployee} - \textsf{Researcher}) \bowtie_{x \neq x'} \rho(x \rightsquigarrow x')(\textsf{UEmployee} - \textsf{Researcher})].$$

where x is the sole attribute of UEmployee and Researcher.

- The $\exists^{+,\neq}$ sentence stating that there are two entities that are either researchers or lecturers could be expressed in $USPJ^{\neq}$ as:

$$\pi_{\emptyset}[(\textsf{UEmployee} \cup \textsf{Researcher}) \bowtie_{x \neq x'} \rho(x \rightsquigarrow x')(\textsf{UEmployee} \cup \textsf{Researcher})].$$

◁

Example 1.14. Consider the CQ in Example 1.11, asking for researchers that are also lecturers. This could be written as the SPJ query:

$$\textsf{Researcher} \bowtie \textsf{Lecturer}.$$

◁

Figure 1.2 shows the fragments of RQFO (left) that we consider in this text, along with the corresponding fragments of relational algebra (right).

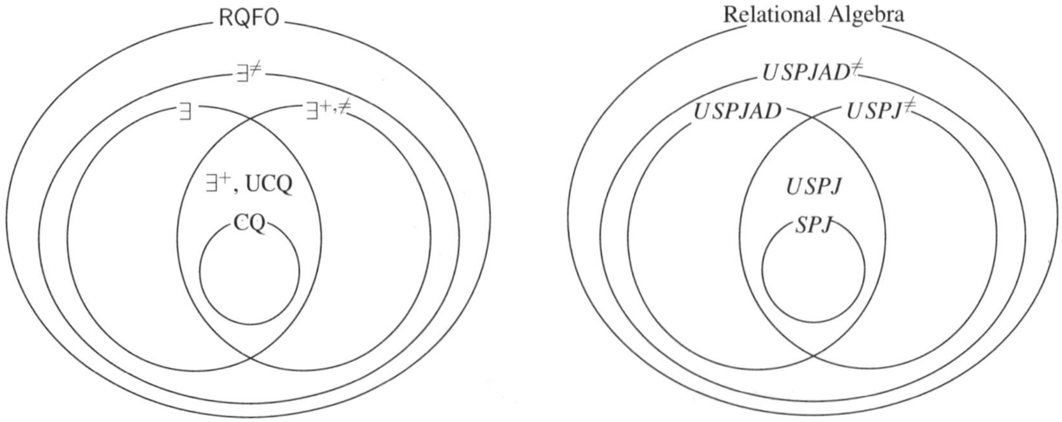

Figure 1.2: Fragments of RQFO and corresponding relational algebra fragments.

Range of free variables in formulas. We have already discussed two issues that need to be addressed in order to talk about an equivalence between first-order logic formulas and relational algebra queries: adjusting the range of quantification in logical formulas to match that of relational algebra, and looking at equivalence up to the distinction between named vs. positional notation. This allowed us to claim a correspondence between *boolean* relational algebra queries and RQFO *sentences*. We next deal with a final distinction between logic-based queries and relational algebra that arises only in the context of non-boolean queries: the range of free variables.

Non-boolean relational algebra queries return only tuples consisting of elements within the active domain of the input instance or schema constants, while first-order logic formulas can hold of arbitrary bindings. To extend this correspondence we could restrict the semantics of logical formulas to bindings whose values are either schema constants or lie in the active domain. With this caveat, the correspondence given in Figure 1.2 extends to non-boolean queries.

Another way to extend the logic/relational algebra correspondence is to deal with RQFO formulas that can only be satisfied by active domain elements or schema constants. A formula is *semantically active domain* if it holds only on bindings for which the values are either in the active domain or are schema constants. Since we assume that our set of schema constants is finite, formulas that are semantically active domain are *safe*, in that for each finite input instance, the corresponding query outputs a finite relation instance. Some of the fragments we have already defined contain only safe formulas. For example, in defining UCQs, we enforced that every CQ had the same free variables, and this suffices to ensure safety. All relational algebra formulas are semantically active domain, and hence safe.

RQFO formulas, even those in fragments such as $\exists^+$, are not necessarily safe: for example the $\exists^+$ formula $A(x) \vee B(y)$ can return infinitely many pairs. However, safety is known to be the only obstacle to converting logical formulas to relational algebra queries:

Theorem 1.1 *The following are equivalent in expressiveness:*

- *safe* RQFO *formulas and relational algebra queries;*
- *safe* $\exists^{\neq}$ *formulas and* $USPJAD^{\neq}$ *queries;*
- *safe* $\exists$ *formulas and* $USPJAD$ *queries;*
- *safe* $\exists^{+,\neq}$ *formulas and* $USPJ^{\neq}$ *queries;*
- *safe* $\exists^{+}$ *formulas and* $USPJ$ *queries.*

Further, an RQFO *formula is safe if and only if it is semantically active domain. In each case above, the equivalence is up to mappings between named and positional notation, and assumes that the formulas use only interpreted constants.*

The proof of the first item can be found in [Abiteboul et al., 1995], which further provides effective transformations that realize the equivalence. The other items can be proven using the same transformations. In particular, if we restrict to safe formulas, the correspondences given in Figure 1.2 extend to non-boolean queries. For the majority of this text, we will deal with RQFO formulas which are safe by construction, such as UCQs. By Theorem 1.1, these formulas can all be translated to relational algebra.

Constraints of particular interest. The problems we look at will have as input both a query and a set of constraints. For queries we focus on CQs or on UCQs, as mentioned above. For constraints, we will sometimes consider general RQFO sentences. We also give particular attention to constraints given by *tuple-generating dependencies* (TGDs), given syntactically as

$$\forall \vec{x}\ [\varphi(\vec{x}) \rightarrow \exists \vec{y}\ \rho(\vec{x}, \vec{y})]$$

where φ and ρ are conjunctions of relational atoms, possibly including constants.

A special subclass consists of *Guarded TGDs* (GTGDs), in which φ is of the form $R(\vec{x}) \wedge \varphi'$ where $R(\vec{x})$ contains all the variables of φ'. These in turn subsume *inclusion dependencies* (IDs): where φ and ρ are single atoms in which no variables are repeated and there are no constants. IDs are also-called "referential constraints."

Example 1.15. Recall the integrity constraints from Example 1.2.

$$\forall \mathsf{deptid}\ \forall \mathsf{dname}\ \forall \mathsf{mgrid}\ \mathsf{Department}(\mathsf{deptid}, \mathsf{dname}, \mathsf{mgrid}) \rightarrow \exists N\ \mathsf{Employee}(\mathsf{mgrid}, N, \mathsf{deptid})$$
$$\forall \mathsf{eid}\ \forall \mathsf{ename}\ \forall \mathsf{deptid}\ \mathsf{Employee}(\mathsf{eid}, \mathsf{ename}, \mathsf{deptid}) \rightarrow \exists D \exists M\ \mathsf{Department}(\mathsf{deptid}, D, M).$$

Both of these are IDs. ◁

Relationships between instances. In reformulation problems we often have some "visible" information, and have to consider what underlying structure is consistent with that. The notion of superinstance captures that an instance I' is consistent with the information provided by another instance I. If we have two instances I and I', and for every relation R, $[\![R]\!]_I \subseteq [\![R]\!]_{I'}$, then we say that I is a *subinstance* of I', and I' is a *superinstance* of I. If $\mathsf{adom}(I)$ is the active domain of I, we say that I is an *induced subinstance* of I' if I consists of exactly those facts of I' whose values lie in $\mathsf{adom}(I)$. I being an induced subinstance can be restated as: I is a subinstance of I' and for each fact F of I', if all values in F lie in some fact of I, then F is in I.

Computational problems involving logic. In this work we will make use of basic results about computational problems associated with logical formulas. A first-order logic sentence is *satisfiable* if there is some instance that satisfies it, and *finitely satisfiable* if there is some finite instance that satisfies it. The problem of determining whether an FO sentence is satisfiable is undecidable, and the same is true for determining finite satisfiability [Abiteboul et al., 1995]. Some expressive sublanguages of FO are known to have a decidable satisfiability problem. We will discuss one such, the guarded negation fragment, later in the text. Satisfiability is a special case of the entailment problem, which is discussed in the next section.

1.3 ENTAILMENT AND PROOFS

We will need some results about reasoning with formulas of first-order logic. A basic reasoning problem is to determine whether a sentence λ *entails* another sentence ρ, meaning: in any structure where λ holds, ρ holds. If λ and ρ are RQFO sentences without uninterpreted constants, then we can freely replace "any structure" above with "any instance," since the truth of λ and ρ in a structure only depends on the facts that make up the instance. More generally, we can talk about a formula $\lambda(\vec{x})$ entailing another formula $\rho(\vec{x})$: this means that in any structure and any binding of the variables $\vec{x}$ to elements, if $\lambda(\vec{x})$ holds then $\rho(\vec{x})$ holds.

We write $\lambda \models \rho$ to indicate that λ entails ρ. We often use the following basic fact: when λ and ρ are formulas with free variables, $\lambda \models \rho$ holds exactly when $\lambda' \models \rho'$, where λ' is formed from λ by replacing the free variables with fresh uninterpreted constants, and similarly for ρ'. Thus we can treat free variables in an entailment as if they were uninterpreted constants. In the definition of entailment, we consider *all structures* (in the case of RQFO sentences, *all instances*) whether they are finite or infinite. Throughout the text, by default we use this notion of entailment, and allow our instances or structures to be either finite or infinite. Of course, in databases one is interested only in finite instances. We will use a "trick" to convert results that quantify over arbitrary instances to results that refer only to finite instances later in the text (see, for example, Section 2.8).

We recall that *proof systems* for logics are formal systems for showing that an entailment holds in the logic. A proof system is *complete* if every entailment that is true has a proof. There are many complete proof systems for first-order logic. We now present a sound and complete proof system for first-order logic which is used throughout this work. Following Fitting [1996], we will start with a *tableau proof system*, which is a proof system that assumes classical semantics. We present this for equality-free FO formulas to begin with, discussing the extension to equality later.

Tableau proofs. Our tableau system will work with first-order formulas that are in negation normal form (NNF), i.e., formulas that are built up from atomic formulas and their negations using conjunction, disjunction, existential quantification, and universal quantification. Every first-order formula is equivalent to a formula in NNF that can be obtained by pushing all negations inside as far as possible and applying the rule $\neg\neg\varphi \leftrightarrow \varphi$ to eliminate double negations. Occasionally we will have to talk about "negating" a formula in a tableau, and need to deal with the fact that general negation is not allowed in NNF. If φ is a formula in NNF, we denote by $\sim\varphi$ the formula in NNF obtained by negating φ and pushing the negations inside as far as possible.

Intuitively, a tableau proof is a demonstration that a formula φ is unsatisfiable that consists of a tree of sets of formulas. We start with a root containing φ, and we grow the tree downward, at each stage picking a leaf node and then a formula within the node, generating one or more child nodes which add on consequences of the formula, with the goal of generating a contradiction. Consequences of a formula are generated by breaking down the top-level connective or quantifier in the formula. If the top-level connective is a disjunction, we expand the tableau node containing the formula with two children, representing a case analysis of both options in the disjunction. For other connectives and the quantifiers, the expansion process generates a single child. We make a node a leaf when it has an explicit contradiction, such as an atomic formula and its negation in the same node. When every path ends in a contradiction, we have proven that the root formula is unsatisfiable.

Formally, a *tableau* is a finite tree in which every node is labeled by a finite set of formulas of equality-free first-order logic, and such that each node other than the root is formed from its parent by applying the replacement given by a *tableau expansion rule*.

- The *conjunction rule* states that if we have a leaf node labeled by a set of formulas that includes a conjunction, we can create a single child of that node, whose set of formulas contains all formulas of the parent and in addition both conjuncts of the conjunction. This rule is abbreviated:

$$\frac{\varphi \wedge \psi}{\begin{array}{c}\varphi \\ \psi\end{array}}$$

- The *existential quantifier rule* states that if a leaf node is labeled by a set of formulas that include a block of existential quantifiers, we can create a single child of that node whose set of formulas adds on a subformula formed by replacing the quantified variables by constants that do not occur in any formula of the node. The rule is represented:

$$\frac{\exists \vec{x}\ \varphi(\vec{x}, \vec{t})}{\varphi(\vec{a}, \vec{t})}$$
$$(\vec{a} \text{ fresh uninterpreted constants})\,.$$

- The *disjunction rule* states that if a leaf node is labeled by a set of formulas that includes a disjunction, we can create two children of that node, where each child adds on one of the disjuncts. We represent the rule as:

$$\frac{\varphi \vee \psi}{\varphi \mid \psi}\,.$$

- The *universal quantifier rule* states that if a leaf node is labeled by a set of formulas that includes a universally quantified formula, we can create a child of that node whose set of formulas adds a formula that is an "instantiation" of the universally quantified formula. That is, the new formula is obtained from the universally quantified one by replacing the universally quantified variable by a constant that occurs in some other formula of the node.

$$\frac{\forall \vec{x}\ \varphi(\vec{x},\vec{t})}{\varphi(\vec{v},\vec{t})}$$
($\vec{v}$ constants occurring in the tableau node).

Above, $\varphi(\vec{v},\vec{t})$ indicates substituting any set of constants $\vec{v}$ for $\vec{x}$ in $\varphi(\vec{x},\vec{t})$. Note that *we always interpret the rules as adding formulas to the child*, based on formulas that were present in the parent.[3] Note also that the disjunction rule is the only rule that creates two children.

A branch of a tableau is *closed* if it ends in a leaf node that contains a *clash*, which is either the formula False, or a pair of formulas ψ and $\neg\psi$ for some atomic formula ψ. Otherwise the branch is said to be *open*. A tableau is closed if all of its branches are closed. A *tableau for* $\lambda(\vec{x}) \models \rho(\vec{x})$ is a tableau whose root node is labeled by $\{\lambda(\vec{a}), \sim\rho(\vec{a})\}$ for fresh uninterpreted constant symbols $\vec{a}$. A *closed tableau for* $\lambda \models \rho$ is also known as a *tableau proof of* $\lambda \models \rho$. The basic result that underlies the use of tableau proofs is that they form a complete proof system.

Theorem 1.2 Completeness of tableaux. *If λ, ρ are equality-free first-order formulas in negation normal form, then $\lambda \models \rho$ if and only if there is a tableau proof of $\lambda \models \rho$.*

In particular a first-order formula ρ is valid *(holds in every structure) if and only if there is a closed tableau rooted at $\sim\rho$.*

We sketch the proof only for the second statement, since the first can be reduced to it, proving it only in the case where φ has no free variables.

Proof. For the *soundness* direction: if there is a structure M where ρ does not hold, we claim that every tableau rooted at $\sim\rho$ must have some branch that is not closed, and thus we cannot have a tableau proof of $\models \rho$. The branch in question can be found inductively by starting at the root and traveling downward, mapping the generated constants to elements of M as we do so. The only choice to be made is in nodes where the disjunction rule is applied, and in this case we use the counterexample structure to guide the choice for left-child or right-child, according to which one holds in M.

For the *completeness* direction, we assume a tableau construction process that is *fair*, in the sense that every possible application of a tableau expansion rule is eventually performed. Consider any tableau (possibly infinite) produced by such a fair tableau construction process, and assume that the tableau never closes. Then the tableau would contain a maximal open branch. Take the structure whose facts are precisely the ground facts on the branch in question. Then we can show by induction that every formula on the branch is true in the structure. In particular, the structure satisfies $\neg\rho$ and hence ρ is not valid. □

[3]Copying all formulas from the parent to the child is not necessary in every rule. For example, in the disjunction rule above, we do not need to copy the original disjunction to each child node.

Example 1.16. Figure 1.3 shows a tableau proof witnessing

$$\exists x\ A(x) \land \neg B(x) \land C(x) \models \neg(\forall y\ [(\neg A(y) \land E(y)) \lor B(y)]).$$

In the figure, only a subset of the formulas in non-root nodes are shown, omitting certain formulas that are copied from the parent of the nodes.

The proof creates a tree "top-down," starting with a root node containing the left of the entailment and the negation of the right. In the first step, we proceed by instantiating the existential quantifier in the left to become a new uninterpreted constant c. This creates the node that is the child of the root below. In the next step we break down the conjunctions, resulting in a grandchild of the root.

We can then instantiate the universal quantifier $\forall y$ to any constant. We have only one constant mentioned in the proof at this point, the constant c. Instantiating with c generates a leaf node containing a disjunction, namely $[(\neg A(c) \land E(c)) \lor B(c)]$. We can break down the disjunction to get two children, one in which the disjunction is replaced by $\neg A(c) \land E(c)$, the other where it is replaced by $B(c)$. Finally in the left hand disjunct we can break down the conjunction.

At this point we have a tree with two leaf nodes. In each node we have a clash showing a contradiction. In the left leaf, this is a clash between $A(c)$ and $\neg A(c)$, while in the rightmost leaf this is a clash between $B(c)$ and $\neg B(c)$. Since every branch has a contradiction, we have a complete proof.

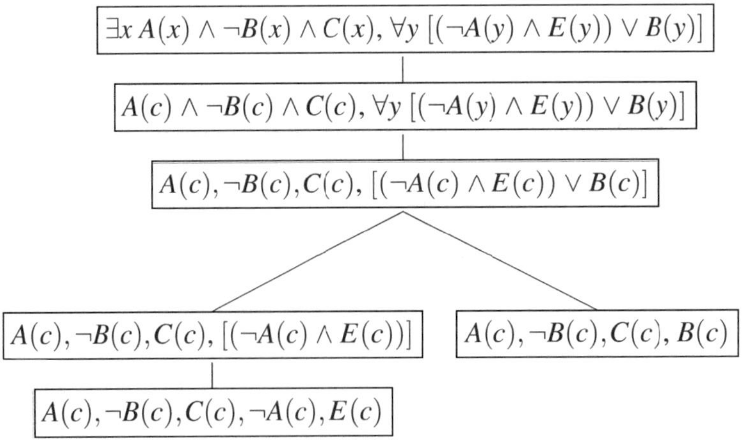

Figure 1.3: A proof of $\exists x\ A(x) \land \neg B(x) \land C(x) \models \neg(\forall y\ [(\neg A(y) \land E(y)) \lor B(y)])$.

◁

Tableaux for relativized-quantifier logic. Recall that in RQFO, quantification is always over elements stored in relations.

$$\exists \vec{x}\ R(\vec{x}, \vec{s}) \wedge \varphi$$

and

$$\forall \vec{x}\ R(\vec{x}, \vec{s}) \rightarrow \varphi.$$

Like general first-order formulas, RQFO formulas can be put into a negation normal form, where we do not have any negation except on atomic formulas. For equality-free RQFO, NNF formulas could be built up from True and False using quantifiers, $\wedge$ and $\vee$. We will also allow atoms and negated atoms as primitive formulas in NNF for equality-free RQFO, since they are useful in tableau proofs.

We do not need a new proof system to capture entailments between RQFO formulas; we can just consider them as specialized classical formulas. However, it will be convenient to have specialized tableau proof rules just for these new quantifiers. The modified quantifier proof rule for existential quantification is simple:

$$\frac{\exists \vec{x}\ (R(\vec{s}, \vec{x}) \wedge \varphi(\vec{s}, \vec{x}, \vec{t}))}{\begin{array}{c} R(\vec{s}, \vec{a}) \\ \varphi(\vec{s}, \vec{a}, \vec{t}) \end{array}} \quad (\vec{a} \text{ fresh uninterpreted constants}) .$$

The rule for relativized universal quantification is:

$$\frac{\forall \vec{x}\ (R(\vec{s}, \vec{x}) \rightarrow \varphi(\vec{s}, \vec{x}, \vec{t})) \quad R(\vec{s}, \vec{v})}{\varphi(\vec{s}, \vec{v}, \vec{t})} .$$

The reader will see that each of these can be thought of as "macros": they are what we would get if we wrote out the relativized formulas as classical formulas, applied the old rules, and immediately eliminated some nodes that had clashes. However, we can show that if we are interested in entailments involving only relativized formulas, the rules are complete. For convenience, we state the result only for sentences:

Theorem 1.3 *For λ, ρ equality-free* RQFO *sentences in NNF we have $\lambda \models \rho$ if and only if there is a closed tableau starting from $\lambda \wedge \sim\rho$, where the classical quantifier rules are replaced by the relativized-quantifier rules above.*

The proof is a variation of the proof of Theorem 1.2, building a counterexample witness from a non-closed tableau proof by combining formulas along a branch.

Entailment in Theorem 1.3 refers to what holds in all *structures*. But since satisfaction of an RQFO sentence depends only on the underlying instance, when λ and ρ are RQFO sentences without constants we can restate an entailment $\lambda \models \rho$ as: every *instance I* satisfying λ also satisfies ρ. If ρ and λ contain schema constants, the same holds provided that λ and ρ contain the necessary "background axioms": all inequalities between distinct schema constants. If λ and ρ do not contain equality, these additional axioms can be dropped. With this disclaimer about constants in mind, we can freely apply tableaux to reason about assertions that an RQFO holds on all instances. When we use tableaux to reason about integrity constraints and queries involving schema constants, we will often assume that the integrity constraints are enhanced with the necessary inequalities.

TGDs and the chase. Tableau proofs form a reasoning system to decide arbitrary first-order entailments. In much of this work, we are interested in special kinds of entailments, of the form

$$Q \wedge \Sigma \models Q^*$$

where Q and Q^* are conjunctive queries and Σ is a conjunction of TGDs.

This entailment problem is often called "query containment with constraints" in the database literature. We often say that Q is *contained in* Q^* *w.r.t. constraints* Σ. A specialized method has been developed to prove these entailments, called *the chase* [Abiteboul et al., 1995, Maier et al., 1979]. The idea in the chase is to

1. start with the assumption Q;
2. iteratively derive consequences with the constraints Σ;
3. stop and declare success if we have generated a set of consequences which "match" Q^*.

We will now describe these steps more precisely.

A proof in the chase consists of a sequence of database instances, beginning with the *canonical database* $\mathsf{CanonDB}(Q)$ of conjunctive query Q: the instance whose elements are the schema constants of Q plus distinct elements c_i for each variable x_i in Q and which has a fact $R(c_1 \ldots c_n)$ for each atom $R(x_1 \ldots x_n)$ of Q. These databases evolve by *firing rules*. Given a set of facts I and a TGD $\delta = \forall x_1 \ldots x_j \; \varphi(\vec{x}) \rightarrow \exists y_1 \ldots y_k \; \rho(\vec{x}, \vec{y})$, a *trigger for* δ is a tuple $\vec{e}$ such that $\varphi(\vec{e})$ holds. If there is no $\vec{f}$ such that $\rho(\vec{e}, \vec{f})$ holds in I, the trigger is *active*. A *rule firing* for a trigger adds facts to I that make $\rho(\vec{e}, \vec{f})$ true, where $f_1 \ldots f_k$ are new values ("chase constants") distinct from any values in I and any schema constants. Such a firing is also called a *chase step*. If the trigger was an active trigger, it is a *restricted chase step*. The definition of a valid chase step depends on a set of schema constants (used in defining the notion of newness), but we will usually omit this, since the set can be inferred from context. A *chase sequence* following a set of TGDs Σ is a sequence of instances where an instance is related to its successor by a rule firing of a dependency in Σ. We refer to the instances in the sequence as *chase configurations*.

Recall that a variable binding that witnesses that a CQ Q^* holds in an instance I is also called a homomorphism of Q^* in I. If I has elements corresponding to the free variables of Q^*, then a homomorphism of CQ Q^* into I that maps each free variable to the corresponding element is called a *match* for Q^* in I. Given CQs Q and Q^*, a *chase proof witnessing the entailment* $Q \wedge \Sigma \models Q^*$ is a sequence beginning with the canonical database of Q, proceeding by applying chase steps with Σ, and ending in a configuration having a match for Q^*.

We can utilize chase proofs for a slightly broader set of entailments than query containment with constraints. For a finite instance I and conjunction of constraints Σ, we abbreviate the sentence $(\bigwedge_{F \in I} F) \wedge \Sigma$ by $I \wedge \Sigma$. Given a CQ Q^* and a finite instance I containing elements for each free variable of Q^*, a *chase proof* for the entailment $I \wedge \Sigma \models Q^*$ is a chase sequence following Σ, beginning with I and ending in a configuration having a match for Q^*.

The following well-known result says that the chase is a complete proof system for these entailments:

Theorem 1.4 *[Fagin et al., 2005, Maier et al., 1979] For any CQ Q^* and finite instance I containing elements for the free variables of Q^*, and any TGD constraints Σ, the entailment $I \wedge \Sigma \models Q^*$ holds if and only if there is a chase proof of this entailment. In particular, chase proofs form a complete proof system for containment of a CQ Q in a CQ Q^* w.r.t. Σ.*

Example 1.17. We recall the schema from Example 1.2, containing information about employees and departments. The constraints Σ were the following two TGDs:

$$\forall \mathsf{deptid}\ \forall \mathsf{dname}\ \forall \mathsf{mgrid}\ \mathsf{Department}(\mathsf{deptid}, \mathsf{dname}, \mathsf{mgrid}) \rightarrow \exists N\ \mathsf{Employee}(\mathsf{mgrid}, N, \mathsf{deptid})$$
$$\forall \mathsf{eid}\ \forall \mathsf{ename}\ \forall \mathsf{deptid}\ \mathsf{Employee}(\mathsf{eid}, \mathsf{ename}, \mathsf{deptid}) \rightarrow \exists D \exists M\ \mathsf{Department}(\mathsf{deptid}, D, M).$$

Consider the following two queries:

$$Q = \{\mathsf{deptid} \mid \exists \mathsf{eid}\ \exists \mathsf{ename}\ \mathsf{Employee}(\mathsf{eid}, \mathsf{ename}, \mathsf{deptid})\}$$
$$Q^* = \{\mathsf{deptid} \mid \exists \mathsf{dname}\ \exists \mathsf{mgrid}\ \mathsf{Department}(\mathsf{deptid}, \mathsf{dname}, \mathsf{mgrid})\}.$$

We claim that Q is contained in Q^* relative to the constraints of the schema. That is, in the more general logical terminology, that:

$$Q \wedge \Sigma \models Q^*.$$

To do this we perform a chase proof. We begin our proof with the "canonical database" of our assumption query $Q = \exists \mathsf{eid}\ \exists \mathsf{ename}\ \mathsf{Employee}(\mathsf{eid}, \mathsf{ename}, \mathsf{deptid})$. That is, we fix constants $\mathsf{eid}_0, \mathsf{ename}_0, \mathsf{deptid}_0$ witnessing the variables to get the "initial database":

$$\mathsf{Employee}(\mathsf{eid}_0, \mathsf{ename}_0, \mathsf{deptid}_0).$$

The second integrity constraint has a trigger on the initial database: the trigger maps variable eid to eid_0, variable ename to constant ename_0, and variable deptid to constant deptid_0. This is an active trigger, since there is no corresponding $\mathsf{Department}$ tuple as required by the constraint. We can now perform a "chase step" with this trigger, to derive a new fact:

$$\mathsf{Department}(\mathsf{deptid}_0, D_0, M_0).$$

where D_0, M_0 are new constants.

We can now match Q^* against the set of facts we have produced, with the homomorphism mapping the free variable deptid in Q^* to the corresponding constant deptid_0. This chase proof witnesses that Q is contained in Q^* $w.r.t.$ Σ. ◁

Tableaux and the chase. We have presented two proof systems, one applicable to arbitrary first-order entailments (tableau proofs) and one that is defined only for a specific kind of entailment. What is the relationship between these two?

It is easy to see that *every chase proof corresponds to a tableau proof.* This has been pointed out before: see, for example, Section 5.4 of Toman and Weddell [2011]. But since we will need to look more closely at this correspondence in Section 4.5, we explain the relationship here, focusing on the case of containment of CQ Q in Q^* under TGDs Σ.

For conjunctive query Q and set of TGDs Σ, a *Q-rooted chase sequence* for Σ is any sequence starting with the canonical database of Q and proceeding by chase steps for Σ. We can make our claimed correspondence precise using a function that maps every Q-rooted chase sequence $\mathsf{config}_0 \dots \mathsf{config}_i$ for Σ to a tableau for $Q \wedge \Sigma \vdash Q^*$, where Q^* is another conjunctive query. Each tableau node will include Q, the formula $\sim Q^*$ formed by converting the negation of Q^* into a RQFO formula, and similarly the RQFO equivalents of all constraints in Σ. For example, if Q^* is

$$\exists \vec{y}\ B_1(\vec{x}_1, \vec{y}_1) \wedge B_2(\vec{x}_2, \vec{y}_2).$$

Then $\sim Q^*$ converted to RQFO will be:

$$\forall \vec{y}\ B_1(\vec{x}_1 \vec{y}_1) \rightarrow \neg B_2(\vec{x}_2, \vec{y}_2).$$

For a TGD

$$\forall x_1 x_2\ U(x_1) \wedge V(x_2) \rightarrow W(x_1, x_2)$$

we would convert it to RQFO as

$$\forall x_1\ U(x_1) \rightarrow [\forall x_2\ V(x_2) \rightarrow W(x_1, x_2)].$$

For each configuration config_i in the chase sequence, we will have a tableau node $\mathsf{TabNode}_i$ containing all of the chase facts in config_i, unioned with Σ and $\sim Q^*$ converted as above.

Consider a chase step that takes configuration config_i to config_{i+1}. This involves a TGD

$$\tau = \forall \vec{x}\ \rho_1(\vec{x}) \rightarrow \exists \vec{y}\ \rho_2(\vec{x}, \vec{y})$$

where the left-hand side has a homomorphism h mapping the variables $\vec{x}$ into config_i. We can mimic this step via two sets of tableau evolution rules in the RQFO variant of the tableau proof system. The first set of rules instantiates all universally quantified variables $\vec{x}$ in τ, using repeated applications of the relativized universal quantifier rule, to get $\rho_2' = \exists \vec{y}\ \rho_2[x_1 := h(x_1) \dots x_n := h(x_n)]$. The next step applies the relativized existential quantification rule repeatedly to instantiate each y_i with a fresh uninterpreted constant c_i.

This process preserves the invariant that the formulas in node $\mathsf{TabNode}_i$ consist of those in config_i unioned with Σ and $\sim Q$. If we have a match h of Q^* in some configuration config_i, we can close this tableau by adding steps that instantiate the universal quantifiers in $\sim Q^*$ using h to get a closed tableau.

Example 1.18. We rephrase the chase proof corresponding to Example 1.17 as a tableau proof. Recall that Q is $\exists \mathsf{eid}\ \exists \mathsf{ename}\ \mathsf{Employee}(\mathsf{eid}, \mathsf{ename}, \mathsf{deptid})$.
In this case, $\sim Q^*$ is

$$\forall \mathsf{dname}\ \forall \mathsf{mgrid}\ \mathsf{Department}(\mathsf{deptid}, \mathsf{dname}, \mathsf{mgrid}) \rightarrow \mathsf{False}.$$

The corresponding tableau proof showing that $Q \wedge \Sigma \vdash Q^*$ is shown in Figure 1.4.

$$\exists \mathsf{eid}\ \exists \mathsf{ename}\ \mathsf{Employee}(\mathsf{eid}, \mathsf{ename}, \mathsf{deptid}),\ \Sigma,\ \sim Q^*$$

$$\mathsf{Employee}(\mathsf{eid}_0, \mathsf{ename}_0, \mathsf{deptid}_0),\ \Sigma,\ \sim Q^*$$

$$\mathsf{Employee}(\mathsf{eid}_0, \mathsf{ename}_0, \mathsf{deptid}_0)\ ,\ \mathsf{Department}(\mathsf{deptid}_0, D, M),\ \Sigma,\ \sim Q^*$$

$$\mathsf{Employee}(\mathsf{eid}_0, \mathsf{ename}_0, \mathsf{deptid}_0)\ ,\ \mathsf{Department}(\mathsf{deptid}_0, D, M),\ \mathsf{False},\ \Sigma,\ \sim Q^*$$

Figure 1.4: Tableau translation of the chase proof for Example 1.17.

◁

In summary, we see that chase proofs are a kind of tableau proof. The tableaux that correspond to chase proofs are very special, in that universal quantification and existential quantification rules occur in tandem, and disjunction plays only a very limited role.

Chasing until termination. One way to find a chase proof is to "chase an initial instance as much as possible." For any set of TGDs Σ and initial instance I, we could just fire rules in an arbitrary order, making sure that any rule that is triggered fires eventually. The union of all facts generated will give an instance that satisfies the constraints, but it may be infinite. We refer to this as *the result of chasing I with Σ*. There will be many such instances depending on the order of rules fired, but they will all satisfy the same conjunctive queries, by Theorem 1.4.

Sometimes one can fully chase an initial instance and get a finite chase sequence and finite final configuration. A *restricted chase sequence* is one that makes only restricted chase steps (i.e., steps using active triggers). One can show that allowing only restricted chase steps does not jeopardize completeness of the chase. An advantage of restricted chase sequences is that we can get to the point where no steps are applicable, and at this point we can cut off the search. A finite restricted chase sequence *terminates* if in the final configuration there are no active triggers, that is, eventually no rules can fire that add new witnesses. If we have a terminating chase sequence beginning with the canonical database of Q, Theorem 1.4 implies that for any conjunctive query Q^*, Q is contained in Q^* *w.r.t.* the constraints if and only if Q^* has a match in the final configuration of the chase sequence. If a set of TGD constraints have the property that for any initial instance every maximal restricted chase sequence is terminating, we say that the constraints *have terminating chase*.

1.4 SUMMARY

We have explained the problems that we focus on throughout the book. We have also gone through definitions of the constraints and queries that we consider, and the systems we use for reasoning with them. We summarize some of the major points to keep in mind in reading the remaining chapters:

- The main integrity constraint languages of interest to us are general RQFO sentences and the subclass of these known as TGDs.
- The main query languages of interest are:
  - queries in Relational Algebra, which have the same expressiveness as safe RQFO formulas;
  - $USPJAD$ queries, which have the same expressiveness as safe $\exists$ formulas;
  - $USPJ$ queries, which have the same expressiveness as safe $\exists^+$ formulas.

  There are also variations of these languages in the presence of equality. The main impact of these variations is that they allow us to express inequalities (e.g., there are three distinct elements in relation U).
- Integrity constraints and queries can make use of interpreted constants from the schema. Constants used in tableau proofs are uninterpreted; this implies that distinct constants need not be equal, and we must assign a value to a constant to know whether a formula containing it is true. In contrast, constants mentioned in a schema are interpreted; they are assumed to represent some fixed value, and distinct constants are assumed to represent distinct values.
- We will need to be able to reason about queries and constraints, and in particular to look at entailments between formulas.
  - To reason about general first-order formulas or about RQFO formulas, we can use the tableau proof system.
  - To reason about containment of CQs under TGDs we can use the chase, which can be seen as a special form of tableau.
  - Entailment is always considered over all structures (or all instances, for RQFO) finite or infinite. This is not the same as reasoning over all finite instances, but for some specialized classes of formulas and constraints (discussed later in the text), the two notions will turn out to be equivalent.

1.5 BIBLIOGRAPHIC REMARKS

A fundamental reference for the foundations of databases is Abiteboul, Hull, and Vianu [Abiteboul et al., 1995]. It covers database schemas as well as the use of first-order logic as a query language. The material on first-order languages includes classical first-order logic, fragments of first-order logic, and relational algebra. The text also goes into detail on the key issues arising in applying first-order logic within databases, which we have discussed only briefly here:

- the "notation mismatch": the fact that variable bindings and reference to positions with a tuple are used in logic, while named attributes are used in relational algebra and all practical database query languages;
- the range of quantified variables: as we have mentioned, the classical semantics of first-order logics quantifies over domains, while the common database approach quantifies over the active domain of the database;
- the treatment of constant symbols: classical logic deals with uninterpreted constants, while for database applications interpreted constants are more convenient;
- the range of free variables: the fact that database query languages such as relational algebra always return elements from the active domain unioned with a set of constants that is independent of the input, while first-order formulas can hold of infinitely many bindings.

The material on tableau proofs can be found in a number of textbooks on logic for computer science, such as [Ben-Ari, 2012]. Our presentation of tableau proof systems follows the approach outlined by Smullyan, found in Fitting's textbook [Fitting, 1996]. A full proof of completeness of the method can be found there.

Two standard references for the chase method are [Fagin et al., 2005, Maier et al., 1979], and overviews can be found in Deutsch and Nash [2009], Deutsch et al. [2008]. A longer introduction to the chase method can be found in the survey of [Onet, 2013]. The chase has many applications in data management—see, e.g., [Haas et al., 2005]. The prior texts distinguish several specialized notions of chase sequence, while we focus on the restricted chase here. We have defined the notion of a class of constraints "having terminating chase" to mean that for any initial instance *all* chase sequences terminate. But in all of the decidability results in this text it would suffice to have the weaker requirement that for any initial instance *some* chase sequence terminates. This is a strictly weaker requirement, as shown in [Onet, 2013].

The book by Toman and Weddell [2011] includes an overview of tableau proofs and the relationship of the chase to tableaux.

We refer to the complexity of computational problems throughout the text, in terms of standard complexity classes (for example NP, EXPTIME). The definitions of these classes can be found in a textbook such as [Papadimitriou, 1994]. We do not use any non-trivial theorems from complexity theory.

CHAPTER 2

Vocabulary-based Target Restrictions

In this chapter we look at the problem of query reformulation in the presence of integrity constraints, where a query is defined over a *source* vocabulary, the goal is to translate it into a query over a *target* vocabulary, and the constraints relate tables in the source vocabulary to the target vocabulary. This relates to a broad range of problems in databases, including view-based query reformulation, data integration, and query optimization. We will show how this problem can be approached via the technique of interpolation.

We first explain what the interpolation-based approach is and connect it with results from mathematical logic. We then go through the application of interpolation to reformulation in detail, first in the case where the goal is a reformulation as a restricted-quantifier first-order query, then varying the target of reformulation to fragments of first-order logic. After completing our application of the technique, we provide an analysis of how it can be used to get effective reformulation for restricted classes of constraints.

Reformulating queries. Let $\mathcal{S}$ be a collection of relations, Σ a set of integrity constraints, and $\mathcal{T}$ a subset of $\mathcal{S}$. Given a query Q specified by a logical formula with n free variables over $\mathcal{S}$, our first goal will be to get a *first-order reformulation of Q over $\mathcal{T}$ with respect to Σ*. This means a query $Q_{\mathcal{T}}$ given by a relativized-quantifier first-order formula using only the relations in $\mathcal{T}$ such that for every instance I satisfying Σ,

$$\forall x_1 \ldots x_n \; Q(x_1 \ldots x_n) \leftrightarrow Q_{\mathcal{T}}(x_1 \ldots x_n)$$

holds in I. We use the same notation when Q is a relational algebra query, identifying its output attributes with free variables. Thus a reformulation is another query $Q_{\mathcal{T}}$ that is *equivalent to Q w.r.t. Σ* or *answers Q w.r.t. Σ*, meaning that they have the same output on instances satisfying Σ.

2.1 REFORMULATING QUERIES USING INTERPOLATION

We begin our exposition of the interpolation-based approach with the connection between interpolation and reformulation discovered by Segoufin and Vianu in [Segoufin and Vianu, 2005] and explored further in [Nash et al., 2010].

2.1.1 FROM A SEMANTIC PROPERTY TO A FIRST-ORDER REFORMULATION

Let us return to the "meta-algorithm" for reformulating a query Q with respect to a target language and a set of constraints, mentioned in the introduction. Recall that step (1) is to identify a property that Q must have in order to admit the desired reformulation. Clearly, for Q to have any reformulation over $\mathcal{T}$, its output should depend only on the interpretations of the relations in $\mathcal{T}$. This has been formalized by the notion of *determinacy* for database views and queries, and we extend the definition here to the setting where there are constraints given by RQFO sentences.

If Σ is a collection of RQFO constraints, we say that an RQFO query Q over $\mathcal{S}$ is *determined over $\mathcal{T}$ relative to Σ* if:

> For any two instances I and I' that satisfy Σ and have the same interpretation of all relations in $\mathcal{T}$ (that is, they have the same T-facts for each $T \in \mathcal{T}$) $[\![Q]\!]_I = [\![Q]\!]_{I'}$.

Example 2.1. We return to the schema of Example 1.2, where the vocabulary consists of the Department and Employee relations, the constraints Σ are inclusion dependencies from Employee to Department (on deptid) and from Department to Employee (on mgrid and deptid), while the target signature $\mathcal{T}$ consists of only Department.

Suppose our query Q asks for the ids of all employees. We claim that Q is *not* determined over $\mathcal{T}$ relative to Σ. To see this, consider two instances I and I', such that I consists of facts:

$$\{\text{Employee}(123, \text{"Jones"}, 1112), \text{Employee}(134, \text{"Smith"}, 1112), \\ \text{Department}(1112, \text{mathematics}, 134)\}$$

and I' consists of facts

$$\{\text{Employee}(134, \text{"Smith"}, 1112), \text{Department}(1112, \text{mathematics}, 134)\}$$

I and I' both satisfy the schema constraints, and they have the same restriction to Department, but the output of Q on I includes employee id 123, while Q evaluated on I' does not.

We have shown via witnesses I and I' that Q is not determined over $\mathcal{T}$ *w.r.t.* Σ. ◁

A special case of interest is where the relations in the restricted vocabulary $\mathcal{T}$ are "virtual tables" defined by *view definitions*. For each $V \in \mathcal{T}$ of arity n there is a corresponding query $Q_V(x_1 \ldots x_n)$, while the constraints Σ consist only of the statements that a view contains exactly those tuples that satisfy its definition: $\forall \vec{x}\ V(\vec{x}) \leftrightarrow Q_V(\vec{x})$. In this case, determinacy of another query Q with respect to $\mathcal{T}$ and Σ can be rephrased as:

> For any two instances I and I', if I and I' yield the same results for each Q_V, then they yield the same results for Q.

Segoufin and Vianu use the terminology "Q is determined by the views $\{Q_V : V \in \mathcal{T}\}$." We will apply our methodology to the semantic property of determinacy, turning it into a proof goal, and showing that reformulations can be read off from these proofs witnessing the proof goal. In the process we will re-prove the following result of Segoufin and Vianu:

Theorem 2.1 *[Segoufin and Vianu, 2005] If* RQFO *query Q is determined over $\mathcal{T}$ with respect to constraints Σ in* RQFO, *then Q has an* RQFO *reformulation over $\mathcal{T}$ with respect to Σ.*

In particular, if Q is determined over views $\{Q_V : V \in \mathcal{T}\}$, there is an RQFO *query Q' mentioning only the view relations $V \in T$ such that evaluating Q' with V replaced by the output of Q_V gives the same result as evaluating Q on the input instance.*

Translating the semantic property to an entailment. Returning to Step (2) of our "meta-algorithm" from Chapter 1, we write out the semantic property (in this case, determinacy) as a proof goal. We now formalize what this means.

Recall from Section 1.3 that an *entailment* is a statement of the form $\lambda(\vec{x}) \models \rho(\vec{x})$, which means that for every instance I and any binding bind of $\vec{x}$, if instance I with binding bind satisfies λ then it satisfies ρ. By convention, we write $\models \rho$ to mean True $\models \rho$: that is, ρ holds in every structure. Let us extend our original signature for the constraints Σ and the query Q by making a copy R' of every relation $R \in \mathcal{S}$. Let Q' be the copy of Q on the new relations, and Σ' be the copy of the constraints Σ on the new relations. Our assumption of determinacy of Q can be restated as an entailment:

$$\models \forall \vec{x}\ [\Sigma \wedge \Sigma' \wedge (\bigwedge_{T \in \mathcal{T}} \forall \vec{y}\ T(\vec{y}) \leftrightarrow T'(\vec{y})) \wedge Q(\vec{x}) \rightarrow Q'(\vec{x})]$$

Or, rewriting,

$$\Sigma \wedge Q(\vec{x}) \models [(\bigwedge_{T \in \mathcal{T}} \forall \vec{y}\ T(\vec{y}) \leftrightarrow T'(\vec{y})\ ) \wedge \Sigma'] \rightarrow Q'(\vec{x})$$

This is the *entailment associated with determinacy.*

How interpolation for the entailment gives a reformulation. Going back to our general plan:

1. We have isolated a *semantic property* that an input query Q must have with respect to the target $\mathcal{T}$ and constraints Σ in order to have a relativized-quantifier first-order reformulation: it must be determined over $\mathcal{T}$ w.r.t. Σ.

2. We have expressed this property as an entailment:

$$\Sigma \wedge Q(\vec{x}) \models [(\bigwedge_{T \in \mathcal{T}} \forall \vec{y}\ T(\vec{y}) \leftrightarrow T'(\vec{y})) \wedge \Sigma'] \rightarrow Q'(\vec{x}).$$

We now relate this to *interpolants.*

If $\lambda \models \rho$ is an entailment, an *interpolant* is a formula χ, such that:

- $\lambda \models \chi$ and $\chi \models \rho$
- Every relation in χ occurs in both λ and ρ.

Interpolation theorems state that any entailment for formulas in a logic L has an interpolant in logic L, possibly satisfying additional conditions.

We will complete the plan by:

- showing that an interpolant for this entailment gives the desired reformulation;
- developing an algorithm to extract these interpolants.

We start with the first item, showing that an interpolant for the entailment above represents the first-order reformulation we want:

Proposition 2.2 *[Craig, 1957b] Suppose Q is a first-order logic formula and Σ is a first-order sentence. Let χ be any interpolant for the entailment*

$$\Sigma \wedge Q \models [(\bigwedge_{T \in \mathcal{T}} \forall \vec{y}\, T(\vec{y}) \leftrightarrow T'(\vec{y})) \wedge \Sigma'] \rightarrow Q'.$$

Then χ uses only the relations in $\mathcal{T}$, and is equivalent to Q for structures that satisfy Σ.

Proof. Note that on the right side of the entailment the only relations from the left that occur are in $\mathcal{T}$. Thus any relation common to the left and right must be contained in $\mathcal{T}$. We conclude that the interpolant χ can use only relations in $\mathcal{T}$, as desired.

Since $\Sigma \wedge Q \models \chi$, we know that for instances satisfying the constraints Σ, we have $Q \rightarrow \chi$.

We argue that $\chi \models \Sigma \rightarrow Q$. Fix instance I and binding bind for the free variables of χ such that $\chi \wedge \Sigma$ holds in I with bind. Let $I + I'$ be formed by adding, for each relation R, a relation R' with $[\![R]\!]_{I+I'} = [\![R']\!]_{I+I'} = [\![R]\!]_I$. The instance $I + I'$ with the binding bind satisfies $\chi \wedge [(\bigwedge_{T \in \mathcal{T}} \forall \vec{x}\, T(\vec{x}) \leftrightarrow T'(\vec{x})) \wedge \Sigma']$. Since $\chi \models [(\bigwedge_{T \in \mathcal{T}} \forall \vec{x}\, T(\vec{x}) \leftrightarrow T'(\vec{x})) \wedge \Sigma'] \rightarrow Q'$, we know that $I + I'$ with binding bind satisfies Q'. By the construction of $I + I'$, this means $I \models Q$. This completes the argument that $\chi \models \Sigma \rightarrow Q$.

We have shown that for an instance satisfying Σ, Q holds of a binding for the free variables if and only if χ holds of the binding, as required in the proposition. □

2.1.2 CRAIG INTERPOLATION AND BETH DEFINABILITY

We have thus completed all the steps of the meta-algorithm, provided that we have a way to get RQFO interpolants from an entailment between RQFO formulas. As a "warm-up," we first prove the following, which shows how to extract classical FO interpolants from an entailment between classical FO formulas:

Theorem 2.3 *[Craig, 1957a] If λ and ρ are first-order logic formulas and $\lambda \models \rho$, then there is an interpolant χ in classical first-order logic. If λ and ρ do not contain equality, then the interpolant does not contain equality either.*

Theorem 2.3 is known as the *Craig Interpolation Theorem* (CIT below), and a χ having the required properties is called a *Craig Interpolant* for the entailment. We will reprove the CIT, and then prove a variant of the CIT for RQFO, which will complete the proof of Theorem 2.1, giving our first instantiation of the meta-algorithm.

Proving the CIT. Recall that we had a complete proof system for the classical semantics of first-order logic, the tableau proof system. In tableau proofs for $\lambda \models \rho$, we have a tree of formulas whose root is labeled with $\lambda \wedge \sim\rho$. Our goal will be to read off interpolants from these proof trees.

To do this, we label our tableau proof trees with "provenance" information, tracking which component of the root was responsible for a derivation. A *labeled tableau* will be a finite tree in which every node contains a finite set of labeled formulas, where the label of the formula is LEFT or RIGHT. We write a labeled formula as LEFT : φ or RIGHT : φ. We sometimes refer to LEFT or RIGHT as a "bias" and say that a labeled formula LEFT : φ has LEFT as its bias and a labeled formula RIGHT : φ has RIGHT as its bias.

We revise the rules for growing a tableau to include the bias labels. Using the same notation for presenting rules as in Section 1.3, the revision is:

$$\frac{X : \varphi \wedge \psi}{\begin{array}{c} X : \varphi \\ X : \psi \end{array}} \qquad\qquad \frac{X : \exists \vec{x}\ \varphi(\vec{x}, \vec{t})}{X : \varphi(\vec{a}, \vec{t})}\ (\vec{a}\text{ fresh})$$

$$\frac{X : \varphi \vee \psi}{X : \varphi \mid X : \psi} \qquad\qquad \frac{X : \forall \vec{x}\ \varphi(\vec{x}, \vec{t})}{X : \varphi(\vec{v}, \vec{t})}.$$

Above X can be either LEFT or RIGHT. The formula labels play no role in the soundness and completeness arguments for the tableau calculus, but they are important for the interpolant calculation rules.

Recall that a node of a tableau is closed if it either contains X : False, or it contains $X : \alpha$ and $Y : \neg\alpha$, for some $X, Y \in \{\text{LEFT}, \text{RIGHT}\}$ and for some atomic formula α. A tableau is closed if all its branches lead to a closed node. A *labeled tableau for* $\lambda(\vec{x}) \models \rho(\vec{x})$ is a tableau whose root node is labeled by LEFT : $\lambda(\vec{a})$, RIGHT : $\sim\rho(\vec{a})$ for fresh constants $\vec{a}$.

Informally, a formula labeled with LEFT is derived from the LEFT-labeled formulas in its ancestors, and hence in particular is derived from the left side of the entailment. A formula labeled with RIGHT is derived from the RIGHT-labeled formulas in its ancestors, and hence is ultimately derived from the negation of the right side of the entailment. So the bias of a labeled formula within a node of a tableau proof of $\lambda \models \rho$ tells whether it is derived from the assumption λ or from the assumption $\sim\rho$. Note that the formulas in tableau nodes for $\lambda \models \rho$ will be subformulas of λ or ρ, possibly with variables instantiated with (uninterpreted) constants. The proof rules only deal with formulas of a given bias, which is what makes it possible to assign a unique bias to each derived formula. The only interaction between LEFT- and RIGHT-labeled formulas comes from getting a contradiction.

Example 2.2. We go back to Example 1.16, which gave a tableau proof witnessing

$$\exists x\ A(x) \land \neg B(x) \land C(x) \models \neg(\forall y\ [(\neg A(y) \land E(y)) \lor B(y)]).$$

In Figure 2.1, we color the RIGHT-annotated formulas from the proof in blue, while keeping the LEFT formulas in black. We see how the annotations propagate downward with the proof rules.

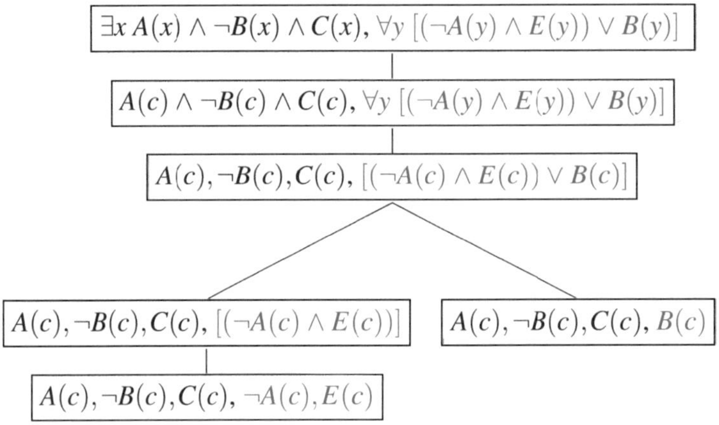

Figure 2.1: Labeling a proof with biases.

◁

Given the completeness of the proof system, we can state an effective version of Theorem 2.3 for classical first-order semantics:

Theorem 2.4 Effective Craig Interpolation. *There is a polynomial time function that takes as input a labeled tableau proof witnessing that $\lambda \models \rho$ (λ, ρ first-order formulas), producing a classical first-order χ such that $\lambda \models \chi \models \rho$, where χ uses only relations that occur in both λ and ρ.*

Further, if λ and ρ are both equality-free, then χ does not use equality either.

We begin the proof with an algorithm that takes as input an equality-free λ and ρ and then explain how to extend to deal with equality. For this we need some additional terminology. We say that a formula χ is an interpolant for a set of biased formulas $\Sigma = \{\text{LEFT} : \lambda_1, \ldots, \text{LEFT} : \lambda_n, \text{RIGHT} : \rho_1, \ldots, \text{RIGHT} : \rho_m\}$ if χ is an interpolant for the entailment

$$(\lambda_1 \land \cdots \land \lambda_n) \models \sim(\rho_1 \land \cdots \land \rho_m) .$$

We say that χ is an interpolant for a node of the tableau if it is an interpolant for the set of all biased formulas in the node. Observe that under this definition an interpolant for the root node of the tableau is precisely an interpolant for the original entailment.

We compute, by induction starting at the leaves, an interpolant for each node of the closed tableau. We use

$$\Gamma \xrightarrow{\text{int}} \chi$$

to indicate that χ is the interpolant calculated for a node for which the set of labeled formulas is Γ. To make the induction work, we will ensure an additional property "interpolating over constants":

Every constant used in χ occurs in both LEFT- and RIGHT-labeled formulas of Γ.

Recall that for a closed tableau, the leaves must contain a clash: either False or a pair of contradictory atomic formulas α and $\neg\alpha$. We can apply the following interpolant calculation rules to leaf nodes:

$$\begin{array}{lcl}
\Sigma \cup \{\text{LEFT} : \alpha, \text{LEFT} : \neg\alpha\} & \xrightarrow{\text{int}} & \mathsf{False} \\
\Sigma \cup \{\text{LEFT} : \alpha, \text{RIGHT} : \neg\alpha\} & \xrightarrow{\text{int}} & \alpha \\
\Sigma \cup \{\text{LEFT} : \neg\alpha, \text{RIGHT} : \alpha\} & \xrightarrow{\text{int}} & \neg\alpha \\
\Sigma \cup \{\text{RIGHT} : \alpha, \text{RIGHT} : \neg\alpha\} & \xrightarrow{\text{int}} & \mathsf{True} \\
\Sigma \cup \{\text{LEFT} : \mathsf{False}\} & \xrightarrow{\text{int}} & \mathsf{False} \\
\Sigma \cup \{\text{RIGHT} : \mathsf{False}\} & \xrightarrow{\text{int}} & \mathsf{True}.
\end{array}$$

We claim that if Γ is associated with a closed leaf node and $\Gamma \xrightarrow{\text{int}} \chi$ is calculated by the rules above, then χ is an interpolant for Γ. This can be verified directly case by case.

We move to a discussion of the inductive rules for propagating the interpolant up the tableau proof tree. We start with the induction step for the conjunction and existential quantification tableau expansion rules. These rules are quite simple: they just copy the interpolant from the child to the parent:

$$\frac{\Sigma \cup \{X : \varphi,\ X : \psi\} \xrightarrow{\text{int}} \chi}{\Sigma \cup \{X : \varphi \wedge \psi\} \xrightarrow{\text{int}} \chi}$$

$$\frac{\Sigma \cup \{X : \varphi(\vec{a}, \vec{t})\} \xrightarrow{\text{int}} \chi}{\Sigma \cup \{X : \exists \vec{x}\ (\varphi(\vec{x}, \vec{t}))\} \xrightarrow{\text{int}} \chi}\ (\vec{a} \text{ fresh uninterpreted constants}) .$$

We see that the orientation of the above interpolant calculation rules is the inverse of the orientation of the corresponding tableau expansion rules. The proof proceeds top-down starting with a tableau composed only of a root node, while the interpolation calculation proceeds bottom up starting from the leaves of the closed tableau.

In stating our interpolation rules we have abbreviated the proof rule a bit, by omitting the copying of the formula that caused the expansion step of the proof. For example, the full labeled proof rule for conjunction expands a node with $\Sigma \cup \{X : \varphi \wedge \psi\}$ by adding a child containing $\Sigma \cup \{X : \varphi \wedge \psi,\ X : \varphi,\ X : \psi\}$. So in the reversed interpolation rule we should have seen

$$\Sigma \cup \{X : \varphi \wedge \psi, X : \varphi,\ X : \psi\} \stackrel{\text{int}}{\longrightarrow} \chi.$$

But we have written

$$\Sigma \cup \{X : \varphi,\ X : \psi\} \stackrel{\text{int}}{\longrightarrow} \chi$$

for brevity. We will continue to abbreviate in the same way for all the other rules below.

The conjunction rule preserves the correctness of the interpolant. That is, whenever $\Sigma \stackrel{\text{int}}{\longrightarrow} \chi$ holds then the conjunction of the LEFT-labeled formulas of Σ entails χ, χ entails the negation of the RIGHT-labeled formulas, χ has the "correct signature" and the "correct set of constants." For the existential rule, we make use of the invariant on constants. In the case of $X = \text{RIGHT}$, we know by induction that:

$$\Sigma_{\text{LEFT}} \models \chi \models \neg(\Sigma_{\text{RIGHT}} \wedge \varphi(\vec{a}, \vec{t}))$$

where Σ_X denotes the formulas occurring in Σ with bias X for $X \in \{\text{LEFT}, \text{RIGHT}\}$. We need to conclude that:

$$\Sigma_{\text{LEFT}} \models \chi \models \neg(\Sigma_{\text{RIGHT}} \wedge \exists \vec{x}\ \varphi(\vec{x}, \vec{t})).$$

This follows as long as we know that χ cannot contain $\vec{a}$. But this is guaranteed by the fact that χ has only constants occurring in Σ_{LEFT}, while $\vec{a}$ cannot occur in Σ_{LEFT}, since it was a fresh constant. The case of $X = \text{LEFT}$ similarly makes use of the fact that χ contains only constants occurring on the right.

The induction step for the disjunction tableau expansion rule is not much harder, although we need to make a case distinction with respect to the bias of the formulas involved:

$$\frac{\Sigma \cup \{\text{LEFT} : \varphi\} \stackrel{\text{int}}{\longrightarrow} \chi_1 \qquad \Sigma \cup \{\text{LEFT} : \psi\} \stackrel{\text{int}}{\longrightarrow} \chi_2}{\Sigma \cup \{\text{LEFT} : \varphi \vee \psi\} \stackrel{\text{int}}{\longrightarrow} \chi_1 \vee \chi_2}$$

$$\frac{\Sigma \cup \{\text{RIGHT} : \varphi\} \stackrel{\text{int}}{\longrightarrow} \chi_1 \qquad \Sigma \cup \{\text{RIGHT} : \psi\} \stackrel{\text{int}}{\longrightarrow} \chi_2}{\Sigma \cup \{\text{RIGHT} : \varphi \vee \psi\} \stackrel{\text{int}}{\longrightarrow} \chi_1 \wedge \chi_2}.$$

Again the soundness of these rules is straightforward. For the first rule, the intuition is: for any $\alpha_1, \alpha_2, \beta, \chi_1, \chi_2$, if $\alpha_1 \models \chi_1 \models \beta$ and $\alpha_2 \models \chi_2 \models \beta$, then $\alpha_1 \vee \alpha_2 \models \chi_1 \vee \chi_2 \models \beta$. For the second rule, the intuition is that for any $\alpha, \chi_1, \chi_2, \beta_1, \beta_2$, if $\alpha \models \chi_1 \models \neg\beta_1$ and $\alpha \models \chi_2 \models \neg\beta_2$, then $\alpha \models \chi_1 \wedge \chi_2 \models \neg(\beta_1 \vee \beta_2)$.

Thus far the interpolants have not introduced quantification at all. The induction step for the universal quantification rule will introduce both existential and universal quantification. The rule requires a case distinction again, based on the bias label of the formula used in the tableau expansion rule. The case where the universal quantification is annotated with bias RIGHT is handled by the rule:

$$\frac{\Sigma \cup \{\text{RIGHT} : \varphi(\vec{v}, \vec{t})\} \xrightarrow{\text{int}} \chi}{\Sigma \cup \{\text{RIGHT} : \forall \vec{x}\ \varphi(\vec{x}, \vec{t})\} \xrightarrow{\text{int}} \exists x_{m_1} \ldots x_{m_k}\ \chi[v_{m_1} := x_{m_1} \ldots v_{m_k} := x_{m_k}]}$$

where $v_{m_1} \ldots v_{m_k}$ are the subset of the v_i occurring in χ that do not occur in a RIGHT formula of Σ.

We now show that this induction step gives an interpolant. The relations occurring in the interpolant are exactly the relations occurring in χ. From the inductive hypothesis we can see that these must occur in both LEFT-and RIGHT-annotated formulas as required. We also need to check that the constants occurring in the interpolant also occur in both a LEFT-and RIGHT-annotated formula in the tableau node. But the v_i's occurring in the interpolant occur in a RIGHT-annotated formula by definition, while all v_i from χ occur in a LEFT-annotated formula by induction. The constants other than those in $\vec{v}$ satisfy this condition by induction.

To complete the argument for correctness, we need to show that the interpolant is implied by the LEFT-annotated formulas and that it implies the negation of the RIGHT-annotated formulas in the parent tableau node. Let λ stand for the LEFT-annotated formulas of Σ and ρ stand for the RIGHT-labeled formulas in Σ.

Then by induction we know that the following implications are valid:

$$\lambda \rightarrow \chi \rightarrow \neg(\varphi(\vec{v}, \vec{t}) \wedge \rho).$$

From this we can infer validity of

$$\lambda \rightarrow \exists \vec{x}\ (\bigwedge_i x_i = v_i \wedge \chi[\vec{v} := \vec{x}])$$

regardless of what the indices i range over. From the hypothesis on χ, φ, ρ we also can conclude

$$\chi \rightarrow \neg((\forall \vec{x}\ \varphi(\vec{x}, \vec{t})) \wedge \rho).$$

For the v_i's in χ that do not occur in ρ, we can replace them by existentially quantified variables, which gives

$$\exists x_{m_1} \ldots x_{m_k}\ \chi[v_{m_1} := x_{m_1} \ldots v_{m_1} := x_{m_k}] \rightarrow \neg((\forall \vec{x}\ \varphi(\vec{x}, \vec{t})) \wedge \rho).$$

This completes the argument that the formula produced in this step is an interpolant.

The second case of interpolation for the universal quantifier rule, where the universal quantification occurs with bias LEFT, is similar:

$$\frac{\Sigma \cup \{\text{LEFT} : \varphi(\vec{v}, \vec{t})\} \xrightarrow{\text{int}} \chi}{\Sigma \cup \{\text{LEFT} : \forall \vec{x}\ \varphi(\vec{x}, \vec{t})\} \xrightarrow{\text{int}} \forall x_{m_1} \ldots x_{m_k}\ \chi[v_{m_1} := x_{m_1} \ldots v_{m_k} := x_{m_k}]}$$

where $v_{m_1} \ldots v_{m_k}$ are the subset of the v_i occurring in χ that do not occur in a LEFT-annotated formula of Σ. Again, the fact that this obeys the requirement for interpolants is easy. The condition on indices guarantees that the invariant on constants is preserved.

For future reference we put the full interpolation algorithm for equality-free classical first-order logic in Figure 2.2. For brevity, we abbreviate the universal quantifier rules slightly, dropping the occurrence of $\forall \vec{x}\ \varphi(\vec{x}, \vec{t})$ in the premise of the interpolation. We will also perform this abbreviation for the variations of the algorithm we present later on.

Example 2.3. Returning to Example 1.16, we calculate the interpolants bottom-up, starting at the leaves in Figure 2.3, with the interpolant shown in red. Each clash involved a mix of LEFT and RIGHT formulas, so each one produced an atom, with the atom matching the LEFT formula.

We can then begin propagating upward, with the first results shown in Figure 2.4. Whenever we have a parent-child connected by a conjunction, we do nothing. The interpolation rule for disjunction used the fact that disjunction was introduced on the right, and hence introduced a conjunction.

The final propagation steps are shown in Figure 2.5. The universal quantifier step uses the fact that the universal quantifier being instantiated occurred in a RIGHT-labeled formula, and hence the corresponding interpolation step introduced an existential quantifier. Since no constants were common to the LEFT and RIGHT-labeled formulas, the substitution eliminated all constants. The interpolation rule for existential quantification, analogous to the rule for conjunction, introduced nothing new.

◁

2.1.3 HANDLING EQUALITY

Up until this point, we have ignored the presence of equality atoms both in proof rules and in interpolation. In addition, we have generated equality atoms even when the entailment does not involve equalities, which does not meet the full requirements of Theorem 2.4. We address these issues now.

We begin by expanding the proof rules. Figure 2.6 shows additional tableau expansion rules to handle equality. These rules express that the equality relation is a congruence, i.e., an equivalence relation that satisfies "replacement of equals by equals" within all relations. Note that the transitivity of the equality relation is captured by the last rule (where α is the equality relation). In the figure, we have included the bias in the tableau rules. For the commutativity rules the bias of the conclusion is just propagated from the hypothesis. The bias of the conclusion in the congruence is chosen to match the bias of the atom α, and the reason for this will be explained below.

$$\Sigma \cup \{\textsc{left} : \varphi, \textsc{left} : \neg\varphi\} \xrightarrow{\text{int}} \mathsf{False}$$
$$\Sigma \cup \{\textsc{left} : \varphi, \textsc{right} : \neg\varphi\} \xrightarrow{\text{int}} \varphi$$
$$\Sigma \cup \{\textsc{right} : \varphi, \textsc{left} : \neg\varphi\} \xrightarrow{\text{int}} \neg\varphi$$
$$\Sigma \cup \{\textsc{right} : \varphi, \textsc{right} : \neg\varphi\} \xrightarrow{\text{int}} \mathsf{True}$$
$$\Sigma \cup \{\textsc{left} : \mathsf{False}\} \xrightarrow{\text{int}} \mathsf{False}$$
$$\Sigma \cup \{\textsc{right} : \mathsf{False}\} \xrightarrow{\text{int}} \mathsf{True}$$

$$\frac{\Sigma \cup \{X : \varphi, X : \psi\} \xrightarrow{\text{int}} \chi}{\Sigma \cup \{X : \varphi \wedge \psi\} \xrightarrow{\text{int}} \chi}$$

$$\frac{\Sigma \cup \{X : \varphi(\vec{a}, \vec{t})\} \xrightarrow{\text{int}} \chi}{\Sigma \cup \{X : \exists\vec{x}(\varphi(\vec{x}, \vec{t}))\} \xrightarrow{\text{int}} \chi} \ (\vec{a} \text{ fresh})$$

$$\frac{\Sigma \cup \{\textsc{left} : \varphi\} \xrightarrow{\text{int}} \chi_1 \quad \Sigma \cup \{\textsc{left} : \psi\} \xrightarrow{\text{int}} \chi_2}{\Sigma \cup \{\textsc{left} : \varphi \vee \psi\} \xrightarrow{\text{int}} \chi_1 \vee \chi_2}$$

$$\frac{\Sigma \cup \{\textsc{right} : \varphi\} \xrightarrow{\text{int}} \chi_1 \quad \Sigma \cup \{\textsc{right} : \psi\} \xrightarrow{\text{int}} \chi_2}{\Sigma \cup \{\textsc{right} : \varphi \vee \psi\} \xrightarrow{\text{int}} \chi_1 \wedge \chi_2}$$

$$\frac{\Sigma \cup \{\textsc{right} : \varphi(\vec{v}, \vec{t})\} \xrightarrow{\text{int}} \chi}{\Sigma \cup \{\textsc{right} : \forall\vec{x}\ \varphi(\vec{x}, \vec{t})\} \xrightarrow{\text{int}} \exists x_{m_1} \ldots x_{m_k}\ \chi[v_{m_1} := x_{m_1} \ldots v_{m_1} := x_{m_k}]}$$

where $v_{m_1} \ldots v_{m_k}$ are the v_i in χ that do not occur in a RIGHT formula of Σ.

$$\frac{\Sigma \cup \{\textsc{left} : \varphi(\vec{v}, \vec{t})\} \xrightarrow{\text{int}} \chi}{\Sigma \cup \{\textsc{left} : \forall\vec{x}\ \varphi(\vec{x}, \vec{t})\} \xrightarrow{\text{int}} \forall x_{m_1} \ldots x_{m_k}\ \chi[v_{m_1} := x_{m_1} \ldots v_{m_1} := x_{m_k}]}$$

where $v_{m_1} \ldots v_{m_k}$ are the v_i in χ that do not occur in a LEFT formula of Σ.

Figure 2.2: Interpolation based on tableaux for classical equality-free first-order logic.

The soundness and completeness proof is extended in a straightforward way. For completeness, we modify the construction of Theorem 1.2. There we assumed that there was no tableau proof and from that, found a maximal open branch that is not closed. From that branch, we could "read off" a counterexample structure whose elements are constants found on the branch. In this case, given an open branch of a tableau we form a structure whose elements are equivalence classes

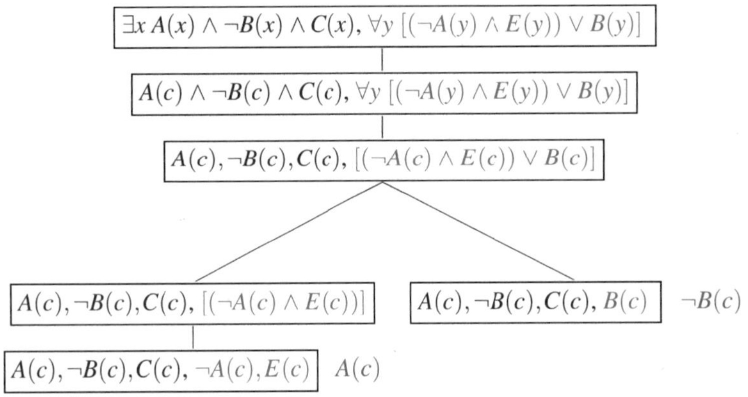

Figure 2.3: Initial steps of interpolation.

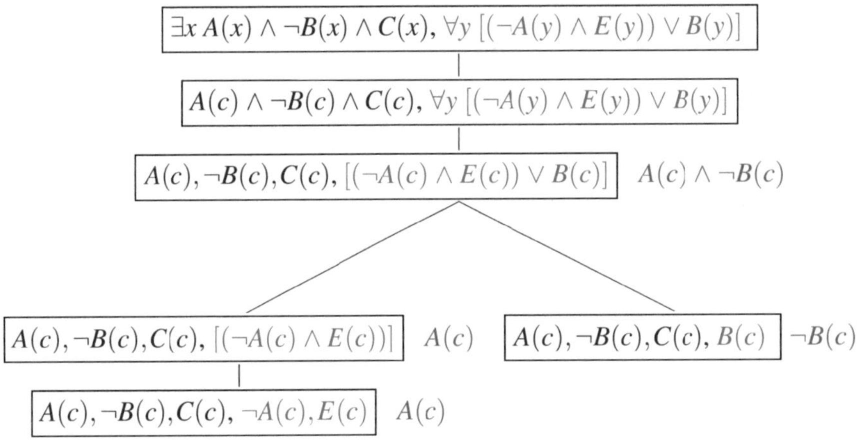

Figure 2.4: First propagation steps of interpolation.

of constants found on the branch, where the equivalence is generated from equalities found on the branch. The rules for equality will guarantee that the structure is well-defined and witnesses that the entailment fails. For example, the equality rules guarantee that the facts holding for an equivalence class are independent of which representative of the equivalence class one picks. The rule (Reflexivity) will guarantee that formulas of the form $\neg a = a$ cannot be generated along a branch. For similar "Henkin-style" constructions, the reader can look at a model theory textbook such as [Chang and Keisler, 1990].

For the interpolant construction, we use the following interpolant calculation rules, which simply propagate the interpolant when one of the simple equality tableau expansion rules is applied.

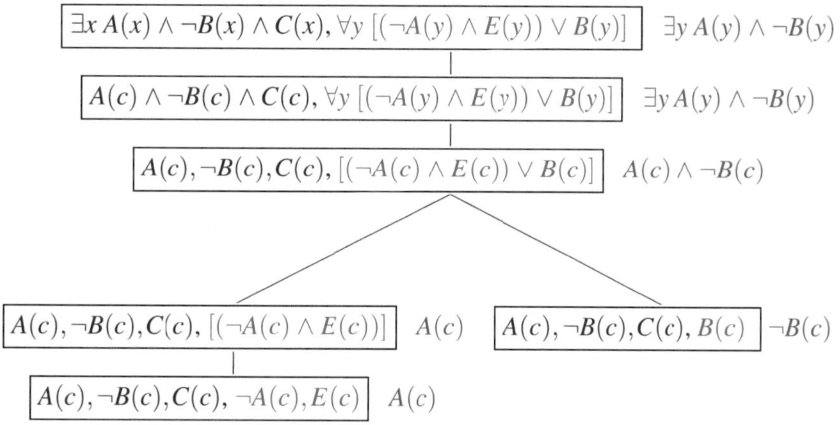

Figure 2.5: Final propagation steps of interpolation.

$$\frac{(a \text{ occurs in an } X\text{-formula in the node})}{X : a = a} \text{ (Reflexivity)}$$

$$\frac{X : a = b}{X : b = a} \text{ (Commutativity)}$$

$$\frac{X : \alpha(a, \vec{t}) \quad Y : a = b}{X : \alpha(b, \vec{t})} \text{ (Congruence)}$$

where α is a relational or equality atom

Figure 2.6: Tableau rules with biases for equality.

$$\frac{\Sigma \cup \{X : a = a\} \xrightarrow{\text{int}} \chi}{\Sigma \xrightarrow{\text{int}} \chi} \ (a \text{ occurs in an } X\text{-formula of } \Sigma)$$

$$\frac{\Sigma \cup \{X : b = a\} \xrightarrow{\text{int}} \chi}{\Sigma \cup \{X : a = b\} \xrightarrow{\text{int}} \chi}$$

The interpolation rules for applications of the congruence rule depend on the bias X of the input $\alpha(a, \vec{t})$ and Y of $a = b$. The rules are shown in Figure 2.7. The idea is that we keep both a and b in the interpolant whenever they are both permitted in the interpolant, and otherwise we will substitute a for b in order to end up with a formula that does not mention b.

Correctness of the interpolation rules for congruence. The interpolation rules corresponding to reflexivity and commutativity of equality are easy to verify. We explain how to derive the interpo-

$$\frac{\Sigma \cup \{\text{LEFT} : \alpha(b,\vec{t})\} \xrightarrow{\text{int}} \chi_1}{\Sigma \cup \{\text{LEFT} : \alpha(a,\vec{t}),\ \text{LEFT} : a = b\} \xrightarrow{\text{int}} \chi_1}$$

$$\frac{\Sigma \cup \{\text{LEFT} : \alpha(b,\vec{t})\} \xrightarrow{\text{int}} \chi_1}{\Sigma \cup \{\text{LEFT} : \alpha(a,\vec{t}),\ \text{RIGHT} : a = b\} \xrightarrow{\text{int}} a = b \rightarrow \chi_1}$$
If b occurs in a LEFT formula of $\Sigma \cup \text{LEFT} : \alpha(a,\vec{t})$

$$\frac{\Sigma \cup \{\text{LEFT} : \alpha(b,\vec{t})\} \xrightarrow{\text{int}} \chi_1}{\Sigma \cup \{\text{LEFT} : \alpha(a,\vec{t}),\ \text{RIGHT} : a = b\} \xrightarrow{\text{int}} \chi_1[b := a]}$$
If b does not occur in a LEFT formula of $\Sigma \cup \{\text{LEFT} : \alpha(a,\vec{t})\}$

$$\frac{\Sigma \cup \{\text{RIGHT} : \alpha(b,\vec{t})\} \xrightarrow{\text{int}} \chi_1}{\Sigma \cup \{\text{RIGHT} : \alpha(a,\vec{t}),\ \text{RIGHT} : a = b\} \xrightarrow{\text{int}} \chi_1}$$

$$\frac{\Sigma \cup \{\text{RIGHT} : \alpha(b,\vec{t})\} \xrightarrow{\text{int}} \chi_1}{\Sigma \cup \{\text{RIGHT} : \alpha(a,\vec{t}),\ \text{LEFT} : a = b\} \xrightarrow{\text{int}} a = b \wedge \chi_1}$$
If b occurs in a RIGHT formula of $\Sigma \cup \{\text{RIGHT} : \alpha(a,\vec{t})\}$

$$\frac{\Sigma \cup \{\text{RIGHT} : \alpha(b,\vec{t})\} \xrightarrow{\text{int}} \chi_1}{\Sigma \cup \{\text{RIGHT} : \alpha(a,\vec{t}),\ \text{LEFT} : a = b\} \xrightarrow{\text{int}} \chi_1[b := a]}$$
If b does not occur in a RIGHT formula of $\Sigma \cup \{\text{RIGHT} : \alpha(a,\vec{t})\}$

Figure 2.7: Interpolation rules associated with application of the congruence rule for equality.

lation rules in Figure 2.7 associated with applying the (Congruence) expansion rule in a tableau proof.

Let us consider treating the congruence rule as an additional "hidden" universal subformula of the form:

$$X : \forall x_a\ x_b\ \vec{y}\ (\alpha(x_a, \vec{y}) \wedge \mathsf{Equal}(x_a, x_b) \rightarrow \alpha(x_b, \vec{y}))$$

where X is chosen to match the bias of a formula $X : \alpha(a,\vec{t})$ in the same node. All of the rules in Figure 2.7 can be derived by tracing through what would happen if the ordinary interpolation algorithm were applied to a node supplemented with this additional labeled subformula, where Equal is treated as an ordinary relation. If we have a tableau node n_0 containing $X : \alpha(a,\vec{t})$ and

$Y : a = b$, we apply the derived rule by converting it to negation normal form:

$$X : \forall x_a \; x_b \; \vec{y} \; (\neg\alpha(x_a, \vec{y}) \vee \neg\mathsf{Equal}(x_a, x_b) \vee \alpha(x_b, \vec{y})).$$

We could next apply the universal quantification rule of tableaux, instantiating x_a to a, x_b to b, $\vec{y}$ to $\vec{t}$, obtaining a node n'_0. We then apply the disjunction rule twice, generating one child node c_1 that is immediately contradictory with $X : \alpha(a, \vec{t})$, another c_2 that is immediately contradictory with Y : Equal(a,b), and another c_3 that includes $X : \alpha(b, \vec{t})$. In each case, the nodes also include the remaining biased subformulas. We generate an interpolant for c_3 by induction, and generate interpolants for c_1 and c_2 using our existing policies, treating Equal(a,b) as any other relation.

Recall that we chose the bias X for this derived rule to be the same as the bias of $\alpha(a, \vec{t})$. In doing this, we ensure that the child node containing $X : \neg\alpha(a, \vec{t})$ and $X : \alpha(a, \vec{t})$ will not generate any occurrence of the relation α in the interpolant. The child node containing $X : \neg\mathsf{Equal}(a, b)$ and $Y : \mathsf{Equal}(a, b)$ may generate an interpolant with Equal, if $Y \neq X$. But this is not a problem, since equality is permitted in an interpolant.

We will give a detailed derivation of the second case in Figure 2.7 using the idea of reducing to interpolation for equality-free first-order logic. This is the case where $X = \text{LEFT}$, $Y = \text{RIGHT}$ and b occurs in a LEFT formula of n_0. Thus we have a node n_0 having LEFT : $\alpha(a, \vec{t})$ and RIGHT : $\mathsf{Equal}(a, b)$ and in addition other formulas Σ. Instantiating the universal quantification in the "hidden rule," we would get a node n'_0 which has, in addition to the formulas of n_0, the labeled formula LEFT : $(\neg\alpha(a, \vec{t}) \vee \neg\mathsf{Equal}(a, b) \vee \alpha(b, \vec{t}))$. Then applying the disjunction rule we would get as children of n'_0 the nodes:

- c_1 containing LEFT : $\alpha(a, \vec{t})$, LEFT : $\neg\alpha(a, \vec{t})$ and other formulas;
- c_2 containing LEFT : $\neg\mathsf{Equal}(a, b)$, RIGHT : $\mathsf{Equal}(a, b)$ and other formulas;
- c_3 containing LEFT : $\alpha(b, \vec{t})$ and other formulas.

We can apply the interpolation rules from before (see Figure 2.2). The interpolation rules applied to c_1 generate interpolant False, the rules applied to c_2 generate interpolant $\neg\mathsf{Equal}(a, b)$, while c_3 inductively generates some interpolant χ_1. We combine these with the rule for $\vee$ introduced with LEFT, which gives us an interpolant for n'_0:

$$\mathsf{False} \vee \neg\mathsf{Equal}(a, b) \vee \chi_1$$

which is the same as $\mathsf{Equal}(a, b) \rightarrow \chi_1$. We must now apply the interpolation rule for universal quantification with bias LEFT from Figure 2.2 to get an interpolant for the original node n_0. Notice that a occurs with both biases in n_0. If b occurs in a LEFT-labeled formula of n_0, then all universally quantified variables that were instantiated occur on both sides, so applying the interpolation rule for universal quantification will just copy the interpolant from n'_0. Thus the final interpolant is $\mathsf{Equal}(a, b) \rightarrow \chi_1$, which matches the second case in Figure 2.7.

Equality-free interpolation and constants. We claim that the basic algorithm we have presented for Craig Interpolation ensures the additional property:

> If $\varphi \models \psi$ and the formulas φ and ψ both do not make use of the equality symbol, then the interpolant will not include equality.

This is the last assertion in Theorem 2.3 and Theorem 2.4. It can be verified by observing that the interpolation rules for connectives, quantifiers, and atomic clashes do not introduce equalities.

The entailments of interest to us will be of the form $Q \wedge \Sigma \models Q'$, where Q, Q' are conjunctive queries and Σ is a set of integrity constraints. When we apply Craig Interpolation to reformulation, we will in principle need to include in our integrity constraints all inequality assertions between schema constants that we know to be unequal. For example, if "Smith" and "Jones" are schema constants, we should include an integrity constraint "Smith" $\neq$ "Jones". Because of this, the reader may worry that the extra condition "the formulas λ and ρ in the entailments do not contain inequalities" will never be satisfied when we apply interpolation. However, we can show that if Q, Q' do not contain equality, and Σ contains equality only in the form of "ground inequalities" (inequalities between constants) then these inequalities can be dropped from the entailment. Thus we can generally weaken conditions of the form "the constraints do not contain equality" to "the constraints do not contain equality except in ground inequalities."

Summary. We have now completed a constructive proof of the CIT for classical first-order logic, Theorem 2.4. We proceed by taking a tableau proof that witnesses the entailment, labeling it with biases, and then creating interpolants "bottom-up." This also can be seen as completing the argument for the first instantiation of the meta-algorithm, in that it gives a recipe for producing a classical first-order logic reformulation from a proof that a query is determined.

We will extend the interpolation theorem and its application to reformulation throughout the rest of this chapter.

2.2 RELATIVIZED-QUANTIFIER INTERPOLATION

We discuss the modification of CIT needed to take a proof witnessing an entailment for relativized-quantifier first-order formulas and produce an RQFO interpolant. This will allow us to instantiate the meta-algorithm for RQFO constraints: (i) we consider again the semantic property of determinacy for a query with respect to the subsignature $\mathcal{T}$ and the constraints Σ; (ii) we formalize determinacy as an entailment as before, but note that if the constraints are RQFO sentences, then the entailment will be between RQFO formulas; (iii) we use relativized-quantifier interpolation to produce an interpolant; (iv) from Proposition 2.2, we know that the interpolant will give us a reformulation. In doing this, we will provide a constructive proof of Theorem 2.1.

The interpolation result we need is a relativized-quantifier version of Craig interpolation, a variant of a result proven originally by Martin Otto.

Theorem 2.5 Relativized-Quantifier Craig Interpolation Theorem. *[Otto, 2000] If λ and ρ are* RQFO *formulas such that $\lambda \models \rho$, then there is an interpolant χ in* RQFO. *Furthermore, if λ and ρ do not use equality, neither does χ.*

For simplicity, in the argument below we assume that the formulas are equality-free. The extension to equality is handled using the same additional axioms as for the classical CIT.

Modifying labeled tableaux and interpolation for RQFO. To extend the proof technique, we start with the tableau proof system for RQFO formulas in NNF outlined in Section 1.3.

The proof system for RQFO differed from the one for classical FO only in the proof rules for quantifiers. Thus we need to extend the quantification rules for RQFO to give a bias labeling to the conclusions.

The existential quantifier rule is:

$$\frac{X : \exists \vec{x}\ (R(\vec{s},\vec{x}) \wedge \varphi(\vec{s},\vec{x},\vec{t}))}{\begin{array}{c} X : R(\vec{s},\vec{a}) \\ X : \varphi(\vec{s},\vec{a},\vec{t}) \end{array}} \quad (\vec{a} \text{ fresh})\ .$$

The relativized universal quantification rule is more interesting, since here we have to deal for the first time with a rule in which two premises—a relativized universally quantified formula $\forall \vec{x}\ (R(\vec{s},\vec{x}) \rightarrow \varphi(\vec{s},\vec{x},\vec{t}))$ and an atomic formula $R(\vec{s},\vec{v})$—possibly with different biases, interact to generate a conclusion. We propagate the bias of the universally quantified formula to the conclusion:

$$\frac{X : \forall \vec{x}\ (R(\vec{s},\vec{x}) \rightarrow \varphi(\vec{s},\vec{x},\vec{t})) \quad Y : R(\vec{s},\vec{v})}{X : \varphi(\vec{s},\vec{v},\vec{t})}\ .$$

We also need to add "bottom-up" interpolation rules for those quantification rules to complete the interpolation algorithm. We present the interpolation rules for the relativized quantifiers in Figure 2.8. The remaining rules are the same as for classical FO. The rules for relativized universal quantification involve a case distinction based on the biases of the two premises. In both of the cases where the two premises have the same bias, we just propagate the interpolant. In the case of distinct biases, we have interpolation rules similar to those associated with instantiating a universal quantifier in classical logic.

Correctness of the modified proof and interpolation rules. We justify the labeling of formulas as well as the interpolation algorithm given in Figure 2.8. To do this we "unwind" the relativized-quantifier rules to see what they would have corresponded to in a classical tableau system.

It is not difficult to see that the rule for existential quantification corresponds to what would happen if the relativized existential quantification were rewritten to a classical formula and the previous interpolation algorithm were applied.

$$\frac{\Sigma \cup \{\text{LEFT} : \varphi(\vec{s},\vec{v},\vec{t})\} \xrightarrow{\text{int}} \chi}{\Sigma \cup \{\text{LEFT} : \forall \vec{x}\ (R(\vec{s},\vec{x}) \rightarrow \varphi(\vec{s},\vec{x},\vec{t})), \text{RIGHT} : R(\vec{s},\vec{v})\} \xrightarrow{\text{int}} \chi'}$$

with $\chi' = \forall x_{m_1} \dots x_{m_k}\ (R(\vec{s},\vec{v}) \rightarrow \chi)[v_{m_1} := x_{m_1} \dots v_{m_k} := x_{m_k}]$ where $v_{m_1} \dots v_{m_k}$ are the v_i in $R(\vec{s},\vec{v}) \wedge \chi$ that do not occur in a LEFT-formula of Σ.

$$\frac{\Sigma \cup \{\text{RIGHT} : \varphi(\vec{s},\vec{v},\vec{t})\} \xrightarrow{\text{int}} \chi}{\Sigma \cup \{\text{RIGHT} : \forall \vec{x}\ (R(\vec{s},\vec{x}) \rightarrow \varphi(\vec{s},\vec{x},\vec{t})), \text{LEFT} : R(\vec{s},\vec{v})\} \xrightarrow{\text{int}} \chi'}$$

with $\chi' = \exists x_{m_1} \dots x_{m_k}\ (R(\vec{s},\vec{v}) \wedge \chi)[v_{m_1} := x_{m_1} \dots v_{m_k} := x_{m_k}]$ where $v_{m_1} \dots v_{m_k}$ are the v_i in $R(\vec{s},\vec{v}) \wedge \chi$ that do not occur in a RIGHT-formula of Σ.

$$\frac{\Sigma \cup \{\text{LEFT} : \varphi(\vec{s},\vec{v},\vec{t})\} \xrightarrow{\text{int}} \chi}{\Sigma \cup \{\text{LEFT} : \forall \vec{x}\ (R(\vec{s},\vec{x}) \rightarrow \varphi(\vec{s},\vec{x},\vec{t})), \text{LEFT} : R(\vec{s},\vec{v})\} \xrightarrow{\text{int}} \chi}$$

$$\frac{\Sigma \cup \{\text{RIGHT} : \varphi(\vec{s},\vec{v},\vec{t})\} \xrightarrow{\text{int}} \chi}{\Sigma \cup \{\text{RIGHT} : \forall \vec{x}\ (R(\vec{s},\vec{x}) \rightarrow \varphi(\vec{s},\vec{x},\vec{t})), \text{RIGHT} : R(\vec{s},\vec{v})\} \xrightarrow{\text{int}} \chi}$$

Figure 2.8: Interpolation rules for RQFO.

We turn to deriving the proof rule and interpolation rule for relativized universal quantification. Consider a classical tableau proof of a contradiction from $\Sigma \cup \{\text{LEFT} : \forall \vec{x}\ (R(\vec{s},\vec{x}) \rightarrow \varphi(\vec{s},\vec{x},\vec{t})), \text{RIGHT} : R(\vec{s},\vec{v})\}$. In the tableau proof system we presented for classical logic, we would need to convert $\forall \vec{x}\ (R(\vec{s},\vec{x}) \rightarrow \varphi(\vec{s},\vec{x},\vec{t}))$ to $\forall \vec{x}\ (\neg R(\vec{s},\vec{x}) \vee \varphi(\vec{s},\vec{x},\vec{t}))$. A proof could proceed by instantiating the universal quantifier to $\vec{v}$ and then spawning two children, one containing:

$$\Sigma \cup \{\text{LEFT} : \neg R(\vec{s},\vec{v})), \text{RIGHT} : R(\vec{s},\vec{v})\}$$

and the other containing:

$$\Sigma \cup \{\text{LEFT} : \varphi(\vec{s},\vec{v},\vec{t}), \text{RIGHT} : R(\vec{s},\vec{v})\}.$$

The first child is contradictory, and the classical construction generates as interpolant $\neg R(\vec{s},\vec{v})$. Assuming the second child also leads to a contradiction, the classical construction would generate some interpolant χ.

Thus the interpolant for the original node would be $\neg R(\vec{s},\vec{v}) \vee \chi$, and applying the rule for universal quantification will give us an interpolant:

$$\forall x_{m_1} \dots x_{m_k}\ (\neg R(\vec{s},\vec{v}) \vee \chi)[v_{m_1} := x_{m_1} \dots v_{m_k} := x_{m_k}].$$

This can be rewritten using our relativized quantifiers as:

$$\forall x_{m_1} \dots x_{m_k}\ (R(\vec{s},\vec{v}) \rightarrow \chi)[v_{m_1} := x_{m_1} \dots v_{m_k} := x_{m_k}].$$

We can capture this process by having the labeled proof rule:

$$\frac{\textsc{left}: \forall \vec{x}\ (R(\vec{s},\vec{x}) \rightarrow \varphi(\vec{s},\vec{x},\vec{t})) \quad \textsc{right}: R(\vec{s},\vec{v})}{\textsc{left}: \varphi(\vec{s},\vec{v},\vec{t})}$$

and then the interpolation rule:

$$\frac{\Sigma \cup \{\textsc{left}: \varphi(\vec{s},\vec{v},\vec{t})\} \xrightarrow{\text{int}} \chi}{\Sigma \cup \{\textsc{left}: \forall \vec{x}\ (R(\vec{s},\vec{x}) \rightarrow \varphi(\vec{s},\vec{x},\vec{t})), \textsc{right}: R(\vec{s},\vec{v})\} \xrightarrow{\text{int}} \chi'}$$

with $\chi' = \forall x_{m_1} \ldots x_{m_k}\ (R(\vec{s},\vec{v}) \rightarrow \chi)[v_{m_1} := x_{m_1} \ldots v_{m_k} := x_{m_k}]$ where $v_{m_1} \ldots v_{m_k}$ are the v_i in $R(\vec{s},\vec{v}) \wedge \chi$ which do not occur in a RIGHT-annotated formula of Σ.

Now consider a classical tableau proof of a contradiction from $\Sigma \cup \{\textsc{right}: \forall \vec{x}\ (R(\vec{s},\vec{x}) \rightarrow \varphi(\vec{s},\vec{x},\vec{t})), \textsc{left}: R(\vec{s},\vec{v})\}$. As before, we would convert the relativized quantifier to

$$\forall \vec{x}\ (\neg R(\vec{s},\vec{x}) \vee \varphi(\vec{s},\vec{x},\vec{t}))$$

and could instantiate the universal quantifier to $\vec{v}$, spawning one child with:

$$\Sigma \cup \{\textsc{right}: \neg R(\vec{s},\vec{v}), \textsc{left}: R(\vec{s},\vec{v})\}$$

and another child with:

$$\Sigma \cup \{\textsc{right}: \varphi(\vec{s},\vec{v},\vec{t}), \textsc{left}: R(\vec{s},\vec{v})\}.$$

The first child is contradictory again, and the classical construction generates as interpolant $R(\vec{s},\vec{v})$. Assuming the second child also leads to a contradiction, the classical construction would generate some interpolant χ for the second child, and then the rule for disjunction in this case will give as interpolant for the original node $R(\vec{s},\vec{v}) \wedge \chi$. Applying the rule for universal quantification will give us an interpolant:

$$\exists x_{m_1} \ldots x_{m_k}\ (R(\vec{s},\vec{v}) \wedge \chi)[v_{m_1} := x_{m_1} \ldots v_{m_k} := x_{m_k}]$$

where the $m_1 \ldots m_k$ are the v_i in $R(\vec{s},\vec{v}) \wedge \chi$ that do not occur in a LEFT-annotated formula of Σ. This can be rewritten using a relativized existential quantifier.

We can capture this process by having the proof rule:

$$\frac{\textsc{right}: \forall \vec{x}\ (R(\vec{s},\vec{x}) \rightarrow \varphi(\vec{s},\vec{x},\vec{t})) \quad \textsc{left}: R(\vec{s},\vec{v})}{\textsc{right}: \varphi(\vec{s},\vec{v},\vec{t})}$$

along with the interpolation rule:

$$\frac{\Sigma \cup \{\textsc{right}: \varphi(\vec{s},\vec{v},\vec{t})\} \xrightarrow{\text{int}} \chi}{\Sigma \cup \{\textsc{right}: \forall \vec{x}\ (R(\vec{s},\vec{x}) \rightarrow \varphi(\vec{s},\vec{x},\vec{t})), \textsc{left}: R(\vec{s},\vec{v})\} \xrightarrow{\text{int}} \chi'}$$

with $\chi' = \exists x_{m_1} \dots x_{m_k} \; (R(\vec{s}, \vec{v}) \rightarrow \chi)[v_{m_1} := x_{m_1} \dots v_{m_k} := x_{m_k}]$ where $v_1 \dots v_{m_k}$ are the v_i in $R(\vec{s}, \vec{v}) \wedge \chi$ that do not occur in a LEFT-annotated formula of Σ.

The other two cases for the proof rule and interpolation rule (where the relativized quantifier and the atom $R(\vec{s}, \vec{x})$ has the same bias) are more straightforward.

We have:

$$\frac{\textsc{left} : \forall \vec{x} \; (R(\vec{s}, \vec{x}) \rightarrow \varphi(\vec{s}, \vec{x}, \vec{t})) \quad \textsc{left} : R(\vec{s}, \vec{v})}{\textsc{left} : \varphi(\vec{s}, \vec{v}, \vec{t})}$$

along with the interpolation rule:

$$\frac{\Sigma \cup \{\textsc{left} : \varphi(\vec{s}, \vec{v}, \vec{t})\} \xrightarrow{\text{int}} \chi}{\Sigma \cup \{\textsc{left} : \forall \vec{x} \; (R(\vec{s}, \vec{x}) \rightarrow \varphi(\vec{s}, \vec{x}, \vec{t})), \textsc{left} : R(\vec{s}, \vec{v})\} \xrightarrow{\text{int}} \chi}$$

and similarly for RIGHT. That is, when both the universal implication and an instantiation of the antecedent have the same bias, then we do not need to generate any quantification in the interpolant. Again this can be seen by translating the entailment to classical logic. The intuition is that we should not be introducing a new relativized quantification over relation R, since in applying this proof rule there is no interaction between an R fact on both the right and left sides.

We have now completed the argument for the relativized-quantifier interpolation theorem, Theorem 2.5.

Application: relativized-quantifier reformulations. We are ready to give the instantiation of the general methodology proposed in this text. Putting together the results of the previous sections, to find an RQFO reformulation of Q with respect to subvocabulary $\mathcal{T}$ and constraints Σ we should:

- Search for a tableau proof that the semantic property determinacy holds. That is, find a proof witnessing

$$\Sigma \wedge Q(\vec{x}) \models [(\bigwedge_{T \in \mathcal{T}} \forall \vec{y} \; T(\vec{y}) \leftrightarrow T'(\vec{y})) \wedge \Sigma'] \rightarrow Q'(\vec{x}).$$

- Use the relativized-quantifier tableau-based interpolation algorithm to produce an interpolant $Q_{\mathcal{T}}(\vec{x})$.
- As shown in Proposition 2.2, such an interpolant will give the reformulation we want.

We also know that to have an RQFO reformulation, Q must be determined over $\mathcal{T}$ *w.r.t.* Σ, and thus there must be a proof of the entailment for determinacy. This means we have proven the following effective version of Theorem 2.1:

Theorem 2.6 *To find a reformulation of an* RQFO *query* Q *with respect to subvocabulary* $\mathcal{T}$ *and* RQFO *constraints* Σ, *it is sufficient to find a proof witnessing the entailment:*

$$\Sigma \wedge Q \models [(\bigwedge_{T \in \mathcal{T}} \forall \vec{y} \; T(\vec{y}) \leftrightarrow T'(\vec{y})) \wedge \Sigma'] \rightarrow Q'$$

where Σ' is formed from Σ by replacing each relation R with R', and Q' is formed similarly from Q. From any such proof, we can effectively produce a reformulation.

Theorem 2.6 reduces searching for a reformulation to searching for a proof. Since the existence of a reformulation implies that the entailment above holds, and the entailment above captures determinacy, we have the following strengthening of Theorem 2.1:

Corollary 2.7 Equivalence of Reformulations, Entailments, and Semantic Properties *An* RQFO *query Q has an* RQFO *reformulation with respect to subvocabulary $\mathcal{T}$ and constraints Σ if and only if Q is determined over subvocabulary $\mathcal{T}$ with respect to Σ if and only if the entailment in Theorem 2.6 holds.*

Segoufin and Vianu's Theorem 2.1 and our Theorem 2.6 are closely related to a theorem in classical logic called the *Projective Beth Definability Theorem*. This theorem states that whenever a certain kind of formula satisfies the semantic property that its truth value is dependent only on a subset of the signature, we can rewrite the formula to use only that subset. The term "projective" refers to the fact that we conclude that the formula can be defined over a subset (projection) of the signature. This theorem was first proven (in a special case) by the logician E. W. Beth [Beth, 1953]. Craig produced a new proof of the theorem [Craig, 1957b], which follows precisely the methodology we advocate in this text. We refer to Theorem 2.6 as the Relativized-Quantifier Projective Beth theorem in the remainder of the text.

2.3 POSITIVE EXISTENTIAL REFORMULATION

Expanding on our general program outlined in the introduction, we show what happens when we restrict the target language for a reformulation. Recall from Section 1.2 that a *positive existential formula with inequalities* ($\exists^{+,\neq}$ formula) is a formula built up using only $\exists$ from atomic relations and inequalities. We also consider the formula False to be positive existential with inequalities.

Given an RQFO formula Q, restricted vocabulary $\mathcal{T}$, and constraints Σ given by RQFO sentences, we are interested in getting a $\exists^{+,\neq}$ reformulation of Q over $\mathcal{T}$ with respect to Σ. This means we want a $\exists^{+,\neq}$ formula over $\mathcal{T}$ that agrees with Q for instances satisfying the constraints.

The semantic property for $\exists^{+,\neq}$ reformulation. Following the "meta-algorithm" from the introduction, we start by finding the appropriate semantic property that an input Q must have to admit a $\exists^{+,\neq}$ reformulation. Nash et al. [2010] isolated such a property, which we call monotonic determinacy.[1] We say that a query Q over schema Sch is *monotonically-determined over $\mathcal{T}$* relative to Σ if:

for any two instances I_1, I_2 that satisfy Σ and such that for all relations $T \in \mathcal{T}$, $[\![T]\!]_{I_1} \subseteq [\![T]\!]_{I_2}$, then $[\![Q]\!]_{I_1} \subseteq [\![Q]\!]_{I_2}$.

[1] Nash et al. [2010] used the term "monotone."

The entailment corresponding to the semantic property. Proceeding to the second step of the meta-algorithm, we will express this semantic property as an entailment. Let Σ' be a copy of the constraints Σ where each occurrence of a relation R in $\mathcal{S}$ has been replaced by a copy R'.

Monotonic determinacy of a first-order query Q over $\mathcal{T}$ relative to Σ can be restated as saying that the following sentence holds on all instances:

$$\forall \vec{x}\ [\Sigma \wedge \Sigma' \wedge (\bigwedge_{T \in \mathcal{T}} \forall \vec{y}\ T(\vec{y}) \rightarrow T'(\vec{y})) \wedge Q(\vec{x})] \rightarrow Q'(\vec{x}).$$

Above, Q' and Σ' are the result of changing unprimed relations R to their primed counterparts R' within Q and within Σ respectively. Observe that if a $\exists^{+,\neq}$ formula over $\mathcal{T}$ is true on an instance I, then it is true on any instance I' which only adds tuples to the relations in $\mathcal{T}$. It is thus easy to see that a sufficient condition for monotonic determinacy of Q over $\mathcal{T}$ w.r.t. Σ is that Σ implies the sentence $\forall \vec{x}\ Q(\vec{x}) \leftrightarrow \varphi(\vec{x})$, where φ is a $\exists^{+,\neq}$ formula mentioning only relations in $\mathcal{T}$.

We highlight the difference from the entailment for determinacy: here we only have implication in the "forward" direction, from unprimed to primed, while for determinacy we have implications in both directions.

Generating $\exists^{+,\neq}$ reformulations from proofs of the entailment. We will show that by applying interpolation to proofs of the entailment for monotonic determinacy, we get $\exists^{+,\neq}$ reformulations. In doing so, we will prove the following analog of Theorem 2.1:

Theorem 2.8 *If the constraints Σ are in* RQFO *and* RQFO *query Q is monotonically-determined over $\mathcal{T}$, then there is a $\exists^{+,\neq}$ formula $\varphi(\vec{x})$ using only relations in $\mathcal{T}$ such that $\Sigma \models \forall \vec{x}\ [Q(\vec{x}) \leftrightarrow \varphi(\vec{x})]$. Furthermore, if the constraints and the query Q do not make use of equality, then χ can be taken to be positive existential (without inequalities).*

We refer to this as the *Projective Monotone Preservation Theorem*. Again, the adjective "Projective" emphasizes that we are dealing with a subset of the signature, as opposed to many preservation theorems one encounters in logic textbooks and papers, which deal with syntactically characterizing a semantic property involving the entire signature.

The steps in proving Theorem 2.8 will follow the meta-algorithm. We will prove a modification of the Craig Interpolation Theorem, the Relativized-Quantifier Lyndon Interpolation Theorem, and our proof will provide an algorithm for generating interpolants of a special form from an entailment. We then show that the interpolants produced by this algorithm, when applied to a re-arrangement of the entailment corresponding to the semantic property of monotonic determinacy, will give us the $\exists^{+,\neq}$ reformulation of our query Q with respect to the constraints.

The interpolants required for $\exists^{+,\neq}$ reformulation. Before giving the argument, we provide some motivation. We can restate the entailment for monotonic determinacy as:

$$\Sigma \wedge (\bigwedge_{T \in \mathcal{T}} \forall \vec{y}\ T(\vec{y}) \rightarrow T'(\vec{y})) \wedge Q(\vec{x}) \models (\Sigma' \rightarrow Q'(\vec{x})).$$

As before, Σ' is a copy of the constraints on primed versions of the relations, and Q' is a copy of the query Q on primed versions of the relations. The common vocabulary on the left and right consists of exactly the relations T' for $T \in \mathcal{T}$.

Further, we note that these common relations only occur on the right of an implication. Writing out the implication $A \rightarrow B$ as $\neg A \vee B$, we see that the common relations would not occur within a negation. Informally, we can say that these relations "occur positively" in the original formula. Thus we want to show that the interpolant will also contain these common relations positively. To do this, we need a formal definition of "occurring positively" that applies to arbitrary first-order formulas, and a version of interpolation that connects the relations occurring positively in the interpolant with those that occur positively in both sides of the entailment.

Formally, we say that a relation *occurs positively* in a first-order formula if it occurs in the scope of an even number of negations, when we rewrite the formula to use only the quantifiers and the connectives $\wedge, \vee, \neg$. A relation occurs negatively in a formula if it occurs in the scope of an odd number of negations. Intuitively if a relation occurs only positively, then the set of solutions to the formula can only increase or stay the same as tuples are added to that relation (this is easy to check if the relation does not appear under any negations at all).

The interpolation theorem that tracks which occurrences are positive is the following result, which is a strengthening of the Relativized-quantifier Craig Interpolation Theorem, Theorem 2.4:

Theorem 2.9 Relativized-quantifier Lyndon Interpolation Theorem. *Suppose λ and ρ are in* RQFO *and $\lambda \models \rho$. Then there is an* RQFO *interpolant χ for the entailment such that a relation occurs positively in χ only if it occurs positively in both λ and ρ, and a relation occurs negatively in χ only if it occurs negatively in both λ and ρ. Furthermore if equality does not occur in λ or ρ, then it does not occur in χ, so in particular χ cannot contain inequalities.*

Again, there is a well-known version of this for the classical semantics of first-order logic, Lyndon's interpolation theorem [Lyndon, 1959].

The construction that witnesses the Relativized-quantifier Lyndon Interpolation Theorem, Theorem 2.9, is identical to the one for the Relativized-quantifier CIT. In the argument for correctness we just add an invariant tracking the polarity of relations in the interpolant. Let us verify this for the base step of the interpolation algorithm. Here a contradiction in a tableau node occurs only when we have an atom $R(\vec{c})$ and its negation $\neg R(\vec{c})$ in the node, or if the node contains False. If the node contains False or if both the atom and its negation have the same bias, then the interpolant produced does not contain any relation at all. In the case where we have a negated atom $\neg R(\vec{c})$ with bias LEFT and a non-negated atom $R(\vec{c})$ with bias RIGHT, the negated atom must necessarily be derived from a negated occurrence of R in λ. Likewise, the non-negated atoms must derive from a non-negated occurrence in the negation of ρ, hence R must occur negatively in ρ. Thus R occurs negatively in both λ and ρ, as required. Similar reasoning applies to the case where the biases of the negated and non-negated atoms are reversed.

Getting $\exists^{+,\neq}$ and positive existential reformulations via interpolants. Theorem 2.9 shows that we can extract a certain kind of interpolant from a tableau proof witnessing an entailment corresponding to monotonic determinacy. We are now ready to instantiate the last step of our meta-algorithm, extracting a reformulation from an interpolant. This will complete the proof of Theorem 2.8.

Apply Theorem 2.9 to the entailment

$$\Sigma \wedge (\bigwedge_{T \in \mathcal{T}} \forall \vec{y}\ T(\vec{y}) \rightarrow T'(\vec{y})) \wedge Q(\vec{x}) \models (\Sigma' \rightarrow Q'(\vec{x})).$$

We can conclude that there is an RQFO interpolant γ mentioning only relations in the primed copy of $\mathcal{T}$, where these relations only occur positively. We can assume γ is built up from True and False via connectives and relativized quantifiers $\forall \vec{x}\ R(\vec{x}) \rightarrow \varphi$ and $\exists \vec{x}\ R(\vec{x}) \wedge \varphi$. We claim that any RQFO formula in which all relations occur positively must be equivalent to a positive existential formula. To see this, convert an RQFO formula to NNF. If the resulting formula γ had any relativized universal quantifier, then consider an outermost quantification of the form $\forall \vec{x}\ (R(\vec{x}) \rightarrow \varphi)$. R must occur negatively in this formula. But then it must occur negatively within γ, since existential quantification and the positive boolean operators preserve the polarity of a subformula, and this contradicts the assumption on γ. Hence the Negation Normal Form of γ cannot contain any relativized universal quantifier, and thus must be $\exists^{+,\neq}$.

We say $\exists^{+,\neq}$ above, rather than positive existential, because the argument applies only to relations R of the schema, not equality. If the equality symbol does not appear in the entailment we know that it is not generated in the interpolant. Therefore when equality does not occur in the constraints or the query, we can strengthen the conclusion to be that the interpolant is positive existential.

This completes the proof of the Projective Monotone Preservation Theorem, Theorem 2.8.

Application to view-based query reformulation. Let us look at the setting where there are no constraints other than those that come from views defined by conjunctive queries. As a corollary of Theorem 2.8 we have:

Corollary 2.10 *Suppose Q is a CQ and $V_1 \ldots V_n$ are views defined by arbitrary equality-free* RQFO *formulas. Then, Q is monotonically-determined in $V_1 \ldots V_n$ if and only if there is a positive existential reformulation of Q in terms of $V_1 \ldots V_n$.*

We will see in Section 2.6 that one can further require that such a reformulation be safe. Since a safe positive existential formula is equivalent to a $USPJ^{\neq}$ relational algebra query and to a UCQ (Section 1.2), we could replace positive existential by $USPJ$ or UCQ in the conclusion.

2.4 EXISTENTIAL REFORMULATION

At this point, we have proven a statement about first-order reformulations and one about positive existential reformulations. What about queries that can be reformulated using *existential formulas*?

That is, formulas that are built up from atoms and negated atoms by positive boolean operators and existential quantification. There are conjunctive queries that are equivalent to existential formulas but not to positive existential ones. For example, in the absence of any constraints $\exists x\ S(x) \wedge \neg R(x)$ is not equivalent to a positive existential formula. Can we use a similar technique to detect which formulas are equivalent to an existential formula with respect to a set of constraints, and if so find such a reformulation? We give a positive answer to this below, restricting for simplicity to equality-free RQFO.

The semantic property for existential reformulation. As before, let Sch be a schema with a set of integrity constraints Σ in equality-free RQFO, and $\mathcal{T}$ a subset of the relations of Sch. We start by isolating a property that Q must have in order to possess an existential reformulation.

We say that a query Q over schema Sch is *induced-subinstance-monotonically-determined over* $\mathcal{T}$ relative to Σ if:

Whenever we have two instances I_1, I_2 that satisfy Σ and such that I_1 is an induced subinstance of I_2 then $[\![Q]\!]_{I_1} \subseteq [\![Q]\!]_{I_2}$.

Recall from Section 1.2 that I_1 being an induced subinstance of I_2 means that I_2 contains all facts of I_1, and I_2 does not add any facts over the active domain of I_1.

Note that if an existential formula over $\mathcal{T}$ is true on an instance I, then it is true on any instance I' which only adds tuples to the relations in $\mathcal{T}$ and never "destroys a negated assertion about a relation of $\mathcal{T}$ holding in I." From this we see that if a formula is equivalent to an existential formula under a set of constraints Σ, then the formula is induced-subinstance-monotonically-determined over $\mathcal{T}$ $w.r.t.$ Σ.

The entailment corresponding to the semantic property. As in the previous cases, we instantiate our meta-algorithm by writing out the semantic property as an entailment.

Let $\mathsf{InDomain}_{\mathcal{T}}(x)$ abbreviate the formula:

$$\bigvee_{T \in \mathcal{T}} \bigvee_{j} \exists w_1 \ldots \exists w_{j-1}\ \exists w_{j+1} \ldots w_{\mathsf{arity}(T)}\ T(w_1, \ldots w_{j-1}, x, w_{j+1}, \ldots, w_{\mathsf{arity}(T)}).$$

So $\mathsf{InDomain}_{\mathcal{T}}$ states that x is in the domain of a relation in $\mathcal{T}$. The entailment we need is:

$$\begin{aligned} Q(\vec{x}) \wedge \Sigma \wedge \Sigma' \wedge \\ \bigwedge_{T \in \mathcal{T}} (\forall \vec{y}\ T(\vec{y}) \rightarrow T'(\vec{y})) \wedge \\ \bigwedge_{T \in \mathcal{T}} (\forall \vec{y} \bigwedge_{i} \mathsf{InDomain}_{\mathcal{T}}(y_i) \wedge T'(\vec{y}) \rightarrow T(\vec{y})\ ) \models \\ Q'(\vec{x}). \end{aligned}$$

Comparing with the two previous entailments, we have the forward implication as before, and a restriction of the backward implication. It is clear that induced-subinstance-monotonicity is equivalent to this entailment holding.

Extracting interpolants from a proof of the entailment: statement of result. We will show later that if we have a "suitable" interpolant for the entailment corresponding to induced-subinstance-monotonicity, then we can extract an existential reformulation from it, completing another instantiation of the meta-algorithm.

This will give us a proof of another analog of Theorem 2.1:

Theorem 2.11 *If the constraints Σ are in equality-free* RQFO, *and* RQFO *query Q is induced-subinstance-monotonically-determined over $\mathcal{T}$, then there is an existential first-order formula $\varphi(\vec{x})$ using only relations in $\mathcal{T}$ such that $\Sigma \models \forall \vec{x}\ Q(\vec{x}) \leftrightarrow \varphi(\vec{x})$.*

A similar theorem will hold if the constraints are in RQFO with equality, with the conclusion being that φ is an existential formula with inequalities.

We defer the proof of Theorem 2.11 for the moment. It will follow from a more general theorem, Theorem 3.11, proved in Chapter 3. The reformulation we need will come from applying an interpolation procedure to the entailment above. But we need a new interpolation result to guarantee that the interpolant will be existential, and this extended interpolation theorem is proven in Theorem 3.12.

Łoś-Tarski. The theorem above is closely related to another result in logic, the Łoś-Tarski preservation theorem. This states that a formula is preserved under extensions exactly when it is equivalent to an existential formula. Roughly speaking, the Łoś-Tarski theorem is a special case of Theorem 2.11, where Σ is empty and $\mathcal{T}$ contains all relations in the schema. The "roughly speaking" disclaimer is because the Łoś-Tarski theorem deals with classical first-order logic formulas rather than for RQFO, and the notion of induced subinstance must be replaced by the analogous notion for structures. But to stress the analogy, we refer to Theorem 2.11 as the *Projective Łoś-Tarski Theorem* further on.

2.5 THE METHODOLOGY IN ACTION

We are ready to give an end-to-end example of reformulation using the methodology outlined in the introduction.

Example 2.4. We review Example 1.2, where the schema contained information about employees and departments. Recall that the constraints were the following two TGDs:

$$\forall \mathsf{deptid}\ \forall \mathsf{dname}\ \forall \mathsf{mgrid}\ \mathsf{Department}(\mathsf{deptid}, \mathsf{dname}, \mathsf{mgrid}) \rightarrow \exists N\ \mathsf{Employee}(\mathsf{mgrid}, N, \mathsf{deptid})$$
$$\forall \mathsf{eid}\ \forall \mathsf{ename}\ \forall \mathsf{deptid}\ \mathsf{Employee}(\mathsf{eid}, \mathsf{ename}, \mathsf{deptid}) \rightarrow \exists D \exists M\ \mathsf{Department}(\mathsf{deptid}, D, M).$$

When this example was introduced, the goal was to take the query:

$$Q = \{\mathsf{deptid} \mid \exists \mathsf{eid}\ \exists \mathsf{ename}\ \mathsf{Employee}(\mathsf{eid}, \mathsf{ename}, \mathsf{deptid})\}$$

and reformulate it over $\mathcal{T} = \{\mathsf{Department}\}$. We are in a position to apply the methodology outlined at the beginning of this chapter to do this.

We begin our proof with the assumption:

$$\exists \mathsf{eid}\ \exists \mathsf{ename}\ \mathsf{Employee}(\mathsf{eid}, \mathsf{ename}, \mathsf{deptid})$$

and fix constants $\mathsf{eid}_0, \mathsf{ename}_0, \mathsf{deptid}_0$ witnessing the variables. We want to give a proof of the desired goal $\mathsf{Employee}'(M, N, \mathsf{deptid}_0)$, using the original constraints, their copies on the primed relations, and the "transfer" axioms, which will include the following "forward transfer" axiom Σ_{AxFor}

$$\mathsf{Department}(\mathsf{deptid}, \mathsf{dname}, \mathsf{mgrid}) \rightarrow \mathsf{Department}'(\mathsf{deptid}, \mathsf{dname}, \mathsf{mgrid}).$$

We start by giving a chase proof. Making use of the second integrity constraint, we can perform a chase step to derive:

$$\mathsf{Department}(\mathsf{deptid}_0, D, M)$$

where D, M are new constants.

We can apply the "forward transfer" axiom Σ_{AxFor} to obtain:

$$\mathsf{Department}'(\mathsf{deptid}_0, D, M).$$

Now we can apply a copy of the first constraint on the primed relations to get:

$$\mathsf{Employee}'(M, N, \mathsf{deptid}_0).$$

Due to the existence of a match of Q' against $\mathsf{Employee}'(M, N, \mathsf{deptid}_0)$ matching the free variable deptid to deptid_0, we have completed the chase proof.

To find the reformulation, we have to rephrase the chase proof as a tableau proof of

$$Q \wedge \Sigma \models (\Sigma_{\mathsf{AxFor}} \wedge \Sigma') \rightarrow Q'.$$

The tableau proof will start with the left of the entailment along with the negation of the right. Putting the negation of the right into our syntax for relativized quantifier tableau proofs, we obtain $\Sigma_{\mathsf{AxFor}} \wedge \Sigma' \wedge \sim Q'$, where $\sim Q'$ is the formula $\forall \mathsf{eid}\ \forall \mathsf{ename}\ \mathsf{Employee}'(\mathsf{eid}, \mathsf{ename}, \mathsf{deptid}_0) \rightarrow \mathsf{False}$.

The chase steps that started the proof above can be mimicked by two steps of tableau expansion. The proof will end not by matching the goal query, as in the chase proof above, but getting a contradiction from the assumption

$$\neg\exists \mathsf{eid}\ \exists \mathsf{ename}\ \mathsf{Employee}'(\mathsf{eid}, \mathsf{ename}, \mathsf{deptid}_0)$$

converting this to NNF as $\forall \mathsf{eid}\ \forall \mathsf{ename}\ \neg\mathsf{Employee}'(\mathsf{eid}, \mathsf{ename}, \mathsf{deptid}_0)$ and then instantiating eid and ename with M and N to get a clash.

Truncating the relation names Employee and Department to Emp and Dept, and coloring the RIGHT-labeled formulas in blue, our labeled tableau proof is as follows:

$$\exists \mathsf{eid}\ \exists \mathsf{ename}\ \mathsf{Emp}(\mathsf{eid}, \mathsf{ename}, \mathsf{deptid}_0), \ldots, \sim Q'$$

$$\mathsf{Emp}(\mathsf{eid}_0, \mathsf{ename}_0, \mathsf{deptid}_0), \ldots$$

$$\mathsf{Emp}(\mathsf{eid}_0, \mathsf{ename}_0, \mathsf{deptid}_0), \mathsf{Dept}(\mathsf{deptid}_0, D, M), \ldots$$

$$\mathsf{Emp}(\mathsf{eid}_0, \mathsf{ename}_0, \mathsf{deptid}_0), \mathsf{Dept}(\mathsf{deptid}_0, D, M), \mathsf{Dept}'(\mathsf{deptid}_0, D, M), \ldots$$

$$\mathsf{Emp}(\mathsf{eid}_0, \mathsf{ename}_0, \mathsf{deptid}_0), \mathsf{Dept}(\mathsf{deptid}_0, D, M), \mathsf{Dept}'(\mathsf{deptid}_0, D, M), \mathsf{Emp}'(M, N, \mathsf{deptid}_0), \ldots$$

$$\mathsf{Emp}(\mathsf{eid}_0, \mathsf{ename}_0, \mathsf{deptid}_0), \mathsf{Dept}(\mathsf{deptid}_0, D, M), \mathsf{Dept}'(\mathsf{deptid}_0, D, M), \mathsf{False}, \ldots$$

We are ready to apply interpolation to get a reformulation. Applying the bottom-up interpolation algorithm, we begin with the contradiction at the leaves, which stems just from the RIGHT formulas. Hence the interpolant is just True. The rule immediately before this involves the integrity constraints Σ', which are rules associated with the RIGHT bias. The relativized universal quantifiers in these rules are applied to facts annotated as RIGHT. Hence in these cases, the corresponding interpolation rule just copies the lower interpolant from child to parent—in this case True.

Working our way upward, we have come to the proof rule which applied the forward transfer axiom Σ_T, and this is where there is an interaction between a formula labeled with RIGHT, namely Σ_T, and a formula labeled with LEFT, namely $\mathsf{Department}(\mathsf{deptid}_0, D, M)$. Using the rule for relativized universal quantification with the universal quantifier labeled with RIGHT, we introduce a relativized existential quantification over Department. Keeping in mind that the constant deptid_0 appears in both LEFT and RIGHT formulas, we get our first non-trivial interpolant:

$$\exists D\ \exists M\ \mathsf{Department}(\mathsf{deptid}_0, D, M) \wedge \mathsf{True}$$

which we can simplify to

$$\exists D\ \exists M\ \mathsf{Department}(\mathsf{deptid}_0, D, M).$$

So far, our bottom-up algorithm has produced the following:

$\exists \mathsf{eid}\ \exists \mathsf{ename}\ \mathsf{Emp}(\mathsf{eid}, \mathsf{ename}, \mathsf{deptid}_0), \ldots, \sim Q'$

$\mathsf{Emp}(\mathsf{eid}_0, \mathsf{ename}_0, \mathsf{deptid}_0), \ldots$

$\mathsf{Emp}(\mathsf{eid}_0, \mathsf{ename}_0, \mathsf{deptid}_0), \mathsf{Dept}(\mathsf{deptid}_0, D, M), \ldots$ — $\exists D\ \exists M\ \mathsf{Dept}(\mathsf{deptid}_0, D, M)$

$\mathsf{Emp}(\mathsf{eid}_0, \mathsf{ename}_0, \mathsf{deptid}_0), \mathsf{Dept}(\mathsf{deptid}_0, D, M), \mathsf{Dept}'(\mathsf{deptid}_0, D, M), \ldots$ — True

$\mathsf{Emp}(\mathsf{eid}_0, \mathsf{ename}_0, \mathsf{deptid}_0), \mathsf{Dept}(\mathsf{deptid}_0, D, M), \mathsf{Dept}'(\mathsf{deptid}_0, D, M), \mathsf{Emp}'(M, N, \mathsf{deptid}_0), \ldots$ — True

$\mathsf{Emp}(\mathsf{eid}_0, \mathsf{ename}_0, \mathsf{deptid}_0), \mathsf{Dept}(\mathsf{deptid}_0, D, M), \mathsf{Dept}'(\mathsf{deptid}_0, D, M), \mathsf{False}, \ldots$ — True

Since the remaining steps do not add to the interpolant, we see we have produced a reformulation that is a renaming of the intuitive result mentioned in Example 1.2:

$$\{z : \exists o\ \exists p\ \mathsf{Department}(z, o, p)\}$$

◁

2.6 SAFETY OF REFORMULATIONS

So far we have looked at producing reformulations whose syntactic form enforces a certain semantic property. An obvious question concerns the semantic property of *safety* which is of considerable interest in databases. Recall from Section 1.2 that a formula is *safe* if for each finite input instance, it returns a finite output instance. This will hold if the query is *semantically active domain*, meaning that it returns only tuples composed of elements that are either schema constants or in the active domain. One cannot decide whether a first-order formula is semantically active domain, or whether it is safe [Abiteboul et al., 1995]. Therefore syntactic conditions are typically used that enforce these properties. Relational algebra itself can be seen as a syntax for the safe first-order logic formulas. Indeed, relational algebra queries have the property that every subquery is safe, and this allows relational algebra queries to be evaluated "bottom-up" (from inner queries to outer). This prompts the question of whether we can instantiate the meta-algorithm so that it automatically produces reformulations whose syntax enforces safety. Ideally, we would like to go even further, instantiating the meta-algorithm so that it produces relational algebra queries directly, allowing us to evaluate the resulting queries directly using a database manager, rather than via some further translation.

The interpolation algorithm of Figure 2.8 does not necessarily produce a semantically active domain or a safe formula, even when the input query is a CQ and constraints are RQFO sentences.

Example 2.5. Let the integrity constraints Σ in our schema be as follows:

$$\begin{aligned}\forall x \forall y\ P(x,y) \rightarrow (R(x) \vee S(y) \vee E(x,y))\\ \forall x\ R(x) \rightarrow \mathsf{False}\\ \forall y\ S(y) \rightarrow \mathsf{False}\\ \forall x \forall y\ E(x,y) \rightarrow P(x,y).\end{aligned}$$

Note that the constraints are consistent.

Let our query be $P(x,y)$. The entailment/proof goal generated in obtaining a positive existential reformulation of this query over $\mathcal{T} = \{R, S, E\}$ is:

$$P(x,y) \wedge \Sigma \models (\Sigma' \wedge \mathsf{Ax}_{\mathsf{For}}) \rightarrow P'(x,y)$$

where $\mathsf{Ax}_{\mathsf{For}}$ is a conjunction of the "forward axioms" $\bigwedge_{T \in \mathcal{T}} T(\vec{x}) \rightarrow T'(\vec{x})$, and Σ' represents a copy of the constraints on the primed relations.

One tableau proof of this entailment starts by generating $R(x) \vee S(y) \vee E(x,y)$ using the first constraint. It then creates three children, with the first child node N_1 containing $R(x)$ and $P(x,y)$, the second child node N_2 containing $S(y)$ and $P(x,y)$, and the final child N_3 containing $E(x,y)$ and $P(x,y)$. From N_1, we can apply first the forward axioms to get $R'(x)$, and then apply the primed copy of the second constraint to obtain a contradiction.

The corresponding interpolant generated from this branch will be $R(x) \wedge \mathsf{True}$, abbreviated (or simplifying) as $R(x)$. Similarly we can close the second child to obtain an interpolant $S(y)$. We can proceed in the same way with the third child, generating a contradiction with $\neg P'(x,y)$, which will be inherited from the root node. This will yield the interpolant $E(x,y)$ for this third branch. The final interpolant formed by applying the connective rules will be:

$$R(x) \vee S(y) \vee E(x,y).$$

The reader can verify directly that this is a valid reformulation of the query relative to the constraints Σ. But this formula is not semantically active domain and is not safe.

The formula is equivalent (relative to the constraints) to the CQ $E(x,y)$, which is the "obvious" reformulation. And indeed this obvious reformulation could have been obtained via the proof that obtains contradictions in N_1 and N_2 by applying the second and third constraints in Σ, rather than first applying $\mathsf{Ax}_{\mathsf{For}}$ and obtaining a contradiction using Σ'. ◁

Of course, any reformulation $Q_{\mathcal{T}}$ of a query Q must be equivalent to Q on instances that satisfy the constraints, by definition. Assuming that our input queries Q are semantically active domain—for example, if they are CQs—this implies that, in principle, there is no issue with safety:

- On all the database instances we are interested in—namely, those that satisfy the constraints—the $Q_{\mathcal{T}}$ produced by the previous algorithms is semantically active domain. Thus we could evaluate the formula ignoring all bindings that take values outside the active domain and the schema constants.

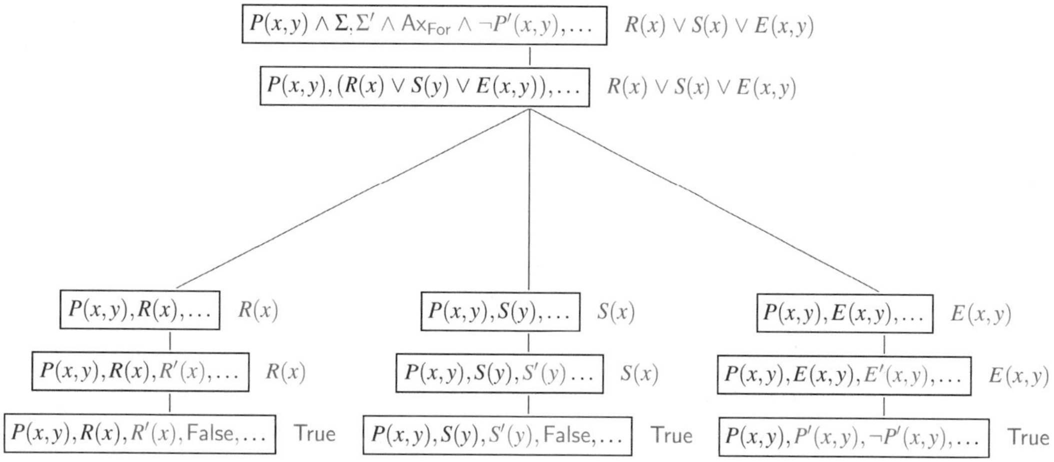

Figure 2.9: A tableau proof and the generated interpolants for Example 2.5.

- We could *post-process* the interpolant to make it safe. For example, we could take the disjunction over queries which guard the output with all possible restrictions to schema constants and projections of relations. The result will necessarily be equivalent to Q on all instances satisfying the constraints.

  A post-processing approach to deal with not only safety but also access restrictions is discussed in [Toman and Weddell, 2011].

If we know that the query is safe, we can effectively covert it to relational algebra: see Theorem 1.1 and the comments afterward. The bottom line is that in all of our theorems, when we have a proof of the appropriate semantic property, we are guaranteed that there is a safe reformulation that can be effectively constructed from the proof.

It would be natural to look for either a restricted form of proof and/or a more specialized interpolation algorithm that would always produce safe reformulations directly, without the need for post-processing. For general first-order queries we do not have such a procedure. But for TGD constraints, we have a specialized interpolation procedure that directly produces a reformulation based on relational algebra queries, hence a safe reformulation. This will be presented in Chapter 4.

2.7 DECIDABLE REFORMULATION

The results in the previous sections reduced determining whether there is a reformulation of query Q over target vocabulary $\mathcal{T}$ with respect to constraints Σ to checking whether an entailment holds. This gives a *semi-decision procedure* for checking existence of a reformulation, and a procedure for finding reformulations whenever one exists: one searches for a proof that witnesses the entailment, and then applies interpolation. However, there is still the question of how to find the proof. There is no way to know when one can safely terminate this search: this follows from the fact that the existence of a reformulation (with respect to general RQFO constraints) is undecidable.

To get *end-to-end decidability*, where we can effectively find the proofs and then apply the interpolation-based method to get a reformulation, we must thus restrict the queries and the constraints to be in a well-behaved fragment of first-order logic.

In this section, we focus only on providing cases where the problem of existence of a reformulation is decidable. In all such cases, there is also an algorithm for obtaining a reformulation whenever one exists, whose worst-case complexity agrees with that of the decision procedure for the existence problem. But we defer treatment of concrete algorithms for reformulation to Chapter 4, where they are discussed in the more general framework of access restrictions. Throughout this section, *the source queries Q to be reformulated will always be CQs*. Several restricted classes of constraints will be considered below.

2.7.1 DECIDABLE END-TO-END REFORMULATION FOR EXPRESSIVE CONSTRAINTS

We start by showing decidability for a very rich class of constraints, those given by sentences in the *Guarded Negation Fragment* (GNF), introduced in [Bárány et al., 2011], a class that subsumes GTGDs (and in particular, referential constraints) as well as many other common constraint classes. GNF is built up inductively according to the grammar:

$$\varphi ::= R(\vec{t}) \mid t_1 = t_2 \mid \exists x\, \varphi \mid \varphi \vee \varphi \mid \varphi \wedge \varphi \mid R(\vec{t}, \vec{y}) \wedge \neg\varphi(\vec{y})$$

where R is either a relation or the equality relation $x = y$, and the t_i represent either variables or constants. Notice that any use of negation must occur conjoined with an atomic relation that contains all the free variables of the negated formula. Such an atomic relation is a *guard* of the formula.

Our theorems below will make use of only a few facts about GNF.

- GTGDs can be expressed in GNF. Recall from Section 1.2 that GTGDs are constraints of the form
$$\forall \vec{x}\ [G(\vec{x}) \wedge \varphi(\vec{x}) \rightarrow \exists \vec{y}\ \rho(\vec{x}, \vec{y})]$$
where G is an atom containing all variables occurring in φ. By simply writing out a GTGD using $\exists, \neg, \wedge$, one sees that these are convertible to GNF. When we look at the entailments generated for our reformulation problems, we see that they will involve only copies of the original constraints and also additional axioms saying that certain relations are preserved between the primed and unprimed copies. Note that these additional axioms are GTGDs, and hence they are expressible in GNF.

- GNF contains all boolean combinations of boolean conjunctive queries.

- We often use the fact that GNF is "tame," encapsulated in the following result of Bárány, ten Cate and Segoufin:

Theorem 2.12 *[Bárány et al., 2011] Satisfiability for* GNF *sentences is decidable, and is in fact* 2EXPTIME-*complete.*

We show that reformulation of a CQ over GNF constraints is decidable, with the same complexity as the satisfiability problem for GNF:

Theorem 2.13 *The following problem is* 2EXPTIME-*complete:*

input: *a vocabulary* Sch, Σ *a collection of constraints in* GNF, Q *a conjunctive query over* Sch, *and* $\mathcal{T}$ *a target vocabulary,*

output: *whether* Q *has an* RQFO *reformulation over* $\mathcal{T}$ *with respect to* Σ.

The same holds for positive existential reformulation and for existential reformulation.

Proof. We first give the upper bound argument for RQFO reformulation. By the "active domain Projective Beth Definability Theorem," Theorem 2.1, we know that such a reformulation exists iff the sentence γ defined by

$$Q \wedge \Sigma \wedge \Sigma' \wedge (\bigwedge_{T \in \mathcal{T}} \forall \vec{x}\ T(\vec{x}) \leftrightarrow T'(\vec{x})) \rightarrow Q'$$

is valid, where the free variables of Q are treated as constants, while Q' and Σ' are obtained by replacing each relation R by a copy R'. But the closure properties of GNF guarantee that γ can be rewritten as a sentence of GNF. Hence the validity of such a sentence is decidable in double exponential time, by Theorem 2.12. The variant for positive existential reformulation is analogous, since here we just replace part of the statement by the conjunction $\bigwedge_{T \in \mathcal{T}}(\forall \vec{x}\ T(\vec{x}) \rightarrow T'(\vec{x}))$, which is clearly in GNF. For existential reformulation the corresponding conjunction can be rewritten, using additional relations and additional GNF constraints defining these relations, in the form $\forall \vec{x}\ [A_1(x_{j_1}) \wedge \ldots \wedge A_m(x_{j_m}) \wedge T(\vec{x}) \rightarrow T'(\vec{x})]$, which is again in GNF.

For the hardness, we give a reduction from unsatisfiability for GNF sentences, which is known to be 2EXPTIME-hard (Theorem 2.12). Given GNF sentence φ, let $\mathcal{T}$ consist of the empty set of relations, and let R be a new nullary relation not mentioned in φ. Our reduction produces the query Q consisting of only the atom R and constraint set consisting only of φ. Obviously if φ is unsatisfiable, then the query can vacuously be reformulated as True (or as any conjunctive query) with respect to φ. On the contrary, if φ is satisfiable, then Q is not determined over $\mathcal{T}$ (since on a satisfying instance we can make R true or false, and hence Q cannot be reformulated in any language). □

Theorem 2.13 deals only with the complexity of the *decision problem*: does there exist an RQFO reformulation of Q over the subvocabulary with respect to the constraints? The proof does not immediately imply a bound on the complexity of obtaining a reformulation, since the decidability techniques from [Bárány et al., 2011] do not use the tableau decision procedure that we used to extract our reformulation. However, there are decision procedures for the guarded fragment with optimal complexity that go via tableau proofs [Hirsch and Tobies, 2000], and these can be extended to GNF [Benedikt et al., 2014c].

Some care must be taken in applying this result to reformulation of a query with respect to views. Recall that the setting of constraints subsumes the setting of views, since the view definitions can be seen as special kinds of constraints. If we take a set of view relations defined by GNF formulas, the corresponding set of constraints expressing the view definitions may not be in GNF: indeed, even if the views are defined by conjunctive queries this still might not be the case. We can apply Theorem 2.13 to reformulating queries with respect to a set of GNF-defined views and GNF integrity constraints, provided that the GNF views are *answer-guarded*, meaning that each view relation $V(\vec{x})$ is associated with a formula of the form $R(\vec{x}) \wedge \varphi(\vec{x})$, where R is a relational atom or equality. In this case, the constraints expressing the relationship of a view to its definition are in GNF.

We turn to lower bounds for reformulation with more specialized constraints, GTGDs. The above results give the idea that the reformulation problem is generally as hard as the problem of query containment under constraints for the corresponding constraint language. We can formulate this using the following reduction, which works for GTGDs and inclusion dependencies:

Given a containment problem: "for boolean conjunctive queries Q, Q', does $Q \subseteq Q'$ hold under TGD constraints Σ," produce reformulation problem: "does $A \wedge Q'$ have an RQFO reformulation over $\mathcal{T} = \{A\}$ with respect to constraints $\Sigma^* = \Sigma \cup \{A \to Q\}$." Here A is a nullary relation not present in Q or Q'.

It is not difficult to see that this reduction is correct. If $Q \subseteq Q'$ holds under constraints Σ, then Q' is equivalent to A on all instances satisfying Σ^*. If containment under constraints Σ fails, there is a witness instance I where Σ holds, Q is true, and Q' is false. Expand I by making A true. Consider any instance I' formed from the canonical database of Q' unioned with the canonical database of Q by closing under constraints in Σ and making A true. Then I and I' satisfy the constraints in Σ^*, agree on A, but disagree on $A \wedge Q'$, thus witnessing that Q' is not determined. Hence (by Corollary 2.7) Q' cannot be reformulated. The same reduction works for positive existential and existential reformulation. Using this and prior results, we get:

Proposition 2.14 *Checking whether a conjunctive query has an* RQFO *(positive existential, etc.) reformulation over subvocabulary $\mathcal{T}$ with respect to GTGDs is* 2EXPTIME*-complete, with the lower bound holding even when the arity of the relations is fixed.*

Proof. The upper bounds follow from the upper bounds for GNF given in Theorem 2.13. The lower bounds follow from the reduction above, and the fact that query containment under GTGDs is 2EXPTIME even for arity two [Lutz, 2007, 2008]. □

2.7.2 REFORMULATION WITH INCLUSION DEPENDENCIES

We turn to the case where the constraints are inclusion dependencies, which correspond to SQL referential constraints. We first note that we need only consider the case of $\exists^+$ reformulation:

Proposition 2.15 *For any conjunctive query Q, if it has an* RQFO *reformulation over a subvocabulary $\mathcal{T}$ w.r.t. a set of inclusion dependencies Σ, then it has a positive existential reformulation over $\mathcal{T}$ w.r.t. Σ.*

Proof. For simplicity, we deal with the case where Q is boolean. Assume that Q has an RQFO reformulation over $\mathcal{T}$ *w.r.t.* Σ. By Corollary 2.7 we know Q is determined over $\mathcal{T}$ with respect to Σ. We also know, by Theorem 2.8, that to get a $\exists^+$ reformulation it suffices to show that Q is monotonically-determined over $\mathcal{T}$ w.r.t. Σ. So fix I and I' satisfying Σ, such that I satisfies Q, and the $\mathcal{T}$ facts of I are contained in those of I'. Let I^+ be formed by unioning the facts of I and I'. Then I^+ satisfies Σ, since satisfaction of a set of IDs is preserved under union. Q is preserved in moving from I to I^+, since Q is a conjunctive query. But I^+ and I' share the same $\mathcal{T}$ facts, and so by determinacy we have that Q holds in I'. Thus we have proved monotonic determinacy. □

The following proposition isolates the complexity of detecting existence of reformulations when constraints consist only of inclusion dependencies.

Proposition 2.16 *Checking whether a conjunctive query has an* RQFO *reformulation (equivalently, by the proposition above, a positive existential reformulation) over subvocabulary $\mathcal{T}$ with respect to a set of inclusion dependencies is* PSPACE*-complete, and is* NP*-complete when the arity of relations involved is fixed.*

Proof. The lower bounds in the second part follow from known lower bounds on query containment with inclusion dependencies [Casanova et al., 1984], using the reduction in the proof of Proposition 2.14. To see the upper bounds, recall that the corresponding constraints for RQFO reformulation are of the form:

$$\Sigma^* = \Sigma \cup \Sigma' \cup \{\forall \vec{x}\ (T(\vec{x}) \leftrightarrow T'(\vec{x})) : T \in \mathcal{T}\}$$

where Σ' is a copy of Σ. Since the bi-implication can be rewritten as two inclusion dependencies, this is again a set of inclusion dependencies. Hence the upper bounds follow from those for query containment under inclusion dependencies, which is known to be in PSPACE in general and in NP for fixed arity [Johnson and Klug, 1984]. □

2.7.3 TGDS WITH TERMINATING CHASE: POSITIVE EXISTENTIAL REFORMULATION

From Theorem 2.13 we see that for GTGDs, existence of a reformulation is decidable. But there are many classes of TGDs that are well-behaved with respect to decidability but which are not contained in GTGDs—see, e.g.,the survey [Onet, 2013]. In particular, conjunctive query containment with constraints is decidable for TGDs with *terminating chase*, as defined in Section 1.3. We will use our reduction of $\exists^+$ reformulation problems under constraints to conjunctive query containment under constraints, and show that it preserves the property of having terminating chase. From this, we will be able to show decidability of positive existential reformulation for these classes of constraints.

Proposition 2.17 *Let C be any class of TGD constraints having terminating chase and such that one can decide whether a constraint is in C. Then the following problem is decidable: given* Sch *a schema whose constraints are in C, $\mathcal{T}$ a target vocabulary, and Q a conjunctive query, decide if Q has a $\exists^+$ reformulation.*

Proof. We focus on the case where Q is boolean. We show how to decide the entailment corresponding to $\exists^+$ reformulation.

Given Q, let $\mathsf{CanonDB}(Q)$ be the *canonical database of* Q: recall from Section 1.3 that this is the instance having elements for each variable of Q and a fact for each atom of Q. By chasing $\mathsf{CanonDB}(Q)$, we can get an instance I_1 that is a "universal model" for the constraints Σ, in the sense that the boolean conjunctive queries holding in it are exactly those that are entailed by $\mathsf{CanonDB}(Q)$ and Σ. Now consider the "forward transfer axioms" $\forall \vec{x}\ T(\vec{x}) \rightarrow T'(\vec{x})$ for $T \in \mathcal{T}$. These rules in isolation have terminating chase, since after one round of firing all applicable rules the chase will terminate. Hence there is an instance I_2 such that I_2 satisfies exactly the queries that follow from $\mathsf{CanonDB}(Q) \wedge \Sigma$ conjoined with the forward transfer axioms. Letting Σ' be the primed copy of Σ, these constraints also have terminating chase (since Σ does), hence there is I_3 that satisfies exactly the queries that follow from $\Sigma \wedge \mathsf{CanonDB}(Q) \wedge \Sigma'$ and the forward transfer axioms. Thus it suffices to check whether Q', the primed copy of Q, holds in I_3, which can be done by just evaluating Q'. □

In Chapter 4 we will show that for schemas with TGD constraints, if there is a $\exists^{\neq}$ reformulation then there is a CQ reformulation (see Corollary 4.6). It follows that we can replace $\exists^+$ reformulation with $\exists^{\neq}$ reformulation or with CQ reformulation in the proposition above.

We can get a quantitative analog of Proposition 2.17. Given an instance I a *restricted chase round* applies a chase step for each active trigger in I and then takes the union of all resulting facts: thus a chase round applies all active triggers in parallel. The argument in Proposition 2.17 shows that if we have a uniform bound n on the number of chase rounds needed to achieve termination for a class of constraints Σ, then the corresponding constraints for the auxiliary schema for $\exists^{+,\neq}$ reformulation will terminate within $3n$ rounds.

We can apply the result above to constraints that come from conjunctive query view definitions. It is well-known that such constraints have terminating chase, but we include an argument for completeness. The following proposition gives a bound on the termination of the chase in this case:

Proposition 2.18 *Let $\mathcal{B}$ be a set of relations and Σ_V a finite set of constraints of the form $V_i \rightarrow \varphi_i$, $\varphi_i \rightarrow V_i$, where each V_i is a relation not in $\mathcal{B}$ and φ_i is a conjunctive query over relations in B. Let* Sch *be the schema with constraints Σ_V, and $\mathcal{T}$ consist of the relations V_i.*

Let I be an instance for this vocabulary such that for every fact $V_i(\vec{c})$, the corresponding formula $\varphi_i(\vec{c})$ holds in I. Then after at most one round of the restricted chase starting at I, there will be no applicable rules. If we start from an arbitrary instance I, then after at most two rounds there will be no applicable rules. In particular, any class of constraints generated from CQ view definitions has terminating chase.

Proof. To see the first item, note that our assumption on I guarantees that in the first round of the chase, no new facts on the relations in $\mathcal{B}$ are generated. New facts of the form $V_i(\vec{c})$ may be generated in the first round, but after the first round no more facts of this form will be generated.

To see the second item, note that after one round of the chase, the resulting instance will satisfy the hypothesis of the first item. □

By combining the proofs of Proposition 2.18 and Proposition 2.17, one can calculate that if we start with constraints generated from conjunctive query view definitions and form the auxiliary schema for monotonic determinacy (with two copies of the constraints and the "forward transfer axioms"), the restricted chase on these new constraints will terminate in at most four rounds.

We will also see (Section 2.8) that whenever the chase terminates for the auxiliary schema, our technique for computing a reformulation is complete for *finite instances*. Combining Proposition 2.18, Proposition 2.17, the observation above, and the fact that for TGD constraints whenever there is a $\exists^{+,\neq}$ reformulation there is a CQ reformulation (Corollary 4.2 proven later on in the text), we obtain end-to-end decidability for CQ reformulation over finite instances:

Theorem 2.19 *Let schema* Sch *have TGD constraints stating that each view relation V_i is equivalent to the result of a conjunctive query Q_i over some base signature $\mathcal{B}$, for $i \leq k$. Then for any conjunctive query Q over $\mathcal{B}$, we can determine whether or not Q can be reformulated as a conjunctive query over $V_i : i \leq n$ (over finite instances, equivalently over all instances) by chasing Q until termination using the two copies of the constraints plus the "forward transfer axioms," and then checking for a match of the primed copy of Q on the result.*

The results above imply that the $\exists^{+,\neq}$ reformulation problem over conjunctive query views is in NP. In the case where the arity of the relations is fixed, this is clear since the entire result of chase rounds can be guessed in NP. In the general case, one can show that only a polynomial-sized subset of each round of the chase is required to ensure a witness to Q', and this subset can be guessed and verified with a non-deterministic polynomial time machine. To see NP-hardness, note that the reduction from Proposition 2.14, applied to the empty set of constraints, reduces the containment problem for boolean CQs to the reformulation problem. The containment problem is known to be NP-hard [Chandra and Merlin, 1977], and so the hardness of reformulation follows.

Putting the arguments together, we get a variant of one of the first key results concerning query reformulation with views, from [Levy et al., 1995]:

Proposition 2.20 *Deciding the existence of a $\exists^{+,\neq}$ reformulation of a CQ Q over a collection of conjunctive query views is* NP*-complete.*

Later we will show that for any schema consisting of TGDs and any CQ Q, Q has a $\exists^{+,\neq}$ reformulation if and only if it has a CQ reformulation (see Corollary 4.2). Therefore in Proposition 2.20, $\exists^{+,\neq}$ reformulation can be replaced by $\exists^{+}$ reformulation or CQ reformulation.

2.7.4 TGDS WITH TERMINATING CHASE: RQFO REFORMULATION

In the previous subsection we have shown that any class with terminating chase has an effective end-to-end $\exists^{+}$ reformulation algorithm. For RQFO reformulations, we cannot argue as before, since the bidirectional "transfer axioms" in the auxiliary schema can cause the chase to fail to terminate. And indeed, the decidability of existence of first-order reformulations over conjunctive query views was open for many years [Nash et al., 2010], but recently Gogacz and Marcinkowski [Gogacz and Marcinkowski, 2015] proved that one cannot decide whether or not a CQ Q is determined over a set of CQ views. This implies that having an RQFO reformulation over all instances is undecidable. However, for many classes of TGDs with terminating chase from the literature, we can obtain decidability results for RQFO reformulation. We demonstrate this by looking at the class of weakly acyclic TGDs, defined in Fagin et al. [2005].

Given a schema Sch whose constraints Σ are TGDs, the associated *dependency graph* is a directed edge-labeled graph $G = (V, E)$, such that the vertices are the positions of relations in Sch—that is, (R, i) such that $i < \text{arity}(R)$. There is an edge $((R, i), (S, j)) \in E$, if there exists a TGD of the form:

$$\forall \vec{x} \vec{y} \; [\alpha(\vec{x}, \vec{y}) \rightarrow \exists \vec{z} \; \beta(\vec{x}, \vec{z})]$$

with variable x appearing in position i of an R-atom in α and one of the following holds:

1. x appears in position j of an S-atom in β. In this case the edge is labeled as *universal.*

2. x is in $\vec{x}$ and there exists variable $z \in \vec{z}$ which occurs in position j of an S-atom of β. In this case the edge is labeled as *existential.*

A set of TGDs is said to be *weakly acyclic* if the corresponding dependency graph does not have any cycle going through an existential edge. It is known that this class has terminating chase [Fagin et al., 2005].

Proposition 2.21 *The following problem is decidable: given a conjunctive query Q, finite collection of weakly acyclic TGDs Σ, and target vocabulary $\mathcal{T}$, determine whether or not Q has an* RQFO *reformulation over $\mathcal{T}$ with respect to Σ.*

Proof. It is easy to see that if Σ is weakly acyclic the set of TGDs:

$$\Sigma \cup \Sigma' \cup \bigcup_{T \in \mathcal{T}} (\forall \vec{x}\ T(\vec{x}) \rightarrow T'(\vec{x})) \cup \bigcup_{T \in \mathcal{T}} (\forall \vec{x}\ T'(\vec{x}) \rightarrow T(\vec{x}))$$

is again weakly acyclic, since we are simply making disjoint copies of the dependency graph and adding universal edges. So the set of constraints above has terminating chase, and decidability follows by simply evaluating the query Q' in the result of chasing the canonical database of Q. □

Similar arguments hold for other classes based on acyclicity conditions. In summary, we see that for constraint classes that are well-behaved in terms of decidability of query containment, the interpolation technique for reformulation can make use of the same decision procedures.

2.8 FINITE INSTANCES AND RESTRICTED CONSTRAINTS

Throughout the text we have dealt with reasoning over all instances, finite and infinite. The results in the previous sections characterized the existence of a reformulation over the target $\mathcal{T}$ that is equivalent to the input query Q over all instances that satisfy the constraints, saying that this was equivalent to an entailment holding over all instances. Since entailment over all instances is captured by the existence of proofs, this was crucial to making use of proofs to get reformulations. We will investigate the situation when looking at reformulations that work only over finite instances. For restricted classes of constraints, we will be able to transfer our semantics-to-syntax theorems to work with "all instances" replaced by "all finite instances," in so doing closing the last of the "gaps" between the classical logic perspective and the database perspective mentioned in Section 1.2. Throughout this section we will restrict, as in the previous section, to the case where Q is a CQ.

Bad behavior over finite instances: some counterexamples. We first show that when restricting to finite instances we do not always get a tight relationship between entailment and reformulations. We note that a query may have a reformulation that works for finite instances but no reformulation that works for all instances.

Theorem 2.22 *There is a set of TGD constraints, a target vocabulary $\mathcal{T}$, and a conjunctive query Q such that there is a positive existential equality-free query over $\mathcal{T}$ that is equivalent to Q over finite instances, but no query equivalent to Q over all instances.*

Proof. Let Sch contain relations M, R, and P, while the target $\mathcal{T}$ consists of only P. Assume we have the following constraints (universal quantifiers omitted):

$$\begin{aligned} M(x) &\rightarrow \exists y\ R(x,y) \\ R(x,y) &\rightarrow \exists z\ R(y,z) \\ R(x,y) \wedge R(y,z) &\rightarrow R(x,z) \\ R(x,x) &\rightarrow P(x) \\ P(x) &\rightarrow M(x). \end{aligned}$$

Then, for the query $\exists x\ M(x)$, there is an SPJ query over $\mathcal{T}$ that works over finite instances (namely, the query that simply tests whether P is non-empty). However, we show that no reformulation over $\mathcal{T}$ answers the same query over all instances. By Corollary 2.7, it suffices to show the query is not determined over $\mathcal{T}$ with respect to the constraints. We create instances I_1 and I_2 whose domain elements are natural numbers. In I_1, R is interpreted by the less-than relation, while both P and M are interpreted by the empty relation. I_2 differs from I_1 only in that M denotes the singleton set $\{0\}$. Both instances satisfy the constraints, and they have the same restriction to $\mathcal{T}$, but I_2 satisfies the query while I_1 does not. □

We show that the characterization theorems relating determinacy and reformulations do not hold in the finite. This has already been shown in the context of views in [Nash et al., 2010]. Recall that our theorems can be seen as relating an entailment, a preservation property, and the existence of a reformulation. This "triple equivalence" is shown, for example, in Corollary 2.7. The equivalence between entailment and preservation still holds for finite instances, using the same proof. Further, the implication from the existence of a reformulation to the entailment will still hold. The remaining piece is the direction from an entailment to a reformulation, which involved interpolation. This may fail, which thus leads to counterexamples for the theorems.

Theorem 2.23 *There is a schema with* RQFO *constraints Σ, target vocabulary $\mathcal{T}$, and conjunctive query Q such that Q is monotonically-determined w.r.t. $\mathcal{T}$ over finite instances (and hence determined over finite instances), but Q does not have any positive existential reformulation over finite instances.*

Proof. Our schema has unary relation P along with binary relations G and H, with the distinguished subsignature $\mathcal{T}$ containing only G. The query Q is $\exists x\ P(x)$. The constraints are:

- $\forall w\ P(w) \rightarrow \exists xy\ G(x,y)$

- $\forall xy\ G(x,y) \wedge P(y) \rightarrow \exists z\ G(y,z)$
- $\forall xy\ G(x,y) \rightarrow H(x,y) \wedge \varphi$, where φ asserts that H is transitive.
- $\forall x\ H(x,x) \rightarrow \exists y\ P(y)$

The first two constraints force, on finite instances, that whenever Q is true, there is a G-cycle. The third constraint forces that if there is a G-cycle, then there is an H-cycle, and hence by transitivity there is an H self-loop. Using the last constraint we get the converse to the statement above, that the existence of any G-cycle implies that Q is true.

Clearly, the query is preserved under adding tuples to G, since once there is a G-cycle it cannot be lost. However, it is not expressible by a first-order query over G since such a formula would have to test the existence of a G-cycle—one can adapt the standard argument in finite model theory that existence of a cycle is not first-order definable [Ebbinghaus and Flum, 1999]. □

Constraints that are well-behaved over finite instances. We will prove that for "tame" constraint classes, "answerability"—both in the form of the semantic notion of determinacy and the syntactic notion of having a reformulation—over all instances and over finite instances coincide, and in particular the main "triple-equivalence" theorems still hold in the finite. The story will mirror the one told for decidability in the previous section: when query answering with the constraint class has the finite model property—that is, when the constraints are "finitely controllable" [Bárány et al., 2010]—the reformulation technique will be complete for creating plans that work over finite instances.

We begin with monotonic determinacy and the accompanying property (for constraints without equality) of having a $\exists^+$ reformulation. For TGDs that have terminating chase, the auxiliary schema associated with monotonic determinacy also has terminating chase, as noted in Proposition 2.17. Using that proposition, we can infer the following general result:

Proposition 2.24 *Let* Sch *be a schema consisting of TGD constraints Σ having terminating chase, Q be a CQ, and $\mathcal{T}$ be a collection of relations. Then Q has a positive existential reformulation w.r.t. $\mathcal{T}$ over finite instances if and only if it has one over all instances.*

Proof. Note that if a set of constraints Σ' has terminating chase and we have a containment $Q \subseteq Q'$ w.r.t. Σ' holding between CQs Q, Q' over all finite instances, then the containment holds over all instances. This is because when such a containment fails to hold, there is a finite instance that is a counterexample, namely the result of chasing the canonical database of Q with the constraints.

Let Σ^* be the constraints formed from Σ in the auxiliary schema associated with monotonic determinacy. As noted in Proposition 2.17 these have terminating chase, thus every containment between CQs that holds over finite instances must hold over all instances. If Q does not have a positive existential reformulation over $\mathcal{T}$ w.r.t. Σ over all instances, then it is not monotonically-determined over $\mathcal{T}$ w.r.t. Σ over all instances, and hence Q is not contained in Q' w.r.t. Σ^*, where Q' is the primed copy of Q. By the above, there is a finite counterexample instance to this containment, which can be converted to a finite counterexample to monotonic determinacy of Q. But then Q cannot have a positive existential reformulation over $\mathcal{T}$ w.r.t. Σ over finite instances, since such a reformulation would be monotone over finite instances as the interpretations of relations in $\mathcal{T}$ increase. □

We can apply Proposition 2.24 to the setting of constraints given by conjunctive query view definitions to infer that for a CQ Q, whenever there is a reformulation over the views equivalent to Q over all finite instances, there is one equivalent to Q over all instances. Using Theorem 2.8, we know that this holds if and only if Q is monotonically-determined. Later in Corollary 4.2 we will show that for TGDs, whenever CQ Q can be reformulated by a positive existential query, it can be reformulated using a CQ. Thus we have shown a semantic characterization of CQ reformulation using monotonic determinacy, applicable to finite instances: if a query Q is monotonically-determined in views $V_1 \dots V_n$ defined by conjunctive queries over all finite instances, then Q can be reformulated in RQFO over finite instances over $V_1 \dots V_n$.[2]

For RQFO reformulation, we do not have any analogous general results about classes with terminating chase, for the reasons mentioned at the beginning of Subsection 2.7.4. We can obtain such results for weakly acyclic TGDs using the argument in Proposition 2.24 and the fact that the auxiliary constraints for RQFO reformulation will again by weakly acyclic, as shown in the proof of Proposition 2.21.

We turn to constraints in GNF. Our proofs below will make use of an additional fact about GNF, again due to [Bárány et al., 2011], building on work of [Bárány et al., 2010]:

Theorem 2.25 *[Bárány et al., 2011] A* GNF *sentence is satisfiable (resp. valid) over all instances if and only if it is satisfiable (resp. valid) over finite instances.*

We will use this to show that there is no gap between reformulations that work over finite instances and those that work over general instances for schemas with GNF constraints. We begin with the easiest case, which concerns positive existential queries. Here, we can say that a reformulation that works over finite instances works over all instances:

Theorem 2.26 *Let* Sch *be a schema whose integrity constraints Σ are in* GNF, *Q be a conjunctive query over* Sch, *and $\mathcal{T}$ be a target vocabulary. Then if Q' is a positive existential query over $\mathcal{T}$ that is equivalent to Q over finite instances, then Q' is equivalent to Q over all instances.*

Proof. We first give the argument when Q is a boolean query. Fix a positive existential query Q' that agrees with Q over finite instances. Consider the property of instances over the schema Sch: if the instance satisfies the constraints, then it satisfies Q' if and only if it satisfies Q. The property

[2]This was also shown in [Nash et al., 2010].

is expressible by a sentence of GNF, since positive existential queries are in GNF, the constraints are in GNF, and GNF is closed under boolean combinations of sentences. Therefore Theorem 2.12 implies that if the property holds on all finite instances, it holds on all instances. Hence Q' answers Q over all instances.

The extension to non-boolean queries is argued by changing the free variables of Q to uninterpreted constants, and then proceeding as in the boolean case. □

In the case of RQFO reformulations, the situation for tame constraints is more complex. We cannot say that for any RQFO Q' that answers Q over finite instances, the same Q answers it over all instances, even for boolean queries. For example, Q' may be true on all finite instances (and hence answer a tautological query) but be false on some infinite instance. However, we can still say that if Q has *some* RQFO reformulation over $\mathcal{T}$ in the finite, it has some (possibly different) query that works over all instances. For this, we will use our characterizations relating semantic and syntactic properties.

Theorem 2.27 *Let* Sch *be a schema whose constraints Σ are in* GNF, *$\mathcal{T}$ be a target vocabulary, and let Q be a conjunctive query. Then there is an* RQFO *query Q' over $\mathcal{T}$ that is equivalent to Q over finite instances satisfying Σ if and only if there is an* RQFO *Q'' equivalent to Q over all instances satisfying Σ. In particular, by Theorem 2.13, we can decide whether this property holds.*

Proof. Suppose there is such a Q' that works over finite instances. Then Q is determined by $\mathcal{T}$ with respect to Σ over finite instances. The following sentence expresses that a pair I, I' witness that Q is not determined over $\mathcal{T}$ with respect to Σ:

> I and I' both satisfy the constraints in Σ, they agree on all relations in $\mathcal{T}$ but they disagree on the truth value of Q for some tuple $\vec{x}_0$.

The property can be expressed as a GNF sentence γ, since it involves combinations of conjunctive queries and GNF constraints. The assumption on Q tells us that γ has no finite instance satisfying it. Since γ is unsatisfiable over finite instances, it is unsatisfiable over all instances by Theorem 2.12. Hence Q is determined over all instances. From Theorem 2.1 Q has an RQFO reformulation over all instances. □

A similar argument works for $\exists^{\neq}$ and $\exists^{+,\neq}$ reformulations.

Theorem 2.28 *Let* Sch *be a schema whose constraints Σ are in* GNF *and let Q be a conjunctive query. Then there is a $\exists^{\neq}$ query over $\mathcal{T}$ that is equivalent to Q over finite instances satisfying Σ if and only if there is such a query that is equivalent to Q over all instances satisfying Σ.*

Similarly, there is a $\exists^{+,\neq}$ query over $\mathcal{T}$ equivalent to Q over finite instances satisfying Σ if and only if there is a $\exists^{+,\neq}$ query over $\mathcal{T}$ equivalent to Q over all instances. Assuming Σ does not contain equality, the same holds for $\exists$ queries.

Proof. We give the proof only for $\exists^{\neq}$, with the second part being analogous. We argue as in Theorem 2.27. Suppose there is an existential Q' that works over finite instances. Consider the following property, stating that I and I' witness that Q is not induced-subinstance-monotonically-determined:

- I and I' both satisfy the constraints in Σ;
- $Q(\vec{x}_0)$ holds in I and $Q(\vec{x}_0)$ does not hold in I';
- for every $T \in \mathcal{T}$, $[\![T]\!]_I$ is contained in $[\![T]\!]_{I'}$; and
- if a tuple $\vec{t}$ is in $[\![T]\!]_{I'}$ and each value t_i of $\vec{t}$ lies in some $[\![T_i']\!]_I$ with $T_i \in \mathcal{T}$, then $\vec{t} \in [\![T]\!]_I$.

The property can be expressed by a GNF sentence γ, and there cannot be a finite instance satisfying it. So γ is unsatisfiable over all instances by Theorem 2.12. This means Q is induced-subinstance-monotonically-determined over all instances. Since Q is induced-subinstance-monotonically-determined over all instances, by Theorem 2.11 there is an existential query with inequalities that is equivalent to it over all instances satisfying the constraints. □

Again, decidability of this property now follows easily from decidability and closure properties of GNF.

2.9 SUMMARY

This chapter has instantiated the "meta-algorithm" mentioned in the introduction to show how we can take an input query Q and generate reformulations $Q_{\mathcal{T}}$ that use a specified set of target relations $\mathcal{T}$. It also has shown how we can vary this process to get queries of different sorts (RQFO, existential, positive existential). In each case, we showed how the problem reduces to searching for a proof that an entailment holds. Each entailment corresponds to verifying that the input query Q has a certain semantic property. The different entailments, the corresponding semantic properties and the comparison with prior results in model theory to vocabulary-based restrictions are summarized in Table 2.1.

On the last row of the table, Γ_{Ind} is an additional axiom stating that for each $R \in \mathcal{T}$, R' has no new facts whose values are all in the domain of R.

Although there can be no computable function that finds proofs that witness these proof goals for first-order logic constraints, we have shown that for many interesting classes of constraints we can find the proofs, and hence get the reformulated queries $Q_{\mathcal{T}}$, effectively. Complexity results for vocabulary-based restrictions are summarized in Table 2.2.

2.10 BIBLIOGRAPHIC REMARKS

As mentioned earlier in this text, the core idea of this work goes back to the logicians E.W. Beth and William Craig [Beth, 1953, Craig, 1957b]. We explain the distinction between the termi-

Table 2.1: Use of interpolation in going from semantic properties to reformulations

Goal	Semantic Property	Proof Goal	Classical Model Theory Analog
RQFO	Determinacy	$Q \wedge \Sigma \wedge \bigwedge_{T \in \mathcal{T}} (\forall \vec{x}\, T(\vec{x}) \leftrightarrow T'(\vec{x}))\ \Sigma' \vdash Q'$	Projective Beth Definability
$\exists^{+,\neq}$	Monotonic Determinacy	$Q \wedge \Sigma \wedge \bigwedge_{T \in \mathcal{T}} (\forall \vec{x}\, T(\vec{x}) \rightarrow T'(\vec{x}))\ \Sigma' \vdash Q'$	(No Exact Analog)
$\exists^{\neq}$	Induced-Subinstance-Monotonic Determinacy	$Q \wedge \Sigma \wedge \bigwedge_{T \in \mathcal{T}} (\forall \vec{x}\, T(\vec{x}) \rightarrow T'(\vec{x}))\ \Gamma_{\mathsf{Ind}} \wedge \Sigma' \vdash Q'$	Łoś-Tarski

Table 2.2: Complexity of reformulation over vocabulary-based restrictions

Constraints	RQFO Reformulation	$\exists^+$ Reformulation	$\exists$ Reformulation
GNF	2EXPTIME	2EXPTIME	2EXPTIME
GTGD	2EXPTIME	2EXPTIME	2EXPTIME
ID	PSPACE	PSPACE	PSPACE
CQ Views	undecidable over unrestricted instances [Gogacz and Marcinkowski, 2015], unknown over finite instances	NP	NP

nology used by Beth and Craig and that used here. A relation R in a relational schema Sch is *implicitly definable over* $\mathcal{T}$ relative to constraints Σ if for any two structures M_1, M_2 that satisfy the constraints of Σ and have the same interpretation of all relations in $\mathcal{T}$, they have the same interpretation of R. What is known as the Projective Beth Definability Theorem is stated as:

Theorem 2.29 *If the constraints Σ are in classical first-order logic, and R is implicitly definable over $\mathcal{T}$, then there is a classical first-order $\varphi(\vec{x})$ using only relations in $\mathcal{T}$ such that $\Sigma \models \forall \vec{x}\ R(\vec{x}) \leftrightarrow \varphi(\vec{x})$.*

This theorem states the same thing as Theorem 2.1 in this text, but for classical first-order logic (hence referring to structures rather than instances) and for a query consisting of a single relation. However, the result implies a similar theorem where R is replaced by a first-order query Q_R. Beth [Beth, 1953] proved the special case of this theorem where the set in $\mathcal{T}$ consists of all relations other than R. Craig [Craig, 1957b] gave a proof of the Projective Beth Theorem, making use of an interpolation theorem that he had proven the same year [Craig, 1957a]. Feferman's article [Feferman, 2008] provides an overview of the development of Craig's interpolation theorem and Beth's definability theorem. Although the original proof of Craig's theorem relies on a proof calculus, as our argument does, there are also proofs that are purely model-theoretic (e.g., [Chang and Keisler, 1990]). Model-theoretic proofs of interpolation theorems have been established for logics much richer than first-order logic, even those for which entailment cannot be captured via an effective proof system (e.g., [Lopez-Escobar, 1965]). Craig's theorem has many applications in computer science—see, e.g., [McMillan, 2005].

Determinacy and relativized-quantifier first-order reformulations. Segoufin and Vianu [Segoufin and Vianu, 2005] were the first to prove Theorem 2.1, the analog of Projective Beth for the active domain semantics. Their proof was non-constructive, using an interpolation theorem of Otto [Otto, 2000], and they do not explore the use of interpolation as a constructive technique to generate reformulations. The use of interpolation algorithms to generate reformulations is mentioned in [Borgida et al., 2010, Franconi et al., 2013, Toman and Weddell, 2011]. The exposition here extends the one in [Benedikt et al., 2014b]. Nash et al. [2010] includes a comprehensive study of determinacy over finite instances. The negative results concerning finite instances in this chapter are extensions of their work.

Nash et al. [2010] poses the question of decidability of the existence of a *relational algebra* reformulation of a conjunctive query with respect to conjunctive query views. Some partial (positive) results on this can be found in [Afrati, 2011, Borgida et al., 2010, Pasailă, 2011]. Still, decidability of "FO reformulation over CQ views" over finite instances remains a major open problem. Recently, Gogacz and Marcinkowski [Gogacz and Marcinkowski, 2015] showed that determinacy of a conjunctive query over conjunctive query views, when general instances are concerned, is undecidable. From this it follows that the corresponding question of existence of an FO reformulation over general instances is undecidable. Related open questions are:

- "Finite controllability of FO reformulation over CQ views": whether the existence of a first-order reformulation over finite instances implies that there is a first-order reformulation that works over all instances.
- "Determinacy-implies-rewritability in the finite over CQ views": if a query Q is determined over finite instances, does it have a first-order reformulation that works over finite instances?

Consider the question of whether determinacy of conjunctive queries Q over CQ views $\vec{V}$ is finitely controllable: is it true that if Q is determined over $\vec{V}$ for finite instances, this holds for all instances? [Nash et al., 2010] noted that if the answer is "yes," then determinacy over CQ views is decidable in both the finite and the unrestricted case. One can search for a finite counter-example to determinacy and in parallel search for a reformulation and a proof that it is equivalent to Q over all instances satisfying the constraints. Finite controllability implies that one of these searches must return successfully. Applying the undecidability result in Gogacz and Marcinkowski [2015], it follows that the answer must be "no."

Monotonic determinacy and positive existential reformulation. The problem of reformulating queries over views has a long history within databases. A key paper in this line is Levy et al. [1995], which proved that one can decide whether a conjunctive query over a set of base tables can be rewritten as a conjunctive query over views. This spawned a line of work on algorithms for rewriting queries using views [Levy et al., 1996, Pottinger and Halevy, 2001].

Rewriting a conjunctive query over base relations in terms of conjunctive query views is a particular case of positive existential reformulation, and so Levy et al. [1995] can be seen as the first complete algorithm for positive existential reformulation in the database context. The results in this chapter on positive existential reformulation using the interpolation-based approach (e.g., Proposition 2.17) can be seen as generalizations of [Levy et al., 1995].

Our notion of monotonic determinacy extends a definition in [Nash et al., 2010] from the setting of views to that of general integrity constraints. The results about positive existential reformulation are from [Benedikt et al., 2014b], although they are very close to statements in [Nash et al., 2010] for the case of views. The study of existential reformulation, its connection to preservation theorems, and the corresponding notion of induced-subinstance-monotonic determinacy appear in [Benedikt et al., 2014b].

Decidability, finiteness, and safety. The idea of proving effective reformulation results using interpolation coupled with a decision procedure for a restricted constraint language is mentioned in [Marx, 2007]. The idea is corrected in [Bárány et al., 2013], which also explores reformulation for the guarded negation fragment. The majority of the decidability results and finite model results in this chapter come from [Bárány et al., 2013] and [Benedikt et al., 2014b]. Safety of reformulations is considered in [Franconi et al., 2013], which presents necessary conditions for existence of a safe reformulation.

CHAPTER 3

Access Methods and Integrity Constraints

In the previous chapter the target of reformulation was specified through vocabulary restrictions. We wanted a query that used a fixed set of target relations, perhaps restricted to be positive existential or existential. In this chapter we deal with a finer notion of reformulation, where the target has to satisfy *access restrictions*, as was illustrated in Examples 1.3 and 1.4.

We begin with the definitions of access methods along with a programming language, the RA-plans, that combines data access by means of a fixed set of access methods with data manipulation using relational algebra queries. Recall that relational algebra represents an algebraic programming language that is equivalent in expressiveness to (safe) first-order logic. Implementation of logic-based languages proceeds by translating a logical formula into relational algebra. RA-plans can be thought of as a variation of relational algebra in which we want to abide by a fixed set of data interfaces given by access methods. They will thus be the new target of reformulation from this point onward. In Section 3.3 we divert from our main thread to investigate RA-plans. We present several alternative formalisms which have the same expressiveness, including one based on logic.

In Section 3.4 we return to our program of going from semantic properties to reformulations, following the methodology outlined in Chapter 2. We present semantic properties that must hold for a query to be implemented using the interface given by a set of access methods, and show that these properties can be captured by entailments. In the remainder of the chapter we explain how proofs of these entailments can be converted into plans within our plan languages. The conversion from proof to plan will again proceed via interpolation. But in this case we need a new interpolation theorem tailored to the setting of access methods.

3.1 BASICS OF TARGET RESTRICTIONS BASED ON ACCESS METHODS

In this chapter we look at a notion of interface that is closer to the traditional notion in programming languages: a set of functions that access the data. A specification of this interface will be an extended set of metadata describing both the format of the data (e.g. the vocabulary that would be used in queries and constraints) and the access methods (functions that interact with the stored data).

An *access schema* consists of:

- A collection of relations, each of a given arity.
- A finite collection C of schema constants ("Smith", 3, ...). Schema constants represent a fixed set of values that will be known to a user prior to interacting with the data. Values that can be used in queries and constraints should be schema constants, as before. In addition, any fixed values that might be used in plans that implement queries should come from the set of schema constants. For example, a plan to answer a query about the mathematics department might involve first putting the string "mathematics" into a university directory service.
- For each relation R, a collection (possibly empty) of *access methods*.[1] Recall from Section 1.2 that a *position* of a relation R is a number between 1 and $\mathsf{arity}(R)$. Each access method mt is associated with a collection (possibly empty) of positions of R—the *input positions* of mt.
- Integrity constraints, which are sentences in relativized-quantifier first-order logic as before.

An *access* (relative to a schema as above) consists of an access method of the schema and a *method binding*—a function assigning values to every input position of the method. If mt is an access method on relation R with arity n, I is an instance for a schema that includes R, and AccBind is a method binding on mt, then the *output* or *result* of the access (mt, AccBind) on I is the set of n-tuples $\vec{t} \in [\![R]\!]_I$ such that $\vec{t}$ restricted to the input positions of mt is equal to AccBind.

An access method may have an empty collection of input positions. In this case, the only access that can be performed using the method is with the empty method binding. When a method has no input positions, we say that the access method is "input-free." In Example 1.3 of Section 1.1, the Udirectory table was assumed to have such an input-free access method.

The goal is to reformulate source queries in a target language that represents the kind of restricted computation done over an interface given by an access schema. We first formalize this operationally, as a language of *plans*. Plans are straight-line programs that can perform accesses and manipulate the results of accesses using relational algebra operators. This language could model, at a high-level, the plans used internally in a database management system. It could also describe the computation done within a data integration system, which might access remote data via a web form or web service and then combine data from different sources using SQL within its own database management system.

All of our plan languages have as a primitive an *access command*. Over a schema Sch with access methods, an access command is of the form:

$$T \Leftarrow_{\mathsf{OutMap}} \mathsf{mt} \Leftarrow_{\mathsf{InMap}} E$$

where:

[1] Our definition of "access methods" is a variant of the terminology "access patterns" or "binding patterns" found in the database literature.

(a) E is a relational algebra expression, the *input expression*, over some set of relations not in Sch (henceforward "temporary tables");

(a) mt is a method from Sch on some relation R;

(a) InMap, the *input mapping* of the command, is a function from the output attributes of E onto the input positions of mt;

(a) T, the *output table* of the command, is a temporary table;

(a) OutMap, the *output mapping* of the command, is a bijection from positions of R to attributes of T.

Note that an access command using an input-free method must take the empty relation algebra expression $\emptyset$ as input.

The manipulation of data retrieved by an access is modeled with the other primitive of our languages, a *middleware query command.* These are of the form $T := Q$, where Q is a relational algebra expression over temporary tables and T is a temporary table. We use the qualifier "middleware" to emphasize that the queries are performed on temporary relations created by other commands, rather than on relations of the input schema.

A *relational algebra-plan* (or simply, *RA-plan*) consists of a sequence of access and middleware query commands, ending with at most one *return command* of the form Return E, where E is an RA expression.

Example 3.1. We return to Example 1.3 of Section 1.1, where we had two sources of information. One was Profinfo, which was available through an access method $\mathsf{mt}_{\mathsf{Profinfo}}$ requiring input on the first position. The second was Udirectory, which had an access method $\mathsf{mt}_{\mathsf{Udirectory}}$ requiring no input. Our query Q asked for ids of faculty named "Smith". One plan that is equivalent to Q would be represented as follows

$$
\begin{aligned}
&T_1 \Leftarrow \mathsf{mt}_{\mathsf{Udirectory}} \Leftarrow \emptyset \\
&T_2 := \pi_{\mathsf{eid}}(\sigma_{\mathsf{lname}=\text{“Smith”}} T_1) \\
&T_3 \Leftarrow \mathsf{mt}_{\mathsf{Profinfo}} \Leftarrow T_2 \\
&\mathsf{Return}\ \pi_{\mathsf{eid}}(T_3).
\end{aligned}
$$

Above we have omitted the mappings in writing access commands, since they can be inferred from the context. We will often do this in plans for brevity. ◁

Semantics of plans. A temporary table is *assigned* in a plan if it occurs on the left side of a command, and otherwise is said to be *free*. The semantics of plans is defined as a function that takes as input an instance I for Sch and interpretations of the free tables. If the plan has no Return statement, the output consists of interpretations for each assigned temporary table. If the plan contains a statement Return E, the output is an interpretation of a relation with attributes for each output attribute of E. In the latter case, we refer to this as the *output* of the plan.

An access command $T \Leftarrow_{\mathsf{OutMap}} \mathsf{mt} \Leftarrow_{\mathsf{InMap}} E$ is executed by evaluating the expression E on I and "accessing mt on every result tuple." That is, each output tuple of E is mapped to a tuple $t_{j_1} \dots t_{j_m}$ using the input mapping InMap. For each tuple $\vec{t} = t_1 \dots t_n \in R$ that "matches" (i.e., that extends) $t_{j_1} \dots t_{j_m}$, $\vec{t}$ is transformed to a tuple $\vec{t}'$ using the output mapping OutMap. The interpretation of T is then the union of all such tuples $\vec{t}'$. A middleware query command $T := E$ executes query E on the contents of the temporary tables mentioned in E, and then assigns the result to temporary table T.

A plan is executed by evaluating its commands in sequence, with each command operating on the instance formed from the input instance, adding the interpretations of assigned tables produced by earlier commands. For a plan having as its final command Return E, the output of the plan is the evaluation of E on the instance formed as above.

We usually assume (without loss of generality) that each table is only assigned once within a plan. Given plan PL, temporary table T that occurs in PL, and an instance I for the schema Sch, we let $[\![T \mid \mathsf{PL}]\!]_I$ be the content of T when PL is run on I. For plan PL including a Return statement, we let $[\![\mathsf{PL}]\!]_I$ be the output of PL on I. Similarly, given a relational algebra expression E over temporary tables $T_1 \dots T_n$ of PL and instance I, $[\![E \mid \mathsf{PL}]\!]_I$ represents the result of E when run on $[\![T_1 \mid \mathsf{PL}]\!]_I \dots [\![T_n \mid \mathsf{PL}]\!]_I$.

Fragments of the plan language. We now define fragments of our plan language, analogs of the fragments of relational algebra and first-order logic discussed in Section 1.2. In RA-plans, we allowed arbitrary relational algebra expressions in both the inputs to access commands and the middleware query commands. We can similarly talk about *$SPJ^{\neq}$-plans*, where the expressions in access and middleware query commands are built up from the $SPJ^{\neq}$ relational algebra operators and *$USPJ^{\neq}$-plans* that allow UNION in addition to $SPJ^{\neq}$ operators. We define *$USPJAD^{\neq}$-plans* as RA-plans in which relational algebra's difference operator only occurs in a *non-membership check*, which tests whether the tuples in a projection of a temporary table are not in a given relation R. Formally, a non-membership check is a sequence of two commands:

$$T' \Leftarrow_{\mathsf{OutMap}} \mathsf{mt} \Leftarrow_{\mathsf{InMap}} \pi_{a_{j_1} \dots a_{j_m}}(T)$$
$$T'' := T - (T \ltimes T').$$

where in the first command:

- mt is an access method on some relation R with input positions $j_1 \dots j_m$;
- the input mapping InMap maps attribute a_{j_i} to position j_i;
- the attributes of the output table T' are a subset of the attributes of T containing each a_{j_i};
- the output mapping OutMap maps j_i back to a_{j_i}.

In the second command, the join condition identifies attributes that have the same name. SPJ-plans, $USPJ$-plans, and $USPJAD$-plans are defined analogously to the classes above, but not allowing inequality conditions in selections or joins.

Plans that answer queries. We now define what it means for a plan to correctly implement a query. Given an access schema Sch, a plan *answers* a query Q *(over all instances)* if for every instance I satisfying the constraints of Sch, the output of the plan on I is the same as the output of Q. We often omit the schema from our notation, since it is usually clear from context, saying that a plan PL answers Q. We say that the plan *answers* Q *over finite instances* if the output of the plan on I is the same as the output of Q for every finite instance I satisfying the constraints. Note that this extends the notion of a query $Q_{\mathcal{T}}$ over a restricted signature $\mathcal{T}$ answering (or reformulating) query Q, as defined at the beginning of Chapter 2.

3.2 NESTED PLANS

It will sometimes be convenient to program plans with a higher-level syntax that allows a notion of subroutine. We formalize this by defining an extension of RA-plans with subroutines, the *nested RA-plans*. We inductively define the syntax of nested plans, along with the definition of a table being *free* or *assigned* within a nested plan, extending the definition for RA-plans given in the previous subsection. While for RA-plans, every temporary table mentioned in the plan will be either free or assigned, this will not be the case for nested plans.

An atomic nested plan is either:

- an access command $T \Leftarrow_{\mathsf{OutMap}} \mathsf{mt} \Leftarrow_{\mathsf{InMap}} E$;
- a middleware query command $T := E$, where E is a relational algebra expression over temporary tables;
- a command Return T, where T is a temporary table.

In each case T is the only assigned temporary table of the plan, and the tables mentioned in E are free tables.

Nested plans are built up via concatenation and subplan calls. If PL_1 and PL_2 are nested plans, then $\mathsf{PL}_1 \cdot \mathsf{PL}_2$ (read as "PL_1 followed by PL_2") is a nested plan. The free tables are the free tables of PL_1 along with any free tables of PL_2 that are not assigned tables of PL_1. The assigned tables of the concatenation are the assigned tables of PL_1 unioned with the assigned tables of PL_2.

If PL_1 is a nested plan which includes a Return command at "top-level" (not nested inside a subplan call), T is a free table in PL_1, E is a relational algebra expression over tables not mentioned in PL_1 whose output matches the attributes of T, and T' is a new temporary table whose attributes are those of the output of PL_1, then

$$T' \Leftarrow \mathsf{PL}_1[T] \Leftarrow E$$

is a nested plan. The assigned tables of this plan are the assigned tables of PL_1 along with T', while the free tables are those of PL_1 minus T along with any temporary tables mentioned in E. Informally, this plan evaluates E to get a set of tuples $[\![E]\!]_I$, performs PL_1 in parallel with the distinguished table T corresponding to $\{\vec{t}\}$ for each tuple $\vec{t}$ in $[\![E]\!]_I$, and sets T' to be the union of each tuple $\vec{o}$ in the output of such a call.

Example 3.2. Let us generalize the plan in Example 3.1 to get a plan $\mathsf{PL}_{\mathsf{lookupname}}$ that looks up all faculty matching the $\mathsf{facultyname}$ field of a tuple in a table $T_{\mathsf{facultynames}}$.

$$
\begin{aligned}
&T_1 \Leftarrow \mathsf{mt}_{\mathsf{Udirectory}} \Leftarrow \emptyset \\
&T_2 := \pi_{\mathsf{eid}}(T_1 \bowtie_{\mathsf{lname}=\mathsf{facultyname}} T_{\mathsf{facultynames}}) \\
&T_3 \Leftarrow \mathsf{mt}_{\mathsf{Profinfo}} \Leftarrow T_2 \\
&\mathsf{Return}\ \pi_{\mathsf{eid}}(T_3).
\end{aligned}
$$

This plan has $T_{\mathsf{facultynames}}$ as a free table, and hence only makes sense as a subplan of another plan. Suppose that a datasource provides an input-free access $\mathsf{mt}_{\mathsf{getnames}}$ returning all names of faculty members. We could create a new nested plan that gets the employee id of every faculty member as follows:

$$
\begin{aligned}
&T_4 \Leftarrow \mathsf{mt}_{\mathsf{getnames}} \Leftarrow \emptyset \\
&T_5 \Leftarrow \mathsf{PL}_{\mathsf{lookupname}} \Leftarrow T_4 \\
&\mathsf{Return}\ T_5.
\end{aligned}
$$

◁

Formally, we can define the result of an assigned temporary table T in a nested plan PL, along with the output of such a plan, when evaluated with respect to an instance I for the Sch relations and all free temporary tables of PL. The evaluation of an access command is as before, the evaluation of a middleware query command is standard. The evaluation of $\mathsf{PL}_1 \cdot \mathsf{PL}_2$ proceeds by first evaluating PL_1 to get interpretations of each assigned table and then evaluating PL_2 on the expansion of the input by these additional interpretations. The evaluation of $T' \Leftarrow \mathsf{PL}_1[T] \Leftarrow E$ is

$$
\bigcup_{\vec{t} \in [\![E]\!]_I} [\![\mathsf{PL}_1]\!]_{I,T:=\{\vec{t}\}}
$$

where $I, T := \{\vec{t}\}$ is the instance formed from I by interpreting T as $\{\vec{t}\}$.

3.3 EXPRESSIVENESS OF PLAN LANGUAGES

In Section 1.2, we reviewed first-order logic and the equivalent operational language Relational Algebra. An RA-plan is a counterpart to relational algebra, but interacting with data only using the access methods. We now present a subset of first-order logic that is equivalent to RA-plans, executable first-order queries. We will also define a logic that is equivalent to SPJ-plans. The equivalence between RA-plans and executable first-order queries gives an alternative way of thinking about the target of reformulation in the presence of access methods: readers who prefer logic can substitute "executable first-order query" whenever they see "RA-plan." The equivalence theorems also provide a justification for our plan languages. The main result of this section used later in the text is Corollary 3.5: it implies that there is an algorithm converting nested plans to ordinary RA-plans, and we make use of this algorithm in our plan-generation algorithms for TGDs in Chapter 4.

Executable logic-based queries. What does it mean for a logical formula to be "implementable" by a set of access methods? In the database literature there is a restricted syntax that enforces conformance with a collection access patterns: the "executable formulas" or "executable queries." It is easiest to explain the idea first for conjunctive queries.

A conjunctive query Q with atoms $A_1 \dots A_n$ is *executable* relative to a schema with access methods [Li and Chang, 2000] if there is an annotation of each atom $A_i = R_i(\vec{x}_i)$ with an access method mt_i on R such that for each variable x of Q, in the first A_i containing x, x occurs only in an output position of mt_i, where an output position is any position that is not an input position. A UCQ $\bigvee_i Q_i$, where Q_i is a CQ, is said to be executable if each disjunct Q_i is an executable CQ.

Example 3.3. Let us go back again to the schema from Example 1.3, which had a Profinfo relation of arity 3 accessible via an access method requiring input on the first position, and also a unary Udirectory relation with an access method requiring no input. The query Q asking for ids of faculty can be written as an executable CQ:

$$\exists \mathsf{onum}\ \exists \mathsf{lname}\ \mathsf{Udirectory}(\mathsf{eid}, \mathsf{lname}) \wedge \mathsf{Profinfo}(\mathsf{eid}, \text{“Smith”}, \mathsf{onum}).$$

Variables eid and lname occur first in the output positions of the unique access method on Udirectory, while variable onum occurs first in an output position of the unique access method on Profinfo. ◁

Every executable UCQ is clearly "implementable with access commands that use the given methods." In fact, every executable conjunctive query Q can be transformed naïvely to an SPJ-plan.

Proposition 3.1 *Every executable CQ can be converted to an SPJ-plan, denoted* PlanOf(Q), *where the number of access commands of the plan is equal to the number of atoms in the query. Similarly every executable UCQ can be converted to a $USPJ$-plan.*

Proof. We inductively translate conjunctions of atoms to plans, with the base case translating the empty conjunction to the empty plan. The inductive rule will remove the Return command in PlanOf($A_1 \ldots A_{i-1}$) and append on (a) the access command $T_i' \Leftarrow \mathsf{mt}_i \Leftarrow E_i(T_{i-1})$ where mt_i is the method annotating A_i and E_i consists of SPJ operations that project onto the input positions of mt_i and enforce repetition of variables and schema constants in input positions of mt_i; (b) the middleware query command $T_i := E_i'(T_i') \bowtie T_{i-1}$ where T_{i-1} is the output table of PlanOf($A_1 \ldots A_{i-1}$), which will have attributes for all variables of $A_1 \ldots A_i$, and E_i' consist of selections that enforce repetition of variables and schema constants in output positions of mt_i; (c) the command Return T_i. A final projection operation will enforce any projections in Q. By translating one disjunct at a time, we see that every executable UCQ translates into a $USPJ$-plan. □

We wish to extend the notion of executability to RQFO formulas. Although a prior definition for first-order formulas exists in the literature [Nash and Ludäscher, 2004a], we will find it useful to build our own for RQFO.

An RQFO formula is *executable for membership checks* (relative to an access schema Sch) if it is built up from equalities and the formula True using arbitrary boolean operations and the quantifiers:

$$\forall \vec{y}\ [R(\vec{x}, \vec{y}) \rightarrow \varphi(\vec{x}, \vec{y}, \vec{z})]$$
$$\exists \vec{y}\ R(\vec{x}, \vec{y}) \wedge \varphi(\vec{x}, \vec{y}, \vec{z})$$

and for any such quantification above, if R is a Sch relation, then R has an access method mt such that all of the input positions of mt are occupied by some x_i (that is: by a free variable or constant).

In the case of a first-order sentence, this definition captures the informal idea that the sentence is compatible with the access methods: we should be quantifying only over the output positions, while the values input positions should be provided. For a formula with free variables, being executable for membership checks is intuitively insufficient for implementation with the access methods: unlike the definition of executable UCQ, there is no restriction on how the free variables relate to positions of the methods. But we will show that a formula executable for membership checks has a weaker property: if we are given a tuple, we can check whether it satisfies the formula using the access methods.

Let $\varphi(\vec{x})$ be a formula using the schema relations and additional tables $\vec{T}$. We say that an RA-plan PL *filters* φ if PL has output attributes for each variable in $\vec{x}$, has free temporary tables contained in $\vec{T} \cup \{T_{\vec{x}}\}$ with $T_{\vec{x}}$ an additional temporary table with attributes for each variable in $\vec{x}$, and φ returns the subset of the tuples in $T_{\vec{x}}$ that satisfy φ. This last property needs to be "up to the distinction between positional and named notation." Formally, it means:

$$[\![\mathsf{PL}]\!]_{I^*} = \{\vec{o}^* \mid \vec{o} \in [\![T_{\vec{x}}]\!]_I \wedge I, \vec{o} \models \varphi\}$$

where for a variable binding $\vec{o}$ with free variables $x_1 \ldots x_n$, $\vec{o}^*$ is the corresponding tuple with attributes $a_1 \ldots a_n$, and I^* is the same as I except that free tables T with arity k are considered as tuples with attributes $\#1 \ldots \#k$. The next proposition says that for any RQFO formula we can find a plan that filters an input table down to the subset satisfying the formula.

Proposition 3.2 *There is a linear time procedure taking as input an* RQFO *formula φ with free variables $x_{a_1} \ldots x_{a_n}$ that is executable for membership checks and producing an RA-plan* Plan_φ *with output attributes $a_1 \ldots a_n$ which filters φ. Furthermore, if the* RQFO *formula is existential with inequalities (resp. existential) the result is a $USPJAD^{\neq}$-plan (resp. $USPJAD$-plan).*

If the formula is positive existential with inequalities (resp. positive existential) the result is a $USPJ^{\neq}$-plan (resp. $USPJ$-plan).

Proof. We create a function $\mathsf{ToPlan}(\varphi(\vec{x}))$ that outputs a plan which filters $\varphi(\vec{x})$. For simplicity, we assume that formula φ does not contain constants. The definition of ToPlan is by induction on the structure of φ.

$\mathsf{ToPlan}(\mathsf{True})$ will be the plan that just returns $T_{\vec{x}}$ while $\mathsf{ToPlan}(x_i = x_j)$ performs a selection on $T_{\vec{x}}$. The boolean operators $\wedge$ and $\vee$ will translate to join and union in the usual way.

Consider the formula $\psi = \exists \vec{y}\ R(\vec{x}, \vec{y}) \wedge \varphi(\vec{x}, \vec{y}, \vec{z})$. Assume for simplicity that $R(\vec{x}, \vec{y})$ has no repetition of variables. $\mathsf{ToPlan}(\psi)$ will be a plan that takes as input $T_{\vec{x} \cup \vec{z}}$ with attributes corresponding to $\vec{x} \cup \vec{z}$, and consists of the concatenation of the following commands:

$$\begin{aligned}
&T_1 \Leftarrow_{\mathsf{OutMap}} \mathsf{mt}_R \Leftarrow_{\mathsf{InMap}} \pi_{\vec{x}}(T_{\vec{x} \cup \vec{z}}) \\
&T_2 := T_1 \bowtie T_{\vec{x} \cup \vec{z}} \\
&T_3 := \mathsf{ToPlan}(\varphi)(T_{\vec{x} \cup \vec{y} \cup \vec{z}} := T_2) \\
&\mathsf{Return}\ \pi_{\vec{x},\vec{z}}(T_3).
\end{aligned}$$

Above

(i) mt_R is any access method on R such that all of its input positions are occupied by an x_i from $R(\vec{x}, \vec{y})$. Such a method exists since φ is executable for membership checks;

(ii) $T_3 := \mathsf{ToPlan}(\varphi)(T_{\vec{x} \cup \vec{y} \cup \vec{z}} := T_2)$ is the set of commands in $\mathsf{ToPlan}(\varphi)$ with the table T_2 substituted for $T_{\vec{x} \cup \vec{y} \cup \vec{z}}$ and an assignment to T_3 replacing the Return command;

(iii) InMap maps attribute a_{x_i} of $T_{\vec{x} \cup \vec{z}}$ to the position of R containing x_i;

(iv) OutMap maps position i of R to attribute x_{a_j} or y_{a_j}, where x_{a_j} or y_{a_j} is in position i of R in $R(\vec{x}, \vec{y})$.

The case where variables are repeated is handled by inserting additional middleware query commands that enforce these repetitions.

To compute $\mathsf{ToPlan}(\forall \vec{y}\ R(\vec{x}, \vec{y}) \rightarrow \varphi(\vec{x}, \vec{y}, \vec{z}))$, it suffices to get a plan for its negation $\exists \vec{y}\ R(\vec{x}, \vec{y}) \wedge \neg\varphi(\vec{x}, \vec{y}, \vec{z}))$. We give a construction for the case of general negation: $\mathsf{ToPlan}(\neg\varphi)$ returns $T_{\vec{x}} - \mathsf{ToPlan}(\varphi)$, where $T_{\vec{x}}$ has attributes corresponding to the free variables of φ. This can be implemented by a plan that first performs the commands in ToPlan(φ), with the output in some table T', and then does a middleware query command subtracting T' from $T_{\vec{x}}$. When φ is a relational atom, this can be implemented as a non-membership check.

The properties of the translation are easily verified. □

We are now ready to present a logical formalism equivalent to RA-plans. An *executable FO query* will be a query that performs an executable UCQ to get a set of tuples, and then filters it using a formula executable for membership checks. Formally such a query consists of:

- a set $x_1 \dots x_k$ of variables;
- a first-order formula $\tau(x_1 \dots x_l)$ with free variables containing $x_1 \dots x_k$, using a distinguished relation $T_{\vec{x}}$ whose arity matches the number of free variables in τ, with τ executable for membership checks;
- an executable UCQ $\epsilon(x_1 \dots x_l)$;

We refer to $x_1 \dots x_k$ as the *return variables*, ϵ as the *output envelope* and τ as the *filter formula*. To evaluate such a query on an instance I, we proceed as follows:

(a) evaluate ϵ over I to get a set of tuples $I_{\vec{x}}$;

(b) evaluate τ over the instance formed from I by making $I_{\vec{x}}$ the interpretation of $T_{\vec{x}}$ to get a subset $I'_{\vec{x}}$ of the tuples in $I_{\vec{x}}$;

(c) project $I'_{\vec{x}}$ on $x_1 \dots x_k$.

Example 3.4. Let our access schema Sch contain relations $R_1(x, y)$ and $R_2(x, y)$ having input-free access methods mt_1 and mt_2 respectively. There is a plan PL that first accesses R_1 using mt_1, putting the output in temporary table T_1, then accesses R_2 using mt_2 placing the output in T_2, and finally returns tuples x lying in the first position of T_1 such that $\forall y\ T_1(x, y) \rightarrow T_2(x, y)$. This can be expressed in the language of RA-plans as:

$$
\begin{aligned}
&T_1 \Leftarrow \mathsf{mt}_1 \Leftarrow \emptyset \\
&T_2 \Leftarrow \mathsf{mt}_2 \Leftarrow \emptyset \\
&\mathsf{Return}\ \pi_{\#1}(T_1) - \pi_{\#1}(T_1 - T_2)).
\end{aligned}
$$

PL can also be expressed by the executable FO query with:

- return variable x
- output envelope $R_1(x, y)$
- filter formula $T_{x,y}(x, y) \wedge \forall y\ (R_1(x, y) \rightarrow R_2(x, y))$

The executable query first gets all tuples $(x, y) \in R_1$, then filters down to those for which $\forall y\ R_1(x, y) \rightarrow R_2(x, y)$ holds, and for all such (x, y) returns x. Since we have input-free access to R_1 and R_2, the output envelope is an executable CQ, and the filter formula is executable for membership checks, as required. $\triangleleft$

Expressive equivalence. We now compare the expressiveness of the languages we have introduced. Using the two propositions above, we see that:

Proposition 3.3 *Every executable FO query can be converted into an RA-plan.*

We show that, conversely, nested RA-plans can be translated into executable FO queries, and hence the same is true for RA-plans. This will imply that RA-plans, nested RA-plans, and executable FO queries have the same expressiveness.

For any nested plan PL and assigned table T in PL, we let PL_T be the plan that is identical to PL except the unique return command is Return T.

Theorem 3.4 *For any nested plan* PL *with free temporary tables $T_1 \dots T_k$, and for any assigned temporary table T of* PL*, there is an executable FO query $\varphi(\vec{x})$ over* Sch $\cup \{T_1 \dots T_k\}$. *with free variables x_a for each output attribute a of* PL *such that φ is equivalent to PL_T. That is, for all instances I interpreting the* Sch *relations and the free temporary tables of* PL*:*

$$I^*, \vec{o}^* \models \varphi \text{ if and only if } \vec{o} \in [\![\mathsf{PL}_T]\!]_I.$$

Similarly for PL *with a top-level* Return, *there is an executable φ that is equivalent to* PL.

In the statement above, I^* is the same as I up to the usual "fine print conversion" between attribute-based and position-based notation discussed in Section 1.2: they are the same except that for each free temporary table T_i, $[\![T_i]\!]_{I^*}$ uses $\mathsf{arity}(T_i)$-tuples (required for an RQFO formula φ), while I uses named attributes (required by PL, which accesses the free tables T_i via relational algebra expressions). We assume that the free temporary tables T_i with arity n have attributes $\#1 \dots \#n$, and that a tuple $(v_1 \dots v_n) \in [\![T_i]\!]_{I^*}$ if and only if the corresponding tuple with attribute $\#i = v_i$ is in $[\![T_i]\!]_I$. Likewise $\vec{o}^*$ is the variable binding with variables $x_{a_1} \dots x_{a_r}$ that corresponds to the tuple $\vec{o}$ with attributes $a_1 \dots a_r$. We often neglect the conversion between positional and named tuples below.

Proof. In this proof, we make use of a few closure properties of executable UCQs and executable FO queries. Executable UCQs are closed under projection (adding existential quantifiers), since one can push the quantification inside the disjunction, and the requirements on the access methods are still satisfied. The formulas that are executable for membership checks are closed under boolean combinations. They are also closed under replacement of relational atoms $R(\vec{w})$ with conjunctions $\bigwedge w_i = y_i$ with y_i variables. Furthermore, for any executable UCQ $\epsilon(\vec{x})$ and formula φ executable for membership checks, the formula $\exists x_1 \dots x_j\ \epsilon \wedge \varphi$ is equivalent to a formula executable for membership checks, by converting $\exists x_1 \dots x_j\ \epsilon$ to a sequence of relativized quantifications. Universal quantifications $\forall x_1 \dots x_j\ \epsilon \rightarrow \varphi$ can be similarly converted.

We provide an inductive translation for both statements in the theorem. We begin with the case for access commands. We can assume that the command is of the form $T \Leftarrow_{\mathsf{OutMap}} \mathsf{mt}_{\mathsf{InMap}} \Leftarrow T'$, since an RA expression on the right can be pushed into a middleware query command. We can also assume that the attributes of T are $\#1 \dots \#n$ and OutMap maps position i of R to attribute $\#i$ of T; an additional middleware query command doing a renaming can be applied to model a nontrivial OutMap. Likewise, we can assume that the attributes of T' are $\#j_1 \dots \#j_m$, where $j_1 \dots j_m$ are the input positions of mt within relation R. We produce $x_1 \dots x_n$ as the return variables, $T'(\vec{y}) \wedge R(\vec{y}, \vec{x})$ as the output envelope, and $T_{\vec{x} \cup \vec{y}}(\vec{x}, \vec{y})$ as the filter formula.

We turn to the inductive case for $\mathsf{PL}^1 \cdot \mathsf{PL}^2$, PL^1 followed by PL^2. By induction, we have an executable FO query specified by $x_1 \dots x_k$, $\epsilon^2(x^2_1 \dots x^2_l)$, $\tau^2(x^1_1 \dots x^1_l)$ for PL^2. For each assigned table T^1_i of PL^1 having k_i attributes, we have an executable FO query for $\mathsf{PL}^1_{T^1_i}$ specified by $x^1_1 \dots x^1_{k_i}$, $\epsilon^1_i(x^1_1 \dots x^1_{l_i})$, and $\tau^1_i(x^1_1 \dots x^1_{l_i})$, where for each m variable x^1_m corresponds to the mth attribute of T^1_i. We create an executable FO query with

- return variables $x^2_1 \dots x^2_k$;
- an output envelope obtained from ϵ^2 by replacing each atom $T^1_i(w_1 \dots w_{k_i})$ with $\exists w_{k_i+1} \dots w_{l_i}\ \epsilon^1_i(\vec{w})$. Since executable UCQs are closed under projection, this can be converted to an executable UCQ;
- filter formula τ obtained from τ^2 by replacing each quantification

$$\exists y_{d_i+1} \dots y_{k_i}\ T^1_i(y_1, \dots y_{d_i}, y_{d_i+1} \dots y_{k_i}) \wedge \gamma$$

by

$$\exists y_{d_i+1} \dots y_{k_i} \dots y_{k_i+1} \dots y_{l_i}\ \epsilon^1_i(\vec{y}) \wedge \tau^1_i(\vec{y}, T_{x^1_1 \dots x^1_{l_i}} := \vec{y}) \wedge \gamma$$

where $\tau^1_i(\vec{y}, T_{x^1_1 \dots x^1_{l_i}} := \vec{y})$ is obtained from τ^1 by replacing the free variables with $\vec{y}$ and replacing every formula $T_{x^1_1 \dots x^1_{l_i}}(\vec{w})$ with $\bigwedge_i w_i = y_i$. Relativized universal quantifications are transformed similarly.

The case of a middleware query command $T := E$ is handled via the standard translation of relational algebra to relational calculus. Since the tables in E are free, and inductively we treat free tables as having input-free access, the filter formula can be an arbitrary relativized-quantifier formula, with no further restrictions on the form of quantification. The fact that the tables in E are free also means that the requirement that the output envelope be executable for membership checks is vacuous. Therefore we can take the output envelope to be a UCQ that returns all tuples over the active domain unioned with schema constants.

We consider a subplan call $T_1 \Leftarrow \mathsf{PL}^2[T^2_{\vec{x}0}] \Leftarrow T_0$, where PL^2 has a distinguished free table $T^2_{\vec{x}0}$ with attributes matching those of T_0. We assume without loss of generality that those attributes are $\#1 \ldots \#n$, and in positional notation we assume that they correspond to positions 1 to n. Again by induction we have an executable formula for PL^2, given by return variables $x^2_1 \ldots x^2_k$, output envelope $\epsilon^2(x^2_1 \ldots x^2_l)$, and filter formula $\tau^2(x^2_1 \ldots x^2_l)$. We form an executable FO query as follows

- the return variables are $x^2_1 \ldots x^2_k$,
- the output envelope $\epsilon(\vec{x}, \vec{y}) = T_0(\vec{y}) \wedge \epsilon^{2+}(x^2_1 \ldots x^2_l, \vec{y})$, where ϵ^{2+} is constructed from ϵ^2 as follows: for each atom of the form $T^2_{\vec{x}}(\vec{w})$, remove the atom and in the remaining collection of atoms substitute each $w_{\#j}$ occurring in the atom by $y_{\#j}$. Note that this substitution is semantically equivalent to the replacement of atoms $T^2_{\vec{x}0}(\vec{w})$ by $\bigwedge_i w_{\#i} = y_{\#i}$. Since $y_{\#i}$ is a free variable that appears first in the relation T_0, which has input-free access, this substitution does not introduce free variables in dangerous positions, and thus does not take us out of executable UCQs.
- the filter formula $\tau(\vec{x}^2, \vec{y})$ is constructed from τ^2 by replacing atoms $T^2_{\vec{x}0}(\vec{w})$ by $\bigwedge_i w_{\#i} = y_{\#i}$. Since this does not introduce quantification, it does not break executability for membership checks.

Above we have handled the inductive cases for the first part of Theorem 3.4. It remains to give the inductive step for the second statement. To get an executable FO query for a plan PL having a top-level statement $\mathsf{Return}\ E$, we transform PL by replacing the Return statement with a final middleware query command $T_{fin} := E$, and take the executable FO query corresponding to T_{fin} in the transformed plan. This completes the proof of Theorem 3.4. □

Putting together Proposition 3.3 and Theorem 3.4, we obtain:

Corollary 3.5 *Nested RA-plans, RA-plans, and executable FO queries have the same expressiveness, and there are computable transformations going from each formalism to an equivalent query in the other.*

For boolean queries, the result implies a simpler equivalence:

Corollary 3.6 *RA-plans with boolean output have the same expressiveness as* RQFO *sentences that are executable for membership checks.*

We will focus on boolean queries in the next sections, and the result above will be useful in allowing us to move freely between RA-plans and RQFO sentences that are executable for membership checks.

3.3.1 RELATIONSHIP OF $USPJAD$-PLANS TO $USPJAD$ QUERIES

We continue our discussion of expressiveness of plan languages by showing that $USPJAD$-plans are the natural analogs of existential formulas in the setting of access restrictions. We begin by proving that $USPJAD$-plans can be converted to $USPJAD$-queries.

Proposition 3.7 *Every $USPJAD$-plan can be translated to a $USPJAD$ query (and hence, by prior results in Section 1.2, to an existential formula).*

Translation. The translation witnessing Proposition 3.7 is an induction on the number of commands in the $USPJAD$-plan PL. It takes as input, in addition to PL, a temporary table T used in PL, and it produces a $USPJAD$ query $\mathsf{ToUSPJ}^{\neg}(T \mid \mathsf{PL})$ over Sch. Since $\mathsf{ToUSPJ}^{\neg}(T \mid \mathsf{PL})$ is in relational algebra, it will work over a schema with a "named version" of each relation R with arity n, which has attributes $\#1 \ldots \#n$.

We aim to maintain the following invariant, for any instance I and any temporary table T of plan PL:

$$[\![\mathsf{ToUSPJ}^{\neg}(T \mid \mathsf{PL})]\!]_I = [\![T \mid \mathsf{PL}]\!]_I \quad (*)$$

Applied to the table in the Return command of PL, the invariant implies the correctness of the translation. The base case of the induction is a single access command, which we translate to an SPJ query in the obvious way. We consider the induction step for a plan PL_i whose last command is a middleware query command $T_i := E_i(T_1^{i-1} \ldots T_k^{i-1})$ where E_i does not include the difference operator and $T_1^{i-1} \ldots T_k^{i-1}$ are temporary tables occurring in the prior command PL_{i-1}. This is straightforward: we first substitute, for each $1 \leq j \leq k$, the inductively-defined $USPJAD$ query $\mathsf{ToUSPJ}^{\neg}(T_j^{i-1} \mid \mathsf{PL}_{i-1})$ for occurrences of table T_j^{i-1} within E_i. We then use the fact that $USPJAD$ queries are closed under each of the $USPJ$ operations to obtain $\mathsf{ToUSPJ}^{\neg}(T_i \mid \mathsf{PL}_i)$.

We turn to the induction step for a plan PL_i consisting of plan PL_{i-1} followed by a non-membership check. Recall that a non-membership check is of the form:

$$\begin{aligned} &T_i' \Leftarrow_{\mathsf{OutMap}} \mathsf{mt} \Leftarrow_{\mathsf{InMap}} \pi_{a_{j_1} \ldots a_{jm}}(T_{i-1}) \\ &T_i := T_{i-1} - (T_{i-1} \ltimes T_i') \end{aligned}$$

where in the first command (1) T_{i-1} is a temporary table produced by PL_{i-1}, (2) mt is an access method on relation R of arity n with input positions $j_1 \ldots j_m$, (3) the input mapping InMap maps attribute a_{j_i} to position j_i, (4) the attributes of the output table T_i' are a subset of the attributes of T_{i-1}, (5) the output mapping OutMap maps position j_i back to a_{j_i}. Let $\mathsf{ToUSPJ}^{\neg}(\mathsf{PL}_{i-1}, T_{i-1})$ be the query formed inductively for PL_{i-1} with temporary table T_{i-1}. We explain the construction of the query $\mathsf{ToUSPJ}^{\neg}(T_i \mid \mathsf{PL}_i)$ for PL_i and T_i, with the construction for the remaining tables being routine. We set:

$$\mathsf{ToUSPJ}^{\neg}(T_i \mid \mathsf{PL}_i) = \mathsf{ToUSPJ}^{\neg}(T_{i-1} \mid \mathsf{PL}_{i-1}) - (\mathsf{ToUSPJ}^{\neg}(T_{i-1} \mid \mathsf{PL}_{i-1}) \ltimes_{\alpha} R)$$

where the join condition α identifies $\#i \in R$ with attribute $\mathsf{OutMap}(i)$ in $\mathsf{ToUSPJ}^{\neg}(T_{i-1} \mid \mathsf{PL}_{i-1})$. Note that this is a $USPJAD$ query, as required.

Correctness. We first show the following alternative characterization of the intermediate expression $T_{i-1} \ltimes T'_i$ that is being removed from T_{i-1} to get T_i in PL_i, where T_{i-1}, T'_i, T_i and PL_i are as in the definition of non-membership check.

Claim 1: On any instance I

$$[\![T_{i-1} \ltimes T'_i \mid \mathsf{PL}_i]\!]_I = \{\vec{t} \in [\![T_{i-1} \mid \mathsf{PL}_{i-1}]\!]_I | \mathsf{OutMap}^{-1}(\pi_{\mathsf{atts}(T'_i)}\vec{t}) \in [\![R]\!]_I)\}$$

where OutMap^{-1} is the inverse of OutMap and $\mathsf{atts}(T'_i)$ are the attributes of T'_i. ■

Proof. It is clear from the definition of T'_i that if $\vec{t} \in [\![T_{i-1} \ltimes T'_i \mid \mathsf{PL}_i]\!]_I$ then $\vec{t}$ is in the expression on the right above.

On the other hand, if $\vec{t}$ is in the expression on the right above, set $\vec{t}' = \pi_{\mathsf{atts}(T'_i)}(\vec{t})$. So $\vec{t} = \vec{t} \bowtie \vec{t}'$, and since $\vec{t} \in [\![T_{i-1} \mid \mathsf{PL}_{i-1}]\!]_I$, it suffices to show $\vec{t}' \in [\![T'_i \mid \mathsf{PL}_i]\!]_I$. We have $\mathsf{OutMap}^{-1}(t') \in [\![R]\!]_I$ by assumption that $\vec{t}$ is in the expression on the right above. In addition, $\vec{t}$ witnesses that $\pi_{a_{j_1} \dots a_{j_m}} \vec{t}'$ is in $\pi_{a_{j_1} \dots a_{j_m}}([\![T_{i-1} \mid \mathsf{PL}_{i-1}]\!]_I)$, and hence the fact that OutMap extends the inverse of InMap guarantees that $\vec{t}' \in [\![T'_i \mid \mathsf{PL}_i]\!]_I$. This completes the proof of the claim. □

We now turn to the proof of the invariant (*).

Suppose tuple $\vec{t}$ is in $[\![\mathsf{ToUSPJ}^{\neg}(T_i \mid \mathsf{PL}_i)]\!]_I$, with the aim of showing that $\vec{t}$ is in $[\![T_i \mid \mathsf{PL}]\!]_I$. From the definition of the translation we have $\vec{t} \in [\![\mathsf{ToUSPJ}^{\neg}(T_{i-1} \mid \mathsf{PL}_{i-1})]\!]_I$, and thus by induction, $\vec{t} \in [\![T_{i-1} \mid \mathsf{PL}_{i-1}]\!]_I$. Recalling that T_i is assigned to $T_{i-1} - (T_{i-1} \ltimes T'_i)$ in the definition of PL, it suffices to rule out the possibility that $\vec{t}$ is in $[\![T_{i-1} \ltimes T'_i \mid \mathsf{PL}_i]\!]_I$. Assume to the contrary that $\vec{t}$ is in $[\![T_{i-1} \ltimes T'_i \mid \mathsf{PL}_i]\!]_I$. Let $\vec{t}'$ be the projection of $\vec{t}$ on the attributes of T'_i. Then $\mathsf{OutMap}^{-1}(\vec{t}')$ is in $[\![R]\!]_I$. We conclude that $\vec{t}$ is in $[\![\mathsf{ToUSPJ}^{\neg}(T_{i\ 1} \mid \mathsf{PL}_{i-1})]\!]_I \ltimes_\alpha [\![R]\!]_I$, which contradicts the assumption that $\vec{t}$ is in $[\![\mathsf{ToUSPJ}^{\neg}(T_i \mid \mathsf{PL}_i)]\!]_I$.

In the other direction, suppose that $\vec{t}$ is in $[\![T_i \mid \mathsf{PL}_i]\!]_I$. Then $\vec{t} \in [\![T_{i-1} \mid \mathsf{PL}_{i-1}]\!]_I$, and hence by induction $\vec{t} \in [\![\mathsf{ToUSPJ}^{\neg}(T_{i-1} \mid \mathsf{PL}_{i-1})]\!]_I$. Suppose by way of contradiction that $\vec{t}$ is in $[\![\mathsf{ToUSPJ}^{\neg}(T_{i-1} \mid \mathsf{PL}_{i-1}) \ltimes_\alpha R]\!]_I$. Then $\mathsf{OutMap}^{-1}(t')$ defined as above is in $[\![R]\!]_I$. Applying Claim 1, $\vec{t} \in [\![T_{i-1} \ltimes T'_i \mid \mathsf{PL}_i]\!]_I$ a contradiction.

This completes the proof of Proposition 3.7.

3.3.2 RELATIONSHIP OF $USPJAD$-PLANS TO OTHER FORMALISMS

Proposition 3.7 shows that $USPJAD$-plans can be translated into $USPJAD$ queries, and hence into existential formulas. We briefly present a converse, stating that the $USPJAD$-plans capture all $USPJAD$ queries/existential formulas that have plans. In the process, we present a logical syntax equivalent to $USPJAD$-plans.

The logical language is the *executable union of conjunctive queries with atomic negation*, defined in [Deutsch et al., 2007]. An executable conjunctive query with negation is a conjunction of formulas α_i that are either of the form $R_i(\vec{x},\vec{c})$ or $\neg R_i(\vec{x},\vec{c})$, such that there is an annotation of each literal S_i with an access method mt_i on R_i, and for each variable x of Q, the first A_i containing x is not negated and x occurs only in an output position of mt_i. An executable union of conjunctive queries with atomic negation is a disjunction of executable conjunctive queries with negation. One can show that each of these can be converted to an executable FO query (as defined in the previous section) in which the filter formula is an existential formula.

We can extend the translation of Proposition 3.1 by adding non-membership checks for the negated atoms, giving a translation from an executable union of conjunctive queries with negation to a $USPJAD$-plan. Theorem 22 in [Deutsch et al., 2007] shows that for every $USPJAD$ query Q that can be implemented with a Turing Machine that can make calls to the methods, Q converted to an executable union of conjunctive queries with negation.[2] Thus in particular, any $USPJAD$ query that has an RA-plan is equivalent to an executable union of CQs with negation, and hence is equivalent to a $USPJAD$-plan. Since a $USPJAD$-plan is equivalent to a $USPJAD$ query (by Proposition 3.7), we can conclude that every $USPJAD$-plan is equivalent to an executable union of conjunctive queries with negation.

We summarize the results in the following theorem:

Theorem 3.8 *Every $USPJAD$-plan is equivalent to an executable union of conjunctive queries with negation, and vice versa. Every access-determined query that is equivalent to a $USPJAD$ query is equivalent to a $USPJAD$-plan.*

Similar results hold for $USPJAD^{\neq}$-plans.

3.4 SEMANTIC PROPERTIES AND ENTAILMENTS RELATED TO PLANS

In the previous sections, we defined the language of RA-plans and argued that it forms a natural counterpart to relational algebra in the setting where the interface to data is given by a set of access methods. We will look at instantiating our meta-algorithm for translating a query into an RA-plan, and similarly for subclasses of RA-plans. We start with the case of generating $USPJ^{\neq}$-plans, looking for an analog to the Projective Monotone Preservation Theorem, Theorem 2.8.

The semantic property for $USPJ^{\neq}$-plans. In order to begin our instantiation of the meta-algorithm for $USPJ^{\neq}$-plans, we need a semantic property corresponding to a plan that only uses "accessible data" and only uses it monotonically.

Given an instance I for schema Sch the *accessible part of I*, denoted $\mathsf{AccPart}(I)$ consists of all the facts over I that can be obtained by starting with empty relations and iteratively entering values into the access methods. If Sch contains no schema constants, this will be an instance containing a set of facts $\mathsf{Accessed}R(v_1 \ldots v_n)$, where R is a relation and $v_1 \ldots v_n$ are values in the

[2] Actually, the proof of Theorem 22 shows that any access-determined $USPJAD$ query can be converted to an executable union of conjunctive queries, where access-determined is defined in Chapter 3.

domain of I such that $R(v_1 \dots v_n)$ holds in I, obtained by starting with relations $\mathsf{Accessed}R_0$ and $\mathsf{accessible}_0$ empty and then iterating the following process until a fixpoint is reached:

$$\mathsf{accessible}_{i+1} = \mathsf{accessible}_i \cup \bigcup_{\substack{R \text{ a relation} \\ j \leq \mathsf{arity}(R)}} \pi_j(\mathsf{Accessed}R_i)$$

and

$$\mathsf{Accessed}R_{i+1} = \mathsf{Accessed}R_i \cup \bigcup_{\substack{(R,\{j_1,\dots,j_m\}) \\ \text{there is a method of Sch on } R \text{ with inputs } j_1,\dots,j_m}} \{(v_1 \dots v_n) \in [\![R]\!]_I \mid v_{j_1} \dots v_{j_m} \in \mathsf{accessible}_i\}.$$

Above $\pi_j(\mathsf{Accessed}R_i)$ denotes projection of $\mathsf{Accessed}R_i$ on the jth position. For a finite instance, this induction will reach a fixpoint after $|I|$ iterations, where $|I|$ denotes the number of facts in I. For an arbitrary instance the union of these instances over all i will be a fixpoint. Assuming Sch does include schema constants, we modify the definition by starting with an $\mathsf{accessible}_0$ consisting of the schema constants, rather than being empty.

Above we consider $\mathsf{AccPart}(I)$ as a database instance for the schema with relations accessible and $\mathsf{Accessed}R$. Below we will sometimes refer to the values in the relation accessible as the *accessible values of I*.

Example 3.5. Suppose our schema has a relation Related of arity 2, with an access method $\mathsf{mt}_{\mathsf{Related}}$ with input on the first position of Related. The schema has exactly one schema constant "Jones". Let instance I consist of facts

$$\{\mathsf{Related}(\text{“Jones”}, \text{“Kennedy”}), \mathsf{Related}(\text{“Kennedy”}, \text{“Evans”}), \mathsf{Related}(\text{“Smith”}, \text{“Thompson”})\}.$$

We construct the accessible part of I. We begin by computing:

$$\mathsf{AccessedRelated}_0 = \emptyset, \quad \mathsf{accessible}_0 = \{\text{“Jones”}\}.$$

That is, initially the accessible part contains no facts and the only accessible constant is the schema constant "Jones".

We can now apply the inductive rules to get:

- $\mathsf{AccessedRelated}_1 = \{(\text{“Jones”}, \text{“Kennedy”})\}$
  $\mathsf{accessible}_1 = \{\text{“Jones”}, \text{“Kennedy”}\}$.

- $\mathsf{AccessedRelated}_2 = \{(\text{“Jones”}, \text{“Kennedy”}), (\text{“Kennedy”}, \text{“Evans”})\}$
  $\mathsf{accessible}_2 = \{\text{“Jones”}, \text{“Kennedy”}, \text{“Evans”}\}$.

At this point, we have reached a fixpoint, so the accessible part of I consists of facts {AccessedRelated("Jones", "Kennedy"), AccessedRelated("Kennedy", "Evans")}. The accessible values of I are {"Jones", "Kennedy", "Evans"}. ◁

In the case of vocabulary-based access-restrictions, the accessible part of an instance just represents the restriction of the instance to the relations in the subsignature $\mathcal{T}$. Thus access determinacy of a query Q in the case of vocabulary-based restrictions is the same as determinacy of Q with respect to the subsignature.

We say Q is access-monotonically-determined over Sch if for all instances I and I' satisfying the constraints of Sch with every fact of AccPart(I) contained in AccPart(I')—that is, AccPart(I) is a subinstance of AccPart(I')—then $[\![Q]\!]_I \subseteq [\![Q]\!]_{I'}$.

The entailment corresponding to the semantic property for $USPJ^{\neq}$-plans. Following our meta-algorithm once again, we translate the semantic property to an entailment. Given schema Sch, the forward accessible schema for Sch, denoted AcSch(Sch), is a schema without access restrictions, defined as follows:

- The constants are those of Sch.
- The relations are those of Sch, a unary relation accessible(x) ("x is an accessible value") plus a copy of each relation R of Sch called InfAcc$R$ (the "inferred accessible version of R").
- The constraints are those of Sch (referred to as "Sch constraints" below) along with the following constraints (dropping universal quantifiers on the outside for brevity)
  - accessibility axioms: for each access method mt on relation R of arity n with input positions $j_1 \ldots j_m$ we have a rule:

    $$\mathsf{accessible}(x_{j_1}) \wedge \ldots \wedge \mathsf{accessible}(x_{j_m}) \wedge R(x_1 \ldots x_n) \rightarrow \mathsf{InfAcc}R(x_1 \ldots x_n) \wedge \bigwedge_j \mathsf{accessible}(x_j).$$

    In addition, we have accessible(c) for each constant c of Sch.
  - A copy of each of the original integrity constraints, with each relation R replaced by InfAcc$R$, denoted "InfAccCopy constraints" below.

Informally, accessible(c) indicates that the value c can be returned by some sequence of accesses. The inferred accessible relations represent facts that can be derived from facts exposed by the access methods using reasoning. Thus the forward accessible schema represents the rules that allow one to move from a "hidden fact" (e.g., $R(c_1 \ldots c_n)$) to a fact that has been exposed (InfAcc$R(c_1 \ldots c_n)$). The copy of the constraints allows us to move from a directly exposed fact InfAcc$R(c_1 \ldots c_n)$ to a derived inferred accessible fact (e.g., $\exists y$ InfAcc$S(c_1 \ldots c_n, y)$). From the structure of the rules one sees that the InfAccCopy constraints can fire based upon facts generated by other kinds of rules, but not vice versa.

Given a query Q, its inferred accessible version $\mathsf{InfAcc}Q$ is obtained by replacing each relation R by $\mathsf{InfAcc}R$. Informally, $\mathsf{InfAcc}Q$ represents the fact that the existence of a witness to Q can be obtained through making accesses and reasoning.

We overload AcSch(Sch) to also refer to the conjunction of axioms in this schema AcSch(Sch). For generating an $SPJ^{\neq}$-plan, the relevant entailment is:

$$Q \wedge \mathsf{AcSch}(\mathsf{Sch}) \models \mathsf{InfAcc}Q.$$

Informally, this means that we can infer from Q holding in a hidden database instance that Q's truth could be made visible to a user through making accesses and reasoning with constraints.

Example 3.6. Recall the setting of Example 1.3, where we had a Profinfo table containing information about faculty, including their last names, office number, and employee id, with a restricted interface that requires giving an employee id as an input, and also a Udirectory table containing the employee id and last name of every university employee, with an input-free access method.

We were interested in the query asking for ids of faculty named "Smith":

$$Q = \exists \mathsf{onum}\ \mathsf{Profinfo}(\mathsf{eid}, \mathsf{onum}, \text{“Smith”}).$$

In this case we have:

$$\mathsf{InfAcc}Q = \exists\ \mathsf{onum}\ \mathsf{InfAccProfinfo}(\mathsf{eid}, \mathsf{onum}, \text{“Smith”}).$$

The forward accessible schema includes rules:

- $\mathsf{Profinfo}(\mathsf{eid}, \mathsf{onum}, \mathsf{lname}) \rightarrow \mathsf{Udirectory}(\mathsf{eid}, \mathsf{lname})$
- $\mathsf{Udirectory}(\mathsf{eid}, \mathsf{lname}) \rightarrow \mathsf{InfAccUdirectory}(\mathsf{eid}, \mathsf{lname}) \wedge \mathsf{accessible}(\mathsf{lname})$
- $\mathsf{Profinfo}(\mathsf{eid}, \mathsf{onum}, \mathsf{lname}) \wedge \mathsf{accessible}(\mathsf{eid}) \rightarrow \mathsf{InfAccProfinfo}(\mathsf{eid}, \mathsf{onum}, \mathsf{lname})$

One can check that $Q \wedge \mathsf{AcSch}(\mathsf{Sch})$ entails $\mathsf{InfAcc}Q$. ◁

There are several intuitions for these auxiliary axioms. Similar axioms have been introduced in prior work [Deutsch et al., 2007, Duschka et al., 2000], as a way of reducing the problem of reformulation under access methods to reasoning just about integrity constraints. The auxiliary schema is a way of capturing some of the semantics of access methods by adding integrity constraints. A second way of motivating the axioms is to think informally of the relations accessible and $\mathsf{InfAcc}R$ as being the subset of the values and facts that would be "visible" to a user via the interface, as opposed to the original relations R which represent the "hidden facts." The axioms give us conditions under which a hidden fact becomes visible. A third way of thinking about these axioms is to relate them to the entailments we saw for vocabulary-based reformulation. The relations $\mathsf{InfAcc}R$ represent copies of the schema relations, analogous to the primed copies used in the vocabulary-based case. In the case of $\exists^{+,\neq}$ vocabulary-based reformulation, we had the axioms:

$$\forall \vec{x} \quad R(\vec{x}) \rightarrow R'(\vec{x})$$

for each "accessible" relation R (that is R in the target vocabulary $\mathcal{T}$. It is easy to see that in the case of vocabulary-based restriction, the accessibility axioms degenerate to exactly this implication.

The following claim shows that the entailment captures the semantic property of access-monotonic determinacy.

Claim 2: The following are equivalent, for any access schema with RQFO constraints and any RQFO query Q:

1. Q entails $\mathsf{InfAcc}Q$ with respect to the rules in AcSch(Sch)

2. Q is access-monotonically-determined w.r.t.Sch ■

Proof. For simplicity we prove this for the case of boolean queries. We start by showing that the first item implies the second. Fix I and I' satisfying the schema with the accessible part of I contained in the accessible part of I', and assume I satisfies Q. Consider the instance I'' for the accessible schema formed by interpreting the relations R as in I, accessible by the accessible values of I, and each $\mathsf{InfAcc}R$ by the interpretation of R in I'. The construction of I'', along with the hypothesis on I and I', easily implies that I'' satisfies the constraints of AcSch(Sch): to check the forward accessibility axioms, we use the fact that the accessible part of I is contained in that of I' and the inductive definition of accessible part. Since I (and hence I'') satisfies Q, the first item now tells us that I'' must satisfy $\mathsf{InfAcc}Q$. Thus Q holds in I' as required.

Arguing from the second item to the first, suppose Q does not imply $\mathsf{InfAcc}Q$ with respect to the rules in AcSch(Sch). This means that there is an instance I^{AcSch} satisfying the rules of AcSch(Sch) and also satisfying $Q \wedge \neg\mathsf{InfAcc}Q$. Let I_1 consist of the restriction of I^{AcSch} to the original schema relations. Let I_2 consist of the inferred accessible relations from I^{AcSch}, renamed to the original schema.

We claim that a fact $R(e_1 \dots e_n)$ in the accessible part of I_1 is in the accessible part of I_2. Note that if $R(e_1 \dots e_n)$ is in the accessible part of I_1, then there is an i such that it is in $\mathsf{Accessed}R_i$. We prove the claim by induction on this i.

In the inductive step, a fact $R(e_1 \dots e_n)$ in the accessible part is generated by an access using elements $e_{j_1} \dots e_{j_m}$ that satisfy accessible facts that were generated earlier in the fixpoint iteration. Thus by induction these earlier facts are in the accessible part of I_2, and in particular $e_{j_1} \dots e_{j_m}$ are accessible values of I_2.

Using the axioms we have that $\mathsf{InfAcc}R(e_1 \dots e_n)$ holds, and thus $R(e_1 \dots e_n)$ holds in I_2. Using the definition of accessible part, we conclude that the fact is in the accessible part of I_2

as required. From this, we can see that I_1 and I_2 witness that Q is not access-monotonically-determined, which completes the argument. □

The semantic property and entailment for RA-plans. We now give the analogous property and entailment for RA-plans. Q is said to be access-determined over Sch if for all instances I and I' satisfying the constraints of Sch with $\mathsf{AccPart}(I) = \mathsf{AccPart}(I')$ we have $[\![Q]\!]_I = [\![Q]\!]_{I'}$. If a query is not access-determined, it is obvious that it cannot be answered through any plan, since it is easy to see that any plan can only read tuples in the accessible part.

Example 3.7. We return to the setting of Example 1.3, where we have a Profinfo table available via a web form, containing information about faculty, including their last names, office number, and employee id, but with only an access method $\mathsf{mt}_{\mathsf{Profinfo}}$ that requires giving an employee id as an input. We consider a query Q asking for ids of faculty named "Smith", where "Smith" is a schema constant.

We show that Q is not access-determined. For this, take I to be any instance that contains exactly one tuple, with lastname "Smith", but with no schema constant as its employee id. Let I' be the empty instance. The accessible parts of I and I' are empty, since in both cases when we enter all the constants we know about in $\mathsf{mt}_{\mathsf{Profinfo}}$, we get the empty response. But Q has an output on I but no output on I'.

I and I' witness that Q is not access-determined. From this we see that Q cannot be implemented by any plan using $\mathsf{mt}_{\mathsf{Profinfo}}$. ◁

Let $\mathsf{AcSch}^{\leftrightarrow}(\mathsf{Sch})$ extend the axioms of $\mathsf{AcSch}(\mathsf{Sch})$ with the following axioms (universal quantifiers omitted):

$$\bigwedge_{i \leq m} \mathsf{accessible}(x_{j_i}) \wedge \mathsf{InfAcc}R(x_1 \ldots x_n) \rightarrow$$
$$R(x_1 \ldots x_n) \wedge \bigwedge_i \mathsf{accessible}(x_i).$$

Above, R is a relation of Sch having an access method with input positions $j_1 \ldots j_m$. Notice that these rules are obtained from those of $\mathsf{AcSch}(\mathsf{Sch})$ by switching the roles of $\mathsf{InfAcc}R$ and R, resulting in a rule set where the Sch relations and their InfAcc copies are treated symmetrically. Again, we show that this entailment captures the proposed preservation property, access determinacy.

Claim 3: The following are equivalent (for any RQFO query Q and access schema consisting of RQFO constraints):

1. Q entails $\mathsf{InfAcc}Q$ with respect to the rules in $\mathsf{AcSch}^{\leftrightarrow}(\mathsf{Sch})$
2. Q is access-determined over Sch ■

Proof. Again we focus on the case where Q is boolean. We prove that the first item implies the second. Fix I and I' satisfying the schema with the same accessible part, and assume I satisfies

Q. Consider the instance I'' for $\mathsf{AcSch}^{\leftrightarrow}(\mathsf{Sch})$ formed by interpreting the relations R as in I, the relation accessible by the accessible values of I, and each $\mathsf{InfAcc}R$ by the interpretation of R in I'. Then one can verify that I'' satisfies the constraints of $\mathsf{AcSch}^{\leftrightarrow}(\mathsf{Sch})$. Since I (and hence I'') satisfies Q, and we are assuming that Q entails $\mathsf{InfAcc}Q$ with respect to $\mathsf{AcSch}^{\leftrightarrow}(\mathsf{Sch})$ we can conclude that I'' must satisfy $\mathsf{InfAcc}Q$. So Q holds in I' as required.

We complete the proof of the claim by arguing from the second item to the first. Suppose Q is not contained in $\mathsf{InfAcc}Q$ with respect to the rules in $\mathsf{AcSch}^{\leftrightarrow}(\mathsf{Sch})$. Hence there is an instance $I^{\mathsf{AcSch}^{\leftrightarrow}}$ satisfying the rules of $\mathsf{AcSch}^{\leftrightarrow}(\mathsf{Sch})$ and also satisfying $Q \wedge \neg\mathsf{InfAcc}Q$. Let I_1 consist of the restriction of $I^{\mathsf{AcSch}^{\leftrightarrow}}$ to the original schema relations. Let I_2 consist of the inferred accessible relations from $I^{\mathsf{AcSch}^{\leftrightarrow}}$, renamed to the original schema.

We claim that a fact $R(e_1 \dots e_n)$ in the accessible part of I_1 is in the accessible part of I_2. This is proven using verbatim the argument in Claim 2, since our axioms contain the forward accessibility axioms. Arguing symmetrically (now using the backward axioms), we find that I_1 and I_2 have the same accessible part, and hence they contradict access determinacy. □

The semantic property and entailment for $USPJAD^{\neq}$-plans. Lastly, we instantiate the first two steps of our meta-algorithm for $USPJAD^{\neq}$-plans. We say that Q is *induced-subinstance-access-monotonically-determined* with respect to Sch if:

> Whenever we have two instances I, I' satisfying the constraints of the schema Sch, and $\mathsf{AccPart}(I)$ is an induced subinstance of $\mathsf{AccPart}(I')$, then $[\![Q]\!]_I \subseteq [\![Q]\!]_{I'}$.

Unwinding the definition of induced subinstance from Section 1.2, we see that $\mathsf{AccPart}(I)$ being an induced subinstance of $\mathsf{AccPart}(I')$ means that: (i) for every fact $\mathsf{Accessed}R(\vec{c})$ of $\mathsf{AccPart}(I)$, $\mathsf{Accessed}R(\vec{c})$ is in $\mathsf{AccPart}(I')$ and (ii) for every $\vec{c}$ with each c_i an accessible value of I, if $R(\vec{c})$ is a fact of $\mathsf{AccPart}(I')$ then $\mathsf{Accessed}R(\vec{c})$ is in $\mathsf{AccPart}(I)$.

To get an entailment that corresponds to this, we look for a set of axioms lying between the two augmented schemas $\mathsf{AcSch}(\mathsf{Sch})$ and $\mathsf{AcSch}^{\leftrightarrow}(\mathsf{Sch})$ presented before. Let $\mathsf{AcSch}^{\neg}(\mathsf{Sch})$ be the restriction of $\mathsf{AcSch}^{\leftrightarrow}(\mathsf{Sch})$ to the case where $m = n$: that is, all x_i are accessible. Equivalently, $\mathsf{AcSch}^{\neg}(\mathsf{Sch})$ extends $\mathsf{AcSch}(\mathsf{Sch})$ with "restricted backward accessibility axioms." For all relations R that have some access method we have the axioms:

$$\forall x_1 \dots x_n \bigwedge_{i \leq n} \mathsf{accessible}(x_i) \wedge \mathsf{InfAcc}R(x_1 \dots x_n) \rightarrow R(x_1 \dots x_n).$$

The reader can check that in the case of vocabulary-based restrictions, this reduces to the entailment used for reformulation with $\exists^{\neq}$-formulas (see Theorem 2.11). This axiom can be rewritten as:

$$\forall x_1 \dots x_n \bigwedge_{i \leq n} \mathsf{accessible}(x_i) \wedge \neg R(x_1 \dots x_n) \rightarrow \neg\mathsf{InfAcc}R(x_1 \dots x_n).$$

Intuitively, the rule says that if the hidden database does *not* include a certain hidden fact, and all the values in the fact are known to a user, then the user can infer that the fact does not hold by making accesses.

The entailment

$$Q \wedge \mathsf{AcSch}^{\neg}(\mathsf{Sch}) \models \mathsf{InfAcc}Q$$

will be what we consider for plans that use only atomic negation. We prove an equivalence of the entailment with the semantic property above.

Claim 4: The following are equivalent (for any RQFO query Q and any access schema containing RQFO constraints):

1. Q entails $\mathsf{InfAcc}Q$ with respect to the rules in $\mathsf{AcSch}^{\neg}(\mathsf{Sch})$.

2. Q is induced-subinstance-access-monotonically-determined w.r.t.Sch. ■

Proof. This is proven analogously to the claim for RA-plans, and again we give the proof only for the boolean case.

We prove that the first item implies the second. Fix I and I' satisfying the schema with $\mathsf{AccPart}(I)$ an induced subinstance of $\mathsf{AccPart}(I')$, and assume I satisfies Q. Again consider the instance I'' for the accessible schema formed as in the proof of Claim 3. From the fact that $\mathsf{AccPart}(I)$ is an induced subinstance of $\mathsf{AccPart}(I')$, we argue that the axioms of $\mathsf{AcSch}^{\neg}(\mathsf{Sch})$ are satisfied by I''.

First consider the "forward accessibility axiom" going from R to $\mathsf{InfAcc}R$. Suppose in I'' we have $R(\vec{c})$ with all c_i in input positions of a method on R satisfying accessible. Then the c_i in input positions are in $\mathsf{AccPart}(I)$, and therefore $R(\vec{c})$ will hold in $\mathsf{AccPart}(I)$. Since $\mathsf{AccPart}(I)$ is a subinstance of $\mathsf{AccPart}(I')$ we can conclude that $\mathsf{InfAcc}R(\vec{c})$ holds, as required.

To see the "backward accessibility axiom" of $\mathsf{AcSch}^{\neg}(\mathsf{Sch})$, assume $\mathsf{InfAcc}R(\vec{c})$ and $\mathsf{accessible}(c_i)$ for $i \leq n$ hold in I'', and that R has at least one access method. Then by definition of I'', $R(\vec{c})$ holds in I'. Using $\mathsf{accessible}(c_i)$ we know that each c_i is an accessible value in I. Since $\mathsf{AccPart}(I)$ is a subinstance of $\mathsf{AccPart}(I')$ each c_i is also an accessible value within I'. Because R has at least one access method, it follows that $\mathsf{Accessed}R(\vec{c})$ holds in $\mathsf{AccPart}(I')$. Now since $\mathsf{AccPart}(I)$ is an induced subinstance of $\mathsf{AccPart}(I')$, applying the definition of induced subinstance, $\mathsf{Accessed}R(\vec{c})$ holds in $\mathsf{AccPart}(I)$ as well. In particular $R(\vec{c})$ holds in I.

We have shown that I'' satisfies $\mathsf{AcSch}^{\neg}(\mathsf{Sch})$. Since I'' satisfies Q, we conclude that I'' must satisfy $\mathsf{InfAcc}Q$. This means that Q holds in I' as required.

We turn to the argument from the second item to the first, which will complete the proof of the claim. Suppose Q does not imply $\mathsf{InfAcc}Q$ with respect to the rules in $\mathsf{AcSch}^{\neg}(\mathsf{Sch})$. Hence there is an instance $I^{\mathsf{AcSch}^{\neg}}$ satisfying the rules of $\mathsf{AcSch}^{\neg}(\mathsf{Sch})$ and also satisfying $Q \wedge \neg\mathsf{InfAcc}Q$. Let I_1 consist of the restriction of $I^{\mathsf{AcSch}^{\neg}}$ to the original schema relations. Let I_2 consist of the inferred accessible relations from $I^{\mathsf{AcSch}^{\neg}}$, renamed to the original schema.

Since $\mathsf{AcSch}^{\neg}(\mathsf{Sch})$ includes all the axioms of $\mathsf{AcSch}(\mathsf{Sch})$, we can use verbatim the argument in the proof of Claim 2 to conclude that a fact $R(e_1 \ldots e_n)$ of the accessible part of I_1 is in the accessible part of I_2 (recalling that this argument used only the forward accessibility axioms).

We will use the rules from $\mathsf{AcSch}^{\neg}(\mathsf{Sch})$ to show that for $e_1 \ldots e_n$ in $\mathsf{AccPart}(I_1)$, and R having at least one access method, a fact $R(e_1 \ldots e_n)$ holding in $\mathsf{AccPart}(I_2)$ is in $\mathsf{AccPart}(I_1)$. By definition of I_2, $\mathsf{InfAcc}R(e_1 \ldots e_n)$ must hold in $I^{\mathsf{AcSch}^{\neg}}$. Using the fact that each of $e_1 \ldots e_n$ is in $\mathsf{AccPart}(I_1)$, R has some access method, and the "restricted backward accessibility axioms" of $\mathsf{AcSch}^{\neg}(\mathsf{Sch})$, we infer that $R(e_1 \ldots e_n)$ holds in $I^{\mathsf{AcSch}^{\neg}}$. From this and the forward accessibility axioms, we derive that $R(e_1 \ldots e_n)$ is in the accessible part of I_1.

Thus we have shown that $\mathsf{AccPart}(I_1)$ is an induced subinstance of $\mathsf{AccPart}(I_2)$. We can conclude that Q is not induced-subinstance-access-monotonically-determined, which completes the argument. □

3.5 STATEMENT OF THE MAIN RESULTS ON ACCESS DETERMINACY AND REFORMULATION

We are now ready to state our main results on the relationship between semantic properties, entailments, and plans. We will state a version for each of the three types of plans mentioned before. We give proofs of the results for boolean queries only, but the results can be extended to non-boolean queries: this will be explained in Section 3.8.

The schema $\mathsf{AcSch}^{\leftrightarrow}$ and RA-plans. For RA-plans, our main result is:

Theorem 3.9 *For any boolean* RQFO *query Q and access schema* Sch *with constraints specified in* RQFO*, there is an RA-plan answering Q (over instances satisfying* Sch*) if and only if* $Q \wedge \mathsf{AcSch}^{\leftrightarrow}(\mathsf{Sch}) \models \mathsf{InfAcc}Q$. *If the query and constraints do not include equality, then the RA-plan will not make use of equality in any of its RA expressions.*

Further, from any tableau proof witnessing $Q \wedge \mathsf{AcSch}^{\leftrightarrow}(\mathsf{Sch}) \models \mathsf{InfAcc}Q$ *we can extract (in linear time) an RA-plan for Q over* Sch.

Using Claim 3, we can restate Theorem 3.9:

> For any boolean RQFO query Q and access schema Sch with constraints specified in RQFO, there is an RA-plan answering Q (over instances of Sch) if and only if Q entails $\mathsf{InfAcc}Q$ with respect to the rules in $\mathsf{AcSch}^{\leftrightarrow}(\mathsf{Sch})$ if and only if Q is access-determined.

In the direction from right to left we are again going from a preservation property to a syntactic restriction. Thus Theorem 3.9 can be considered as an "access-restricted variant" of the Active-domain Projective Beth Definability theorem, Theorem 2.1. We will return to the proof later.

The schema AcSch and $USPJ^{\neq}$-plans. We now state an analogous result for negation-free plans, which will be an access-related variant of the Projective Monotone Preservation Theorem, Theorem 2.8.

Theorem 3.10 *For any boolean* RQFO *query* Q *and access schema* Sch *containing constraints specified in* RQFO, *the following are equivalent:*

- *there is a* $USPJ^{\neq}$*-plan answering* Q *(over instances in* Sch*).*
- Q *entails* $\mathsf{InfAcc}Q$ *with respect to* $\mathsf{AcSch(Sch)}$ *(*$Q \wedge \mathsf{AcSch(Sch)} \models \mathsf{InfAcc}Q$*).*

Furthermore, for every tableau proof witnessing $Q \wedge \mathsf{AcSch(Sch)} \models \mathsf{InfAcc}Q$*, we can extract a* $USPJ^{\neq}$*-plan. If the query and the constraints of* Sch *are specified by* RQFO *formulas without any equalities (e.g., TGDs), then we can replace* $USPJ^{\neq}$*-plan with* $USPJ$*-plan in the above statement. So we do not need inequalities in the reformulation unless we have equalities in the constraints.*

Using Claim 2, the main part of Theorem 3.10 can be restated as:

> For any boolean RQFO query Q and access schema Sch containing constraints specified in RQFO, there is a $USPJ^{\neq}$-plan answering Q (over instances in Sch) if and only if Q entails $\mathsf{InfAcc}Q$ with respect to $\mathsf{AcSch(Sch)}$ if and only if Q is access-monotonically-determined.

The schema $\mathsf{AcSch}^{\neg}$ and $USPJAD^{\neq}$-plans. We now state an extension of the "Projective Łoś-Tarski theorem," Theorem 2.11, to the setting of access methods, again focusing on the case of boolean queries.

Theorem 3.11 *For any boolean* RQFO *query* Q *and access schema* Sch *containing constraints specified in* RQFO, *the following are equivalent:*

- *there is a* $USPJAD^{\neq}$*-plan answering* Q *(over instances for* Sch*).*
- $Q \wedge \mathsf{AcSch}^{\neg}\mathsf{(Sch)} \models \mathsf{InfAcc}Q$*. That is,* Q *entails* $\mathsf{InfAcc}Q$ *with respect to* $\mathsf{AcSch}^{\neg}\mathsf{(Sch)}$.

Furthermore, from every tableau proof witnessing $Q \wedge \mathsf{AcSch}^{\neg}\mathsf{(Sch)} \models \mathsf{InfAcc}Q$*, we can effectively extract a* $USPJAD^{\neq}$*-plan. If the constraints of* Sch *and the query* Q *are specified by equality-free* RQFO *sentences (in particular, TGDs), then we can replace* $USPJAD^{\neq}$*-plan by* $USPJAD$*-plan.*

In the vocabulary-based setting, the entailment $Q \wedge \mathsf{AcSch}^{\neg}\mathsf{(Sch)} \models \mathsf{InfAcc}Q$ reduces to the entailment given in Section 2.4, which was shown there to be equivalent to the query being induced-subinstance-monotonically-determined. And clearly, in the vocabulary-based setting, a $USPJAD^{\neq}$-plan can be expressed as an $\exists^{\neq}$ formula. Thus Theorem 3.11 generalizes the "Projective Łoś-Tarski Theorem," Theorem 2.11, characterizing queries that can be reformulated using $\exists^{\neq}$ formulas.

By Claim 4, the main claim of Theorem 3.11 can be restated as:

Q entails $\mathsf{InfAcc}Q$ with respect to the rules in $\mathsf{AcSch}^{\neg}(\mathsf{Sch})$ if and only if Q is induced-subinstance-access-monotonically-determined w.r.t.Sch if and only if Q has a $USPJAD^{\neq}$-plan.

Note that this result can be seen as a justification of the definition of $USPJAD^{\neq}$-plan, in that the class captures all induced-subinstance-access-monotonically-determined queries.

The proofs of all of the main theorems of this section—Theorem 3.9, Theorem 3.10, and Theorem 3.11—will be given in the next sections.

3.6 ACCESS INTERPOLATION

We have instantiated the first steps of our meta-algorithm for reformulation via access plans. For each target language based on access methods (RA-plans, $USPJAD^{\neq}$-plans, $USPJ^{\neq}$-plans), we have stated a semantic property of a query that is required for it to have an equivalent target plan (e.g., access determinacy, access-monotonic determinacy, etc.). We have shown that each semantic property is equivalent to an entailment. The next ingredient in proving the main results relating plans to proofs of these entailments is an interpolation theorem that tracks the "access methods used in the interpolant."

Interpolation and access methods. Recall Corollary 3.6, which follows from Proposition 3.2 in Section 3.3. It states that boolean RA-plans have the same expressiveness as RQFO sentences that are executable for membership checks. For simplicity, we call these "executable FO boolean queries" below.

By this corollary, we can prove our main results by finding reformulations that are executable FO boolean queries, rather than RA-plans. To find these reformulations, we require a version of Craig interpolation that allows us to relate the "binding patterns"—i.e., the subset of variables that are quantified in each relativized quantification—used in the interpolant χ of the entailment $\lambda \models \rho$ with those used in λ or ρ. When we apply this theorem to the entailment of $\mathsf{InfAcc}Q$ by Q, we can conclude that the interpolant is an executable FO boolean query.

We associate to RQFO formulas the set of binding patterns used in quantification, where a binding pattern is a relation and a subset of the positions. This is done by structural induction on the formula, assuming that the formula is first put into negation normal form.

$$
\begin{aligned}
\mathsf{BindPatt}(\top) = \mathsf{BindPatt}(x = y) &= \emptyset \\
\mathsf{BindPatt}(R(t_1,\ldots,t_n)) &= \{(R,\{1,\ldots,n\})\} \\
\mathsf{BindPatt}(\neg\varphi) &= \mathsf{BindPatt}(\varphi) \\
\mathsf{BindPatt}(\varphi \wedge \psi) &= \mathsf{BindPatt}(\varphi) \cup \mathsf{BindPatt}(\psi) \\
\mathsf{BindPatt}(\varphi \vee \psi) &= \mathsf{BindPatt}(\varphi) \cup \mathsf{BindPatt}(\psi) \\
\mathsf{BindPatt}(\exists \vec{x}\ (R(t_1,\ldots,t_n) \wedge \varphi)) &= \mathsf{BindPatt}(\varphi) \cup \{(R,\{i \mid t_i \notin \vec{x}\})\} \\
\mathsf{BindPatt}(\forall \vec{x}\ (R(t_1,\ldots,t_n) \rightarrow \varphi)) &= \mathsf{BindPatt}(\varphi) \cup \{(R,\{i \mid t_i \notin \vec{x}\})\}
\end{aligned}
$$

For example,

$$\text{BindPatt}(\exists x\ \exists y\ (R(x,y) \wedge \forall z\ (S(x,y,z) \rightarrow U(x,y,z)))) = \{(R,\emptyset),(S,\{1,2\}),(U,\{1,2,3\})\}.$$

We can similarly talk about the *universal binding patterns* of a formula—those that arise from a subformula $\forall\vec{x}\ (R(t_1,\ldots,t_n) \rightarrow \varphi)$—and the *existential binding patterns*—those that arise from a subformula $\exists\vec{x}\ (R(t_1,\ldots,t_n) \wedge \varphi)$. These can be defined formally by modifying the inductive definition above. Note that every binding pattern of a formula is either a universal pattern or an existential pattern, since a non-quantified relation can be considered as a vacuous case of existential quantification (if occurring positively) or universal quantification (if occurring negatively).

Intuitively, $\text{BindPatt}(\varphi)$ describes the kind of access that is used if φ is evaluated in an instance using a straightforward inductive evaluation procedure. For a sentence φ, if for each pattern $(R\{s_1 \ldots s_j\})$ in $\text{BindPatt}(\varphi)$ Sch contains an access method on R whose input positions are contained in $\{s_1 \ldots s_j\}$, then φ is an executable FO boolean query. We say that a binding pattern $(R_1,\{s_1 \ldots s_j\})$ is *covered by* another binding pattern $(R_2,\{t_1 \ldots t_k\})$ if $R_1 = R_2$ and $\{s_1 \ldots s_j\}$ is a superset of $\{t_1 \ldots t_k\}$. To show that a sentence φ_1 is an executable FO boolean query, it suffices to get another executable FO boolean query φ_2 whose binding patterns cover those of φ_2.

Recall that a relation R *occurs positively* (*negatively*) in a formula φ if some occurrence of R in φ is in the scope of an even (odd) number of negations. For the purpose of this definition, we view the implication symbol as a shorthand: $\psi \rightarrow \chi$ stands for $\neg\psi \vee \chi$. For example, in the formula $\forall x\ (P(x) \rightarrow \exists y\ R(x,y))$, the relation P occurs negatively and the relation R occurs positively.

Theorem 3.12 Access interpolation. *Let λ and ρ be* RQFO *sentences such that $\lambda \models \rho$. Then there exists an* RQFO *sentence χ such that*

1. *$\lambda \models \chi$ and $\chi \models \rho$.*
2. *A relation occurs positively (negatively) in χ only if it occurs positively (negatively) in both λ and ρ.*
3. *A constant occurs in χ only if it occurs both in λ and ρ.*
4. *Every existential binding pattern of χ is covered by an existential binding pattern of ρ, and the relation it binds occurs positively in λ. Every universal binding pattern of χ is covered by a universal binding pattern of λ, and the relation it binds occurs negatively in ρ.*
5. *If λ and ρ are both equality-free, then χ is equality-free.*

Furthermore, χ can be computed in polynomial time from a proof (in a suitable proof system) of the entailment $\lambda \models \rho$.

We show how Theorem 3.12 suffices to prove the results of Section 3.5.

The schema $\mathsf{AcSch}^{\leftrightarrow}$ and RA-plans. Recall the statement of Theorem 3.9.

> For any boolean RQFO query Q and access schema Sch containing constraints expressible in RQFO, there is an RA-plan answering Q (over instances in Sch) if and only if Q entails $\mathsf{InfAcc}Q$ with respect to the rules in $\mathsf{AcSch}^{\leftrightarrow}(\mathsf{Sch})$. If the query and constraints do not include equality, then the RA-plan will not make use of equality in any of its relational algebra expressions.

From Claim 3, we obtain the "plan-to-proof" direction of Theorem 3.9. Suppose Q does not imply $\mathsf{InfAcc}Q$ with respect to the rules in $\mathsf{AcSch}^{\leftrightarrow}(\mathsf{Sch})$. By Claim 3, Q is not access-determined, and it follows that no plan can answer Q.

For the "proof-to-plan" direction of Theorem 3.9, we assume Q entails $\mathsf{InfAcc}Q$ and construct an RA-plan that answers Q. We will use a slight modification of the axiom schema $\mathsf{AcSch}^{\leftrightarrow}$, denoted $\mathsf{AltAcSch}^{\leftrightarrow}$ in which the relation accessible does not appear. In every forward accessibility axiom an atom $\mathsf{accessible}(x)$ on the left is replaced by a relation $\mathsf{InfAcc}R(\vec{z})$, where $\vec{z}$ contains x in at least one position (and the other variables are universally quantified). Occurrences of accessible on the right are dropped. For example, the axiom $\mathsf{accessible}(x) \wedge R(x, y) \rightarrow \mathsf{InfAcc}R(x, y) \wedge \mathsf{accessible}(y)$ would be replaced by many axioms, including $\mathsf{InfAcc}S(x, w, z) \wedge R(x, y) \rightarrow \mathsf{InfAcc}R(x, y)$. We also allow all variants of these axioms in which free variables corresponding to input positions on the left are substituted by schema constants. Similarly, in every backward accessibility axiom we replace $\mathsf{accessible}(x)$ on the left by an atom in the original schema containing x, again dropping occurrences of accessible on the right.

Proposition 3.13 *Q proves $\mathsf{InfAcc}Q$ using the axioms of $\mathsf{AcSch}^{\leftrightarrow}$ if and only if Q proves $\mathsf{InfAcc}(Q)$ in the modified schema $\mathsf{AltAcSch}^{\leftrightarrow}$.*

Proof. In one direction, suppose that Q does not prove $\mathsf{InfAcc}Q$ using the axioms of $\mathsf{AcSch}^{\leftrightarrow}$. Then by Claim 3, Q is not access-determined. Fix I and I' instances for the original schema satisfying Σ with the same accessible part, but disagreeing on the output of Q. Without loss of generality, we can assume that there is a tuple $\vec{d}$ in the output of Q on I but not in the output of Q on I'. By applying an isomorphism to non-accessible values of I' and I, we can assume that every non-accessible value of I' is not in I and vice versa. Let I^* be the instance in which relations R are interpreted as in I and relations $\mathsf{InfAcc}R$ are interpreted as in I', a new relation symbol.

We argue that I^* satisfies $\mathsf{AltAcSch}^{\leftrightarrow}$. Clearly both the original relations and the relations $\mathsf{InfAcc}R$ satisfy Σ. Consider a modified forward accessibility axiom (universal quantifiers omitted, and with no schema constants for simplicity):

$$\mathsf{InfAcc}R_{j_1}(\ldots x_{j_1} \ldots) \wedge \ldots \mathsf{InfAcc}R_{j_m}(\ldots x_{j_m} \ldots) \wedge R(\vec{x}) \rightarrow \mathsf{InfAcc}R(\vec{x})$$

where R has an access method on positions $j_1 \ldots j_m$. Suppose we have a tuple $c_1 \ldots c_m$ in I^* satisfying the left-hand side of this implication. Then $c_{j_1} \ldots c_{j_m}$ must be accessible values of I and I'. Since the fact $R(\vec{c})$ holds in I, it must be in the accessible part of I, and hence in the accessible part of I'. So $\mathsf{InfAcc}R(\vec{c})$ holds in I^* as required. The backward accessibility axioms are argued symmetrically.

The tuple $\vec{d}$ is in $[\![Q]\!]_{I^*}$, since it is in $[\![Q]\!]_I$ and Q is a formula using the relations in the original schema. But $\vec{d}$ is not in $[\![Q]\!]_{I'}$. Therefore $\vec{d}$ cannot be returned by $\mathsf{InfAcc}Q$ on I^*. So I^* witnesses that Q does not prove $\mathsf{InfAcc}Q$ in $\mathsf{AltAcSch}^{\leftrightarrow}$.

In the other direction, suppose we have I^* witnessing that Q does not prove $\mathsf{InfAcc}(Q)$ in $\mathsf{AltAcSch}^{\leftrightarrow}$. Expand I^* to an instance I^+ for the signature extended with accessible, by interpreting accessible by all values of schema constants unioned with all values that lie in the domain of some $\mathsf{InfAcc}R$ relation and in the domain of some relation of the original schema. We show that the resulting instance satisfies the constraints of $\mathsf{AcSch}^{\leftrightarrow}$. The accessibility axioms follow directly from the corresponding axioms of $\mathsf{AltAcSch}^{\leftrightarrow}$. Similarly, the output of Q in I^+ is the same as the output of Q in I, while the output of $\mathsf{InfAcc}Q$ on I^+ is the same as the output of $\mathsf{InfAcc}Q$ on I^*. Therefore Q does not prove $\mathsf{InfAcc}Q$ in $\mathsf{AcSch}^{\leftrightarrow}$. □

We can rephrase the modified assumption on Q as:

$$Q \wedge \Sigma_1 \models (\Sigma_2 \rightarrow \mathsf{InfAcc}Q)$$

where Σ_1 contains the Sch constraints along with the "backward" accessibility axioms going from $\mathsf{InfAcc}R$ relations to R relations within $\mathsf{AltAcSch}^{\leftrightarrow}$, while Σ_2 contains the forward accessibility axioms and the InfAccCopy constraints.

By the access interpolation theorem there is an RQFO formula χ in negation normal form such that:

1. $Q \wedge \Sigma_1 \models \chi$.

2. $\chi \models \Sigma_2 \rightarrow \mathsf{InfAcc}Q$.

3. a relation occurs positively (respectively negatively) in χ if and only if it occurs positively (resp. negatively) on both sides of the entailment.

4. for a binding pattern p on a relation U in χ if p is existential, then it is covered by an existential pattern in $\Sigma_2 \rightarrow \mathsf{InfAcc}Q$, and U occurs positively in $Q \wedge \Sigma_1$. If p is a universal pattern, then it is covered by a universal pattern of $Q \wedge \Sigma_1$ and U occurs negatively in $\Sigma_2 \rightarrow \mathsf{InfAcc}Q$.

Because we are dealing with the modified axioms $\mathsf{AltAcSch}^{\leftrightarrow}$, the only relations in the entailment are the original schema relations and their InfAcc copies. Occurrences of the original schema relations R on the right-hand side of the entailment are all in the forward accessibility axioms, and they correspond exactly to access methods of the schema. It follows that every existential pattern over the relations R in χ is of the proper form. Furthermore the relations R occur only positively on the right—since $\Sigma_2 \rightarrow \mathsf{InfAcc}Q$ in negation normal form is $(\sim \Sigma_2) \vee \mathsf{InfAcc}Q$, and $\sim$ applied to a forward accessibility axiom is of the form $\exists \vec{x}\ R(\vec{x}) \wedge \ldots \wedge \neg\mathsf{InfAcc}R(\vec{x})$. So relations R can occur only positively in χ, and hence can occur only in existential patterns of χ. We conclude that all the patterns in χ involving the relations of the original schema must be existential and of the proper form.

Now let us examine occurrences of relations of the form $\mathsf{InfAcc}R$ within χ. The last property of χ above implies that any existential pattern on relations of the form $\mathsf{InfAcc}R$ would need to correspond to a positive occurrence of $\mathsf{InfAcc}R$ in $Q \wedge \Sigma_1$. But there are no such occurrences. Any universal pattern on relations of the form $\mathsf{InfAcc}R$ would need to correspond to a universal pattern in $Q \wedge \Sigma_1$, and hence must be covered by the use of $\mathsf{InfAcc}R$ in a backward axiom. Hence all such occurrences are covered by an access method of the schema.

We conclude that χ is an executable FO boolean query. Let $\mathsf{DeAcc}(\chi)$ be the result of changing all relations of the form $\mathsf{InfAcc}R$ in χ to R. We claim that $\mathsf{DeAcc}(\chi)$ is an executable rewriting of Q (and hence can be converted to an RA-plan using Proposition 3.2).

We justify this by proving containments between Q and $\mathsf{DeAcc}(\chi)$ in both directions. Suppose tuple $\vec{t}$ is returned by Q on an instance I of Sch. Let I' be the instance for the augmented schema in which both $\mathsf{InfAcc}R$ and R relations are interpreted as in I. We can see that I' satisfies the constraints in Σ_1 and Σ_2.

Applying the first condition on an interpolant above, we infer that χ holds of $\vec{t}$ in I', which implies that χ holds of $\vec{t}$ in I. But $\mathsf{DeAcc}(\chi)$ evaluated on I yields the same set of tuples as evaluating χ on I'. So $\vec{t}$ satisfies $\mathsf{DeAcc}(\chi)$ in I.

In the other direction, suppose tuple $\vec{t}$ satisfies $\mathsf{DeAcc}(\chi)$ in I. Then letting I' be as above, we have that $\vec{t}$ satisfies χ in I'. By the second property of an interpolant we have that $\Sigma_2 \rightarrow \mathsf{InfAcc}Q$ holds in I'. Since I' satisfies Σ_2, $\vec{t}$ is returned by $\mathsf{InfAcc}Q$ in I'. This tells us that $\vec{t}$ is returned by Q as required.

This completes the proof of the first assertion in Theorem 3.9. The assertion about equality-free queries and constraints follows since the Access interpolation theorem produces an equality-free interpolant when the entailment involves equality-free formulas, and the other transformations (e.g., from nested plans to RA-plans) do not introduce equality.

The schema AcSch and $USPJ$-plans. We turn to the proof of Theorem 3.10:

> For any boolean conjunctive query Q and access schema Sch containing constraints specified in RQFO (in particular, any TGDs), there is a $USPJ^{\neq}$-plan (in fact, $USPJ$-plan, provided that the constraints are expressible in equality-free RQFO) answering Q (over instances for Sch) if and only if Q entails $\mathsf{InfAcc}Q$ with respect to $\mathsf{AcSch}(\mathsf{Sch})$.

We prove Theorem 3.10, starting again with the direction from plan to proof. Suppose there is a $USPJ^{\neq}$-plan PL that answers Q. We show that Q entails $\mathsf{InfAcc}Q$ using the rules of $\mathsf{AcSch}(\mathsf{Sch})$. By Claim 2, if this is not the case, then Q is not access-monotonically-determined. So there are I and I' satisfying the constraints of Sch with every fact of $\mathsf{AccPart}(I)$ contained in $\mathsf{AccPart}(I')$ but I satisfies Q while I' does not satisfy Q.

Since Q holds on I, PL must return true on I. Since PL is a $USPJ^{\neq}$-plan using only the access methods of schema Sch, the facts witnessing satisfaction of PL must be in the accessible part of I, hence in the accessible part of I'. Therefore PL must also return true on AccPart(I'), and (since PL is $USPJ^{\neq}$) it follows that PL must return true on I', a contradiction of the assumption.

We turn to the direction from proof to plan, assuming Q entails InfAcc$Q$ with respect to AcSch(Sch). We have

$$Q \wedge \Sigma_1 \models \Sigma_2 \rightarrow \mathsf{InfAcc}Q$$

where Σ_1 is the Sch constraints, while Σ_2 contains the "forward accessibility axioms" along with the InfAccCopy constraints.

We can apply the access interpolation theorem to this entailment. We get an interpolant χ which contains only relations in the original schema. These have only existential binding patterns, as before, and the binding patterns conform to the access methods of the schema. Applying Proposition 3.2, we get the required plan.

The assertion about equality-free queries and constraints follows as with Theorem 3.9. This completes the proof of Theorem 3.10.

The schema AcSch$^{\neg}$ and $USPJAD^{\neq}$-plans. Finally, we prove Theorem 3.11:

> For any boolean RQFO query Q and access schema Sch containing constraints specified in RQFO, there is a $USPJAD^{\neq}$-plan answering Q over instances for Sch if and only if Q entails InfAcc$Q$ with respect to AcSch$^{\neg}$(Sch). Furthermore, if the constraints of Sch are specified by equality-free RQFO formulas (in particular, TGDs), then Q can be chosen to be a $USPJAD$-plan.

As before, we start with the direction from plan to proof. By Claim 4 if Q does not imply InfAcc$Q$, Q is not induced-subinstance-access-monotonically-determined w.r.t.Sch. This means we have instances I, I' satisfying the constraints of schema Sch, AccPart(I) is an induced subinstance of AccPart(I'), I satisfies Q and I' does not satisfy Q.

We argue that for every $USPJAD^{\neq}$-plan PL$'$ the tuples in any table returned by PL$'$ on I are contained in the tuples returned by PL$'$ on I'. First observe that since PL$'$ only interacts with the data via accesses using the methods of Sch, its output on I is the same as its output on AccPart(I), and similarly its output on I' is the same as its output on AccPart(I'). Proposition 3.7 shows that a $USPJAD^{\neq}$-plan can be converted to a $USPJAD^{\neq}$ query, and hence to an existential formula. We show that such queries are preserved in moving from AccPart(I) to AccPart(I') when AccPart(I') is an induced subinstance AccPart(I'). Fixing witnesses for the existential quantifiers in Q, we see that positive atoms satisfied by these witnesses are preserved, since AccPart(I) is a subinstance of AccPart(I'). Negated atoms are preserved by the additional properties of an induced subinstance over an arbitrary subinstance. Hence PL also holds in I', and thus Q must hold in I', a contradiction.

We move to the direction from a proof to a plan, assuming Q entails $\mathsf{InfAcc}Q$ w.r.t.$\mathsf{AcSch}^{\neg}(\mathsf{Sch})$. Let $\mathsf{AltAcSch}^{\neg}(\mathsf{Sch})$ be the variant of $\mathsf{AltAcSch}^{\leftrightarrow}$ where the backward accessibility axioms are of the form:

$$\forall x_1 \ldots x_n \bigwedge_{i \leq n} \varphi_i(x_i) \wedge \mathsf{InfAcc}R(x_1 \ldots x_n) \rightarrow R(x_1 \ldots x_n)$$

where R is any relation that has *some* access, and φ_i is any existential quantification of an atom over the original schema relations that contains x_i. That is, $\mathsf{AltAcSch}^{\neg}(\mathsf{Sch})$ is obtained from $\mathsf{AcSch}^{\neg}(\mathsf{Sch})$ in the same way that $\mathsf{AltAcSch}^{\leftrightarrow}(\mathsf{Sch})$ is obtained from $\mathsf{AcSch}^{\leftrightarrow}(\mathsf{Sch})$, by "inlining" the relations accessible.

By the same argument as in the proof of Proposition 3.13, we can see that provability of $\mathsf{InfAcc}Q$ from Q in the schema $\mathsf{AltAcSch}^{\neg}(\mathsf{Sch})$ is equivalent to provability of $\mathsf{InfAcc}Q$ from Q in $\mathsf{AcSch}^{\neg}(\mathsf{Sch})$. We write out the entailment as in the proof of Theorem 3.9, putting the "forward axioms" on the right side of the entailment and the restricted "backward axioms" on the left side of the entailment.

Applying the access interpolation theorem, we get an interpolant χ that will use the relations in the original schema with existential binding patterns, but can also have relations $\mathsf{InfAcc}R$ conforming to the quantification pattern in the backward axioms—that is, not quantified at all. Further, the relations $\mathsf{InfAcc}R$ can occur only negatively in the interpolant, since they occur only negatively on the right hand side. We conclude that χ must be an $\exists^{\neq}$ sentence ($\exists$ sentence when the query and constraints are equality-free) in which the only negated atoms involve relations $\mathsf{InfAcc}R$, such that R has at least one access method. Letting χ' be obtained from converting occurrences of $\mathsf{InfAcc}R$ to R, we get an executable sentence. We can argue as before that χ' has the desired properties.

This completes the proof of Theorem 3.11.

3.7 PROVING THE ACCESS INTERPOLATION THEOREM

In the previous section we showed that from proofs of entailments related to our semantic properties for access schemas we can get plans that fulfill the semantic properties, using a result about the existence of interpolants, the access interpolation theorem (Theorem 3.12). All that remains is to prove Theorem 3.12. Recall the statement:

> Let λ and ρ be RQFO sentences such that $\lambda \models \rho$. Then there exists an RQFO sentence χ such that
>
> 1. $\lambda \models \chi$ and $\chi \models \rho$.
> 2. A relation occurs positively (negatively) in χ only if it occurs positively (negatively) in both λ and ρ.
> 3. A constant occurs in χ only if it occurs both in λ and ρ.

4. Every existential binding of χ is covered by an existential binding pattern of ρ, and the relation it binds occurs positively in λ. Every universal binding of χ is covered by a universal binding pattern of λ, and the relation it binds occurs negatively in ρ.

5. If λ and ρ are both equality-free, then χ is equality-free.

Furthermore, χ can be computed in polynomial time from a proof (in a suitable proof system) of the entailment $\lambda \models \rho$.

We use the same tableau proof calculus as in the proof of the relativized-quantifier version of Craig's Theorem, Theorem 2.5, given in Figure 2.8. The interpolation rules will also be the same as those in the proof of that theorem. What is needed is an analysis of the binding patterns that occur in the interpolants.

Consider the proof rule for existential quantification:

$$\frac{X : \exists \vec{x}\ (R(\vec{s},\vec{x}) \wedge \varphi(\vec{s},\vec{x},\vec{t}))}{\begin{array}{c} X : R(\vec{s},\vec{a}) \\ X : \varphi(\vec{s},\vec{a},\vec{t}) \end{array}} \quad (\vec{a} \text{ fresh})$$

and the corresponding interpolation rule:

$$\frac{\Sigma \cup \{X : R(\vec{s},\vec{a}), X : \varphi(\vec{s},\vec{a},\vec{t})\} \xrightarrow{\text{int}} \chi}{\Sigma \cup \{X : \exists \vec{x}\ (R(\vec{s},\vec{x}) \wedge \varphi(\vec{s},\vec{x},\vec{t}))\} \xrightarrow{\text{int}} \chi} \quad (\vec{a} \text{ fresh}).$$

We see that the binding pattern produced in the interpolant is the same as that in the formula $\exists \vec{x}\ (R(\vec{s},\vec{x}) \wedge \varphi(\vec{s},\vec{x},\vec{t}))$. So the binding pattern portion of the invariant is preserved. In the case of universal quantification, we have four cases, corresponding to the bias of the formulas. In each case, the proof rule is the same:

$$\frac{X : \forall \vec{x}\ (R(\vec{s},\vec{x}) \rightarrow \varphi(\vec{s},\vec{x},\vec{t})) \quad Y : R(\vec{s},\vec{v})}{X : \varphi(\vec{s},\vec{v},\vec{t})}.$$

But the interpolation rule varies. Let us look at the case where $X = \textsc{left}, Y = \textsc{right}$. In this case our interpolation rule was:

$$\frac{\Sigma \cup \{\textsc{left} : \varphi(\vec{s},\vec{v},\vec{t})\} \xrightarrow{\text{int}} \chi}{\Sigma \cup \{\textsc{left} : \forall \vec{x}\ (R(\vec{s},\vec{x}) \rightarrow \varphi(\vec{s},\vec{x},\vec{t})), \textsc{right} : R(\vec{s},\vec{v})\} \xrightarrow{\text{int}} \chi'}$$

with $\chi' = \forall x_{m_1} \dots x_{m_k} \ (R(\vec{s},\vec{v}) \rightarrow \chi)[v_{m_1} := x_{m_1} \dots v_{m_k} := x_{m_k}]$ where $v_{m_1} \dots v_{m_k}$ are the subset of the v_i occurring in $R(\vec{s},\vec{v}) \wedge \chi$ that do not occur in a LEFT-formula of Σ.

We see that the interpolant introduces quantification where the quantified positions are a subset of those positions quantified in the top-most quantifier of the formula $\forall \vec{x} \ (R(\vec{s},\vec{x}) \rightarrow \varphi(\vec{s},\vec{x},\vec{t}))$. Thus the binding pattern is covered by a binding pattern of a LEFT-annotated formula. Further, we are introducing a universal binding pattern, but it corresponds to the interaction of a universal binding pattern on the left, and a positive occurrence on the right (hence a negative occurrence in the formula on the right is obtained). Similarly, in the case $X = \text{RIGHT}, Y = \text{LEFT}$, we had the interpolant rule:

$$\frac{\Sigma \cup \{\text{RIGHT} : \varphi(\vec{s},\vec{v},\vec{t})\} \xrightarrow{\text{int}} \chi}{\Sigma \cup \{\text{RIGHT} : \forall \vec{x} \ (R(\vec{s},\vec{x}) \rightarrow \varphi(\vec{s},\vec{x},\vec{t})), \text{LEFT} : R(\vec{s},\vec{v})\} \xrightarrow{\text{int}} \chi'}$$

with $\chi' = \exists x_{m_1} \dots x_{m_k} \ (R(\vec{s},\vec{v}) \wedge \chi)[v_{m_1} := x_{m_1} \dots v_{m_k} := x_{m_k}]$ where $v_{m_1} \dots v_{m_k}$ are the v_i in $R(\vec{s},\vec{v}) \wedge \chi$ that do not occur in a RIGHT-formula of Σ.

Here the interpolant calculation introduces an existential quantification, but one which results from the interaction of a positive occurrence of the relation R on the left, and a corresponding universal pattern on the right. Hence we have the same existential pattern in the formula being negated on the right.

This completes the proof of the access interpolation theorem, Theorem 3.12. Plugging this interpolation algorithm into the meta-algorithm, as described earlier in this chapter, completes the proof of Theorem 3.10, Theorem 3.9, and Theorem 3.11.

The reader may wonder if the theorem cannot be strengthened by requiring that binding patterns in the interpolant are covered by patterns on *both* sides of the entailment. This is not possible, as the following example shows:

$$\Big(\exists x \ \exists y \ S(x,y) \ \wedge \ \forall x \ \forall y \ (S(x,y) \rightarrow R(x,y))\Big) \ \models \ \exists x \ \exists y \ R(x,y).$$

An interpolant in the stronger sense for this entailment would only be allowed to use the access method $(R,\{1,2\})$, which would preclude the use of any quantifier in the interpolant, but it is easy to see that no quantifier-free interpolant exists for this implication.

3.8 EXTENSION TO NON-BOOLEAN QUERIES

We explain how the major results extend to non-boolean conjunctive queries, without the claims that the plans can be found via interpolation from a proof of the corresponding entailment. We focus on providing a variant of Theorem 3.14 for non-boolean CQs, with the other results being modified similarly.

Theorem 3.14 *For any conjunctive query Q and access schema* Sch *with constraints specified in* RQFO, *there is an RA-plan answering Q (over instances satisfying* Sch*) if and only if $Q \wedge \mathsf{AcSch}^{\leftrightarrow}(\mathsf{Sch}) \models \mathsf{InfAcc}Q$ if and only if Q is access-determined w.r.t.* Sch.

Proof. The direction from a plan to a proof has already been proven, as has the equivalence between the semantic property access determinacy and the entailment. It suffices to show that if Q is access-determined, there is an RA-plan that answers it.

We first claim that if a CQ Q is access-determined, the values in any output tuple of Q on an instance I must lie in the accessible values of I, the active domain of the accessible part of I. Since Q is a CQ, its output must be in the active domain of I unioned with the schema constants. Suppose by way of contradiction that $t_1 \dots t_n$ is an output of Q with $t_i \notin \mathsf{accessible}(I)$. Since schema constants are always in the accessible part, t_i cannot be a schema constant. Let t'_i be some element outside of the active domain of I that is not a schema constant, and let I' be formed by replacing t_i by t'_i in each fact. Clearly I' has the same accessible part as I, but the output of Q on I' contains $t_1 \dots t_{i-1}\ t'_i\ t_{i+1} \dots t_n$, which is not in the output of Q on I. Hence I and I' contradict access determinacy of Q.

Going back to the definition of the accessible values in an instance I, we see that it is the union of inductively-defined sets $\mathsf{accessible}_i(I)$ as i varies over the natural numbers $\mathcal{N}$. For every i, there is an RQFO formula $\rho_i(x)$ that holds in an instance I and an assignment of the variable x to element x_0 exactly when $x_0 \in \mathsf{accessible}_i(I)$: the formula is a union of conjunctive queries corresponding to sequences of at most i accesses that can produce such an x. The compactness theorem of first-order logic [Chang and Keisler, 1990] implies that for first-order formula φ and an infinite sequence $\rho_i : i \in \mathcal{N}$ of formulas such that $\varphi \models \bigvee_i \rho_i$, there must be a k such that $\varphi \models \bigvee_{i \leq k} \rho_i$. We can apply this to the sequence of formulas ρ_i above, concluding that there is k such that for every instance I the output of Q on I is contained in $\mathsf{accessible}_k$, the kth approximation of the accessible values. There is an RA-plan PL_k that produces all tuples in the k-accessible-part, and thus it suffices to create a plan that takes the set of such tuples in the output of PL_k and filters down to the subset which satisfy the query Q. Using the results of Section 3.3, we can see that it is enough to generate a plan that will check, given an instance of the schema enhanced with a relation consisting of a single parameter tuple $\vec{t}$, whether or not $\vec{t}$ is in the output of Q. Further, it is enough to generate such a plan for each fixed equality type of $\vec{t}$ (each decision of which indices are equal): if we can do this, we can split up the tuples by equality type, run the plan corresponding to each equality type separately, and then union the results. For simplicity we argue that there is a plan that will perform this check on a tuple $\vec{t}$ in which all indices have distinct values; the case of more general equality types reduces to this one.

Consider the schema extended with distinct schema constants for each free variable of Q. By replacing each free variable in Q by the corresponding schema constant we obtain a boolean query Q'. Every access that can be performed on an instance I in the original schema can still be performed when I is extended by values for the additional schema constants in this transformed schema. Thus if two instances $I, \vec{t}$ and $I', \vec{t}'$ agree on their accessible part in the extended schema, I and I' must agree on their accessible part in the original schema. From this we see that since Q is access-determined under the original schema, Q' is access-determined in the extended one. By Theorem 3.9, the proof-to-plan result for boolean queries, there is a plan PL' that answers Q'. Such a PL' performs the filtering that we require. □

3.9 DECIDABLE PLAN-GENERATION

In Section 2.7 we obtained end-to-end decidability of reformulation problems for restricted classes of constraints Σ by analyzing the constraints in the "auxiliary schema," which consisted of two copies of Σ and a set of "transfer axioms." We can do the same here, where the accessibility axioms play the role of transfer axioms. Note that in our results here, as with our previous decidability results, our user query Q will be assumed to be a conjunctive query.

We start with the case of GNF constraints, stating the analog of Theorem 2.13:

Theorem 3.15 *The following problem is decidable in* 2EXPTIME, *and is* 2EXPTIME-*complete:*

input: *an access schema including a collection Σ of constraints in* GNF, *Q a conjunctive query.*

output: *whether Q has an RA-plan over the schema.*

The same holds for $USPJ^{\neq}$-plans and $USPJAD^{\neq}$-plans.

The proof mirrors that of Theorem 2.13, since each version of the "accessible schema" will contain only GNF constraints.

For GTGDs, we can again extend the vocabulary-based result:

Proposition 3.16 *Checking whether a CQ has an RA-plan ($USPJ^{\neq}$-plan, etc.) over an access schema with GTGDs is* 2EXPTIME-*complete, with the lower bound holding even when the arity of the relations is fixed.*

The proof is the same as that of Proposition 2.14.

3.9.1 THE CASE OF INCLUSION DEPENDENCIES

We turn to the complexity of access-restriction reformulation in the special case where constraints are inclusion dependencies. Recall that in the case of vocabulary-based restrictions, Proposition 2.15 showed that the existence of a restricted-quantifier FO reformulation coincided with the existence of a CQ reformulation. We do not know if the analogous result holds for reformulation with access restrictions.

We also found (Proposition 2.16) that the complexity of finding reformulations in the presence of inclusion dependencies coincided with the complexity of query answering with inclusion dependencies, which is known to be PSPACE-complete. This was because the "transfer axioms" generated as part of the auxiliary schema are also inclusion dependencies. This phenomenon—"complexity of reformulation = complexity of entailment"—is something that we see often. The meta-algorithm of the last two chapters can be seen as a reduction of reformulation problems to entailment problems involving constraints and a query, and this "Craig reduction" normally preserves the classes of constraints that we are interested in.

The case of access restrictions and inclusion dependencies is an exception. The auxiliary schema adds the accessibility axioms, which are not inclusion dependencies, but rather are a very restricted kind of GTGD. We thus need a more refined analysis to isolate the complexity. One can show:

Theorem 3.17 *The complexity of all our access-related determinacy/answerability problems in the case of inclusion dependencies is in* EXPTIME.

Proof sketch. Notice that in these cases the auxiliary schema contains only GTGDs whose left-hand side consists of one non-unary atom and several unary atoms. An exponential-sized push-down automaton can explore the chase closure, guessing a homomorphism from the query to elements within guarded sets on the stack, and recording in the control state atoms that have already occurred in the pre-image of the homomorphism. Since reachability in a pushdown automaton is in PTIME, we have an EXPTIME upper bound. □

An involved lower-bound argument, sketched in [Bárány et al., 2013], shows that the problem is actually EXPTIME-complete.

3.9.2 CONSTRAINTS WITH TERMINATING CHASE

Recall from Section 2.7 that for TGD constraints with terminating chase, conjunctive reformulation always behaves well (resulting in an implication problem for a set of constraints that also has a terminating chase), while for first-order reformulation this is not necessarily the case. We will see exactly the same phenomena in the case of restrictions based on access methods.

We have the following result, proven exactly as Proposition 2.17:

Proposition 3.18 *Let C be a class of TGDs with terminating chase and with effective syntax. Then the following problem is decidable:*

> *Given* Sch *an access schema whose constraints are in C and Q a conjunctive query, determine if Q has a $USPJ^{\neq}$-plan.*

As will be shown in Chapter 4 (Theorem 4.3) for schemas based on TGDs, any query with a $USPJAD^{\neq}$-plan has an SPJ-plan, hence above we could replace $USPJ^{\neq}$-plan with $USPJAD^{\neq}$-plan or SPJ-plan.

For RA-plans, we do not have general results about classes with terminating chase, but we can get decidability results for classes satisfying acyclicity conditions:

Proposition 3.19 *The following problem is decidable:*

> *Given a query Q, a schema* Sch *with access methods and constraints given by weakly acyclic TGDs Σ, determine whether or not Q has an RA-plan.*

Proof. One can check that $\mathsf{AcSch}^{\leftrightarrow}(\mathsf{Sch})$ is also weakly acyclic, arguing as in Proposition 2.21. □

3.10 FINITE INSTANCES AND ACCESS RESTRICTIONS

The negative results about vocabulary-based reformulation for finite instances, stated in Section 2.8, carry over immediately to the setting with access restrictions.

We now turn to the positive results for "tame" constraint classes. Our goal will be to show that answerability over all instances and answerability over finite instances coincide, and in particular the characterization theorems relating answerability to entailment still hold in the finite. We start with constraints in GNF, proceeding as in the vocabulary-based case.

The following result generalizes Theorem 2.26, which stated that a $\exists^+$ reformulation of a query Q over finite instances must be a reformulation over all instances, provided that the constraints are in GNF.

Theorem 3.20 *Let* Sch *be an access schema whose constraints are in* GNF *and let Q be a conjunctive query. Then if* PL *is a $USPJ$-plan that answers Q over finite instances, then* PL *answers Q over all instances. In particular Q has a $USPJ$-plan that answers it over finite instances if and only if it has one over all instances.*

Proof. We give the argument for Q a boolean CQ, with the extension to the non-boolean case being routine.

Fix $USPJ$-plan PL for Q. There is a $USPJ$ query that holds true on an instance exactly when PL does, just by translating a plan to a query inductively. We argue that the following property of instances over the schema Sch is expressible by a sentence in GNF: if the instance satisfies the constraints, then it satisfies the query given by PL if and only if Q holds in it. The expressibility in GNF follows from the fact that GNF contains $USPJ$ queries and the constraints, and is closed under boolean combinations of sentences. Therefore Theorem 2.12 implies that if the property holds on all finite instances, it holds on all instances. Hence PL answers Q over all instances. □

In the case of RA-plans, we can only transfer statements about the existence of a plan, as in the vocabulary-based case.

The following generalizes Theorem 2.27:

Theorem 3.21 *Let* Sch *be an access schema whose constraints are in* GNF *and let Q be a conjunctive query. Then there is an RA-plan that answers Q over finite instances if and only if there is an RA-plan that answers Q over all instances.*

Proof. We give the proof of this result only when Q is a boolean CQ. However, the argument extends to the non-boolean case, since the main characterization theorems extend to non-boolean CQs, as explained in Section 3.8.

Suppose Q has an RA-plan PL that works over finite instances. Then the entailment corresponding to access determinacy of Q *w.r.t.* Sch is valid over finite instances. Since the entailment holds over finite instances, it holds over all instances by Theorem 2.12. Hence Q is access-determined over all instances. From Claim 3, we conclude that Q entails InfAcc$Q$ over all instances, and hence by Theorem 3.9 Q has an RA-plan over all instances. □

A similar argument works for $USPJAD^{\neq}$-plans and for $USPJ^{\neq}$-plans.

Theorem 3.22 *Let* Sch *be an access schema whose constraints are in* GNF *and let Q be a conjunctive query. Then Q has a $USPJAD^{\neq}$-plan that answers it over finite instances if and only if it has such a plan that answers it over all instances, and similarly for $USPJ^{\neq}$-plans.*

If the constraints do not include equality, the same holds for $USPJAD$-plans and $USPJ$-plans.

Proof. We give only the argument for boolean Q and $USPJAD^{\neq}$-plans, arguing as in Theorem 3.21.

Suppose Q has a $USPJAD^{\neq}$-plan using k access commands that works over finite Sch instances. Then the entailment corresponding to monotonic determinacy must hold over finite instances. The entailment can be expressed as the validity of a GNF sentence. So it holds over all instances by Theorem 2.12. Applying Claim 4, we see that Q is induced-subinstance-access-monotonically-determined over all Sch instances, and hence by Theorem 3.11, Q has a $USPJAD^{\neq}$-plan that answers it over all Sch instances. □

Recall that in Proposition 2.24 of Section 2.8, we showed that for classes with terminating chase, there is a positive existential reformulation over finite instances if and only if there is a reformulation that works over all instances. The argument extends to the setting of access methods, with "a positive existential reformulation" replaced by "a $USPJ$-plan." For existence of an RQFO reformulation we argued for the same conclusion, but only for weakly acyclic TGDs. The argument extends to the setting of access methods with "an RQFO reformulation" replaced by "an RA-plan."

3.11 SUMMARY

In this chapter we have extended our meta-algorithm to interfaces given by access methods. This is an example of how interpolation-based reformulation can be applied to finer-grained interfaces to data. It is also a step toward applying the method with a target that is more like a program, rather than producing a formula as in Chapter 2. This idea will be pursued further in Chapter 4.

The main theorems for restrictions based on access-methods are summarized in Table 3.1. Complexity results for determining existence of a plan are summarized in Table 3.2.

Table 3.1: Proof/Plan correspondence for access-restricted reformulation

Goal	Semantic Property	Proof Goal
RA-plan	Access Determinacy	$Q \wedge \mathsf{AcSch}^{\leftrightarrow}(\mathsf{Sch}) \models \mathsf{InfAcc}Q$
$USPJ^{\neq}$-plan	Access-Monotonic Determinacy	$Q \wedge \mathsf{AcSch}(\mathsf{Sch}) \models \mathsf{InfAcc}Q$
$USPJAD^{\neq}$-plan	Induced-Subinstance-Access-Monotonic Determinacy	$Q \wedge \mathsf{AcSch}^{\neg}(\mathsf{Sch}) \models \mathsf{InfAcc}Q$

Table 3.2: Complexity of reformulation over access methods

Constraints	RA-plan	$USPJ^{\neq}$-plan	$USPJAD^{\neq}$-plan
GNF	2EXPTIME	2EXPTIME	2EXPTIME
GTGD	2EXPTIME	2EXPTIME	2EXPTIME
ID	EXPTIME	EXPTIME	EXPTIME
CQ Views	Undecidable over unrestricted instances [Gogacz and Marcinkowski, 2015], unknown over finite instances	NP	NP

3.12 BIBLIOGRAPHIC REMARKS

Work on querying in the presence of access methods. Work on optimization with access methods was initially motivated by the goal of finding index-only plans over a fixed set of indices in traditional databases [Rajaraman et al., 1995, Ullman, 1989]. Later work considered access methods as a model of the interfaces of datasources such as Web forms, to be used in information integration [Knoblock et al., 1998]. Li [2003], Li and Chang [2001] explored the complexity of determining when a query could be answered in the presence of access methods, where answering the query referred to coming up with an executable query. Extensions to richer queries were considered in [Nash and Ludäscher, 2004a,b]. The implementation of access patterns was investigated in [Florescu et al., 1999], focusing on integrating access restrictions into a cost-based optimizer. None of these papers consider the interaction of integrity constraints with interface restrictions based on access methods.

The approach to reformulating with access methods using interpolation stems from [Benedikt et al., 2014b], but here we include full proofs, extending the sketches provided in [Benedikt et al., 2014b]. The complexity and decidability results are from [Benedikt et al., 2014b] and the earlier conference paper [Bárány et al., 2013]. The latter paper studies reformulations whose target language consists of logical formulas that are evaluated over the accessible part of an instance, rather than defining a plan language as we do, but the arguments are similar.

The work of Deutsch, Ludäscher, and Nash. The first paper on querying with integrity constraints and access methods is [Deutsch et al., 2007]. It does not define a plan language, but rather deals with getting an "executable reformulation": a union of conjunctive queries with atomic negation that can be executed using the access methods in the obvious way. We have shown in Section 3.3 that these correspond to our notion of $USPJAD$-plan in expressiveness. We will show in Theorem 4.3 of Chapter 4 that if one starts with a CQ and the constraints consist only of TGDs, negation and union are not necessary in either an RA-plan or a $USPJAD$-plan. But Deutsch et al. [2007] allow the source query Q to be a $USPJAD$ query, and allow constraints with disjunction and atomic negation on both sides. Thus Theorem 4.3 does not apply to their setting. Although the constraints and source queries considered in [Deutsch et al., 2007] are very rich, the algorithms are specific to the case where the chase terminates.

They give several approaches to the *existence problem*—determining whether a query has a $USPJAD$ executable query—as well as the problem of finding such a query if it exists.

Section 4 of [Deutsch et al., 2007] provides one algorithm for the existence problem:

(i) Apply the chase procedure to the original query Q with the constraints until termination. The algorithm chases the queries directly to get another query, rather than dealing with the corresponding canonical database to get an instance. Thus for them the result of the chase is another query, the "universal plan" Q_1.

(ii) Form a query Q_2 as the "answerable part" of Q_1: this is (informally) a maximal subquery of Q_1 that can be generated using the access methods.

(iii) Chase Q_2 to get a new query Q_3, and check whether Q_3 is contained in Q, which will allow one to conclude that Q_2 is equivalent to Q.

In the case of TGDs with terminating chase, this procedure matches our approach for SPJ-plans. The first step, chasing Q, corresponds in our setting to generating consequences using chase steps for the canonical database of Q_0 with the original copy of the constraints. The second step corresponds to applying our "forward accessibility axioms," or equivalently to taking the accessible part of the instance generated in the first step. The final step corresponds to applying the InfAccCopy constraints and checking for a match of the copy of Q.

Deutsch et al. [2007] utilize a chase-based algorithm above in the setting of constraints and queries with disjunction and negation. They do this by defining a variant of the chase with disjunction and negation, and a notion of "answerable part" of a query that applies to $USPJAD$ queries. This is closely related to the approach for $USPJAD$-plans given here. The extended definition of "answerable part" to handle atomic negation corresponds to applying both the forward accessibility axioms and a restriction of the backward accessibility axioms, with the restriction being that all values occurring in atoms must satisfy accessible, and thus corresponds to the schema $\mathsf{AcSch}^{\neg}(\mathsf{Sch})$.

Section 7 of [Deutsch et al., 2007] provides another approach to the existence problem, which proceeds by augmenting the constraints with a set of auxiliary axioms capturing accessibility (denoted Σ_D), and a derived query (denoted there as $dext(Q)$). The main result is that for some classes of constraints (those with "stratified witnesses") a source query Q has an executable $USPJAD$ rewriting if and only if Q is contained in $dext(Q)$ with respect to the enhanced schema. Again, in the case of TGDs with terminating chase, this coincides with our technique. The authors emphasize the second algorithm as a way of reducing rewriting with access methods and constraints to rewriting under constraints alone.

First-order rewritings, and their distinction from positive rewritings, are not covered in [Deutsch et al., 2007]. Neither do they consider the relationship of rewritability to semantic properties. However, the semantics-to-syntax approach we take here is related to results and discussions in Section 9 of [Deutsch et al., 2007]. In Theorem 22, they prove that their notion of executable query covers all $USPJAD$ queries that could be implemented using the access methods. Although the theorem is phrased using a Turing Machine model, the proof shows that every access-determined $USPJAD$ query has a rewriting that is executable in their sense.

Related work for access interpolation. The access interpolation theorem, Theorem 3.12, generalizes the Craig interpolation theorem and the Lyndon interpolation theorem. It also generalizes Otto's relativized interpolation theorem [Otto, 2000], mentioned in the previous chapter. Theorem 3.12 provides a new constructive proof of the relativized interpolation theorem. In addition, Theorem 3.12 generalizes a known interpolation theorem for the bounded fragment (studied in the context of set theory and bounded arithmetic [Feferman, 1968]) and for hybrid logic [Areces et al., 2001, Blackburn and Marx, 2003]. Theorem 3.12 can also be proven using Otto's relativized interpolation theorem, although the resulting proof would not be constructive.

Related work on complexity of access-related problems. The complexity of reasoning with Guarded TGDs is investigated in [Calì et al., 2008, Lukasiewicz et al., 2012], where tight bounds are given for conjunctive query containment under both Guarded TGDs and Linear Guarded TGDs, including IDs. The application to bounds on the finer access-related problems studied in this chapter is mentioned in [Bárány et al., 2013].

CHAPTER 4

Reformulation Algorithms for TGDs

Let us rephrase the meta-algorithm for reformulating queries that we have referred to throughout the book, adding a bit more generality. It says we should:

1. Isolate a semantic property that any input query Q must have with respect to the target $\mathcal{T}$ and constraints Σ in order to have a reformulation of the desired type.
2. Express this property as a proof goal or entailment.
3. Search for a proof of the entailment within an appropriate proof system.
4. From the proof, extract a plan.

Up until now the last step was always performed through an appeal to an interpolation algorithm. We have shown that this algorithm can be applied to yield optimal worst-case complexity for many reformulation problems—for example, Proposition 2.20 shows that the algorithm achieves this for reformulating over conjunctive query views. Still, there are disadvantages to the use of interpolation. First, since the algorithm goes through first-order logic, it is difficult to get a good grasp on what kinds of plans or reformulations are produced, even in the restricted cases of greatest interest to databases. Secondly, safety of reformulations was not enforced automatically by the algorithms, although in the vocabulary-based setting it could be assured via post-processing (see Section 2.6). Our access-related algorithms were only presented for boolean queries, with the non-boolean case relying on post-processing. We can lift these restrictions in the case of TGD constraints.

In this chapter, we give transformations that take chase proofs of our entailments directly to plans, without going through executable first-order queries. This gives an alternative implementation of the last part of the meta-algorithm in the case of schemas with TGDs.

But all the material in the chapter outside of Section 4.5 is presented independently of interpolation, and thus *to understand the main algorithms of this chapter, one does not need any familiarity with interpolation, or with first-order proof systems such as tableau.*

However, this does not mean that in this chapter we are departing from the interpolation-based approach. In Section 4.5 we will show that *these algorithms are special cases of interpolation.* Our general interpolation-based theorems can be seen as an explanation of why these algorithms work, and as a generalization of these algorithms outside of the TGD case.

In the process, we show that for schemas with TGD constraints stronger claims can be made about the relationship between semantic conditions/entailments and plans:

- For access-monotonically-determined query, we will get an SPJ-plan.
- The gap between access-monotonically-determined queries and induced-subinstance-access-monotonically-determined queries will disappear. Every query that is induced-subinstance-access-monotonically-determined will have an SPJ-plan, and will (by the prior results) thus be access-monotonically-determined.

Throughout this chapter, we restrict the input query Q to be a conjunctive query, but not necessarily boolean. We assume that the constraints in our access schemas consist only of TGDs. As mentioned at the end of Subsection 2.1.3, all the results we present for equality-free constraints, such as TGDs, will continue to hold if the schemas also include inequalities between schema constants. For TGDs, it is not difficult to see that inequalities between constants do not interact with the chase proof system: given queries Q and Q', a collection of TGDs Σ_1, and constant inequalities Σ_2, Q entails Q' *w.r.t.* $\Sigma_1 \cup \Sigma_2$ if and only if Q' has a match in the final configuration of a Σ_1 chase sequence beginning with the canonical database of Q if and only if Q entails Q' *w.r.t.* Σ_1.

4.1 FINDING PLANS THROUGH CHASE PROOFS

Recall from Section 1.3 that for query containment problems using conjunctive queries and TGDs, we can use the proof system known as the chase. In the chase a proof is a sequence of database instances, beginning with the canonical database of query Q, evolving by firing rules—that is, grounding the TGDs.

A proof is a sequence of chase configurations, instances connected by some rule firing of a TGD in Σ. A *full proof* ends with a *match*, i.e., a homomorphism of the target query Q' into the final configuration.

We also know from Section 3.5 that when we apply our methodology for reformulation to a schema based on TGD constraints Σ, we will get a proof goal (prior to re-arranging the left and right sides) of the form:

$$Q \wedge \Gamma \models \mathsf{InfAcc}Q$$

where Q is the query we are trying to reformulate, $\mathsf{InfAcc}Q$ is a query obtained from copying Q on the "inferred accessible" relations, and Γ consists of two copies of Σ—the Sch constraints and $\mathsf{InfAccCopy}$ constraints, as in the previous chapter—along with "accessibility axioms" relating the two copies. In particular, we have a problem of conjunctive query containment with respect to TGD constraints (namely Γ), and hence we can restrict our attention to chase proofs.

We now take a different look at finding reformulations from proofs, focusing first on the case of SPJ-plans and the "forward accessible schema" $\mathsf{AcSch}(\mathsf{Sch})$. Given a chase sequence

$\mathsf{config}_1 \ldots \mathsf{config}_k$ corresponding to a full proof, let $C_{\mathsf{SeqConsts}}$ be the set of chase constants generated by firings of Sch constraints within this sequence. We convert prefixes of our full proof $\mathsf{config}_1 \ldots \mathsf{config}_k$ into plans by induction on the number of accessibility axioms fired in the prefix. We will generate plans PL_i for any prefix $\mathsf{config}_1 \ldots \mathsf{config}_i$ that ends with the firing of an accessibility axiom, where the generated plan PL_i will make use of temporary tables T_i whose attributes correspond to a subset C_i of $C_{\mathsf{SeqConsts}}$. Informally, rows of these tables will store possible homomorphisms that map the chase constants into the instance being queried. Therefore, we interchangeably talk about constants or attributes when referring to the elements of C_i hereafter. The C_i will be monotonic under inclusion as i increases. We will maintain as an invariant that the attributes in C_i are exactly the constants $c \in C_{\mathsf{SeqConsts}}$ such that $\mathsf{accessible}(c)$ holds in the configuration of the last element config_i of the prefix $\mathsf{config}_1 \ldots \mathsf{config}_i$. In the induction step, we consider a chase sequence ending with the firing of a rule:

$$\begin{aligned}\mathsf{accessible}(c_{j_1}) \wedge \ldots \mathsf{accessible}(c_{j_m}) \wedge R(c_1 \ldots c_n)\\ \rightarrow \mathsf{InfAcc}R(c_1 \ldots c_n) \wedge \bigwedge_i \mathsf{accessible}(c_i)\end{aligned}$$

associated with method mt on relation R having input positions $j_1 \ldots j_m$. We say that the rule firing *exposes fact* $R(c_1 \ldots c_n)$. Let config_{i-1} be the chase configuration prior to the firing of this rule. Note that by the inductive invariant, each of $c_{j_1} \ldots c_{j_m}$ must be an attribute of table T_{i-1} associated with the sequence prior to the firing. We now define the *commands that correspond to this rule firing*.

We explain the induction step first in the case where no c_{j_i} are schema constants and no constant is repeated in $R(c_1 \ldots c_n)$. We first generate an access command whose input expression is the projection of T_{i-1} onto $c_{j_1} \ldots c_{j_m}$, with the input mapping InMap taking columns $c_{j_1} \ldots c_{j_m}$ of T_{i-1} to input positions $j_1 \ldots j_m$ of mt. The command's output will be a table T_i' with attributes $C_i = C_{i-1} \cup \{c_1 \ldots c_n\}$, with the output mapping taking position i to c_i. We follow the access command by a middleware query command that sets T_i to the join of T_i' with T_{i-1}.

If we have a full chase proof, the final configuration must have a match for $\mathsf{InfAcc}Q$. Let V be the set of chase constants corresponding to the free variables of Q. We add a last Return command that will return the projection of T_i on V. In the special case that Q is boolean, the final query amounts to checking that the table T_i is non-empty.

Example 4.1. Consider a variant of Example 1.3, using the same schema and the query $Q = \exists \mathsf{eid}\ \exists \mathsf{onum}\ \exists \mathsf{lname}\ \mathsf{Profinfo}(\mathsf{eid}, \mathsf{onum}, \mathsf{lname})$. Using the chase, we get the following **proof**:

1. Create the canonical database, containing the single fact $\{\mathsf{Profinfo}(\mathsf{eid}_0, \mathsf{onum}_0, \mathsf{lname}_0)\}$
2. One of the initial integrity constraints matches $\mathsf{Profinfo}(\mathsf{eid}_0, \mathsf{onum}_0, \mathsf{lname}_0)$, and firing the rule infers $\mathsf{Udirectory}(\mathsf{eid}_0, \mathsf{lname}_0)$.
3. $\mathsf{Udirectory}(\mathsf{eid}_0, \mathsf{lname}_0)$ matches an accessibility axiom, and the rule firing generates $\mathsf{InfAccUdirectory}(\mathsf{eid}_0, \mathsf{lname}_0)$, $\mathsf{accessible}(\mathsf{lname}_0)$, and $\mathsf{accessible}(\mathsf{eid}_0)$.

Algorithm 1: Chase-Proof-to-SPJ-Plan algorithm

Input: full chase proof with configurations $\mathsf{config}_1 \ldots \mathsf{config}_k$

V := attributes for free variables of Q;
PL $:= \emptyset$;
T_0 := table with no columns ;
$numsteps = 0$;
for i = 1 *to* k **do**
  if config_i *is obtained by firing an accessibility axiom exposing fact* $F = R(c_1 \ldots c_n)$ *via method* mt *with inputs* $j_1 \ldots j_m$ **then**
    Append to PL command $T'_i \Leftarrow \mathsf{mt} \Leftarrow \pi_{c_{j_1} \ldots c_{j_m}}(T_{i-1})$;
    Append to PL command $T_i := T'_i \bowtie T_{i-1}$;
    $numsteps++$
Add command "Return $\pi_V(T_{numsteps})$" to PL ;
return Plan

4. An accessibility axiom matches $\mathsf{Profinfo}(\mathsf{eid}_0, \mathsf{onum}_0, \mathsf{lname}_0) \wedge \mathsf{accessible}(\mathsf{eid}_0)$ creating fact $\mathsf{InfAccProfinfo}(\mathsf{eid}_0, \mathsf{onum}_0, \mathsf{lname}_0)$.

5. We now have a match for InfAcc$Q$, so we have a full proof.

Here is the generated **plan**:

1. The firing of the accessibility axiom on the third line above generates access command $T_1 \Leftarrow \mathsf{mt}_{\mathsf{Udirectory}} \Leftarrow \emptyset$, where T_1 is a table with attributes for eid_0 and lname_0.

2. The accessibility axiom on the fourth line generates commands

$$T' \Leftarrow \mathsf{mt}_{\mathsf{Profinfo}} \Leftarrow \pi_{\mathsf{eid}_0}(T_1)$$
$$T_2 := T' \bowtie T_1$$

3. The match at the end generates the command Return $\pi_\emptyset(T_2)$, which returns True if T_2 is non-empty.

   That is, we do an input-free access on Udirectory and put all the results into Profinfo.

◁

Full definition of SPJ-plan generation algorithm. In the first presentation of the algorithm, we did not deal with several "corner cases" concerning these rule firings:

- the fact $F = R(c_1 \ldots c_n)$ may contain not only constants that are produced in the chase proof ("chase constants") but also constants from the schema (e.g., "Smith", 3, etc.),

- the fact may have some chase constants repeated.

Here we complete the description to cover these cases. We first discuss schema constants and repetition of chase constants in *input positions*. If $R(c_1 \dots c_n)$ has some chase constants repeated in an input position and possibly some of $c_{j_1} \dots c_{j_m}$ are schema constants, then in our input expression we perform a projection of T_{i-1} onto the attributes corresponding to the distinct chase constants in $c_{j_1} \dots c_{j_m}$ and then transform every tuple t into a corresponding tuple t' that can be used as an input to the access method mt. We do this transformation by repeating values or filling in positions with constants, using $R(c_1 \dots c_n)$ as a template. That is, if j_i is such that c_{j_i} is a chase constant c, then set t'_{j_i} to be c, while if c_{j_i} is a schema constant d, then set t'_{j_i} to be d. This transformation can be done with an SPJ query.

Example 4.2. Consider an accessibility axiom rule firing at step i of the form

$$\mathsf{accessible}(c_1) \wedge \mathsf{accessible}(\text{“Smith”}) \wedge R(c_1, c_1, \text{“Smith”}, c_2, c_2, \text{“Jones”}) \\ \rightarrow \mathsf{InfAcc}R(c_1, c_1, \text{“Smith”}, c_2, c_2, \text{“Jones”}).$$

Suppose that this rule firing was associated with access method mt on R having inputs on the first three positions of R.

If T_{i-1} is the temporary table produced by the commands associated with the $i-1^{th}$ firing, then T_{i-1} will have an attribute for c_1. We create an SPJ expression E_i that will take as input T_{i-1} and produce a table containing

$$\{(c_1 = v_1, c'_1 = v_1, c_{\text{“Smith”}} = \text{“Smith”}) | v_1 \in \pi_{c_1}(T_{i-1})\}.$$

Such an E_i can be expressed using projection, a self-join, and a constant operator. We then generate an access command

$$T_i \Leftarrow \mathsf{mt} \Leftarrow E_i.$$

◁

The modification of the algorithm that deals with repetition and schema constants in *output positions* (that is, non-input positions of the accessed relation) is similar, being done by post-processing, using a middleware query command to filter the output table down to those tuples that have constants in the proper positions and repeated values as in the fact F. We then apply a projection to obtain a table whose attributes are the distinct chase constants in F.

Example 4.3. In the case of Example 4.2, the output table T_i of the access command $T_i \Leftarrow \mathsf{mt} \Leftarrow E_i$ could have attributes $c_1, c'_1, c_{\mathsf{Smith}}, c_2, c'_2, c_{\mathsf{Jones}}$, and the output mapping would map the positions of R to these attributes. We post-process by performing the middleware query command:

$$T'_i = \pi_{c_1, c_2} \sigma_{c_2 = c'_2 \wedge c_{\mathsf{Jones}} = \text{“Jones”}} T_i$$

◁

4.2 PLAN SEARCH ALGORITHMS

A simple plan-generation algorithm. Algorithm 1, as with our previous algorithms, generates a plan assuming that we already have found a chase proof. We explain how this algorithm can be combined with a search for a proof to get a plan-generation algorithm.

We will restrict our search to *eager proofs*. Informally, in eager proofs, we always fire "cost-free" (i.e., non-accessibility axiom) rules before firing a rule that corresponds to an access. Eager proofs begin with a set of rule firings of Sch constraints; no firings of Sch constraints occur after this initial phase. The proof then proceeds by alternating blocks of accessibility axiom firings A_i and *follow-up rule firings* F_i of InfAccCopy constraints. We require that after block F_i is completed the proof contains no firings of InfAccCopy constraints that were applicable at the end of F_i. It is clear that any proof can be turned into an eager proof by re-arranging the proof steps.

Algorithm 2 summarizes a simple version of the "general methodology" for SPJ-plan generation with respect to TGDs; for brevity it is shown in the basic case without repeated variables and constants, as in Algorithm 1. It combines *searching for a chase proof* and *applying the simplified proof-to-plan algorithm* outlined above.

The search for a proof consists of forming the canonical database of the source query Q and applying chase steps for the Sch constraints (line 4). We proceed by iteratively applying chase steps corresponding to forward accessibility axioms, with each accessibility axiom firing followed by a set of "follow-up chase steps" corresponding to firings of the InfAccCopy constraints. All chase steps add to the configuration, but only the chase steps corresponding to forward accessibility rules add to the resulting plan.

If the chase configuration has a match for InfAcc$Q$, then the proof is complete, and we can return the associated plan. Extensions of this algorithm which take into account cost will be introduced in Chapter 5.

4.3 PROPERTIES OF SPJ PLAN-GENERATION

We now argue for correctness of the algorithm, in thus process establishing additional properties of the algorithm.

Theorem 4.1 *For any conjunctive query Q, for every successful chase sequence proving* InfAcc$Q$ *from Q, the corresponding plan* PL *generated by Algorithm 1 answers Q.*

Further, the following are equivalent:

- *Q is access-monotonically-determined.*
- *Q has a $USPJ^{\neq}$-plan that answers it.*
- *Q has an SPJ plan that answers it.*

The second part follows from the first, since it is argued in the previous chapter that if Q has a $USPJ^{\neq}$-plan it is access-monotonically-determined, and in Claim 2 of Section 3.4 it is

Algorithm 2: *SPJ* plan-generation algorithm for TGD constraints

config := Canonical database of Q;
V = attributes for free variables of Q;
Plan := $\emptyset$;
Chase config with integrity constraints of Σ;
T_0 = table with no columns ;
$i := 0$;
while *there is a rule exposing fact* $F = R(c_1 \dots c_n)$ *via method* mt *with inputs* $j_1 \dots j_m$ **do**
    Choose such a rule;
    Append to Plan command $T' \Leftarrow \mathsf{mt} \Leftarrow \pi_{c_{j_1} \dots c_{jm}}(T_{i-1})$;
    Append to Plan command $T_i = T' \bowtie T_{i-1}$;
    Add InfAcc$F \cup \{\mathsf{accessible}(c_1) \dots \mathsf{accessible}(c_n)\}$ to config;
    Chase config with InfAccCopy integrity constraints ;
    if *there is a match for* InfAcc$Q$ *in* config **then**
        Add command "Return $\pi_V(T_i)$" to Plan ;
        return Plan
    i++
return $\emptyset$

shown that if a query given by an RQFO formula is access-monotonically-determined, then there is a proof of InfAcc$Q$ from Q *w.r.t.* AcSch(Sch).

If config$_i$ denotes the ith configuration in the chase proof, let InfAccQuery(config$_i$) be the conjunctive query formed by taking the conjunction of all facts of the form InfAcc$R(\vec{c})$ in config$_i$ and turning them into an existentially quantified conjunction of facts $R(\vec{w})$, changing the chase constants c that satisfy accessible(c) to free variables and the other chase constants to existentially quantified variables. Observe that if config$_i$ has a match for InfAcc$Q$, then InfAccQuery(config$_i$) entails Q. Recall that our algorithm generated commands for every firing of an accessibility axiom, producing a corresponding plan PL$_i$, which produces a temporary table T_i. The attributes of T_i will be all chase constants such that the relation accessible holds in config$_i$—hence these match the output attributes of InfAccQuery(config$_i$).

Given an instance I, a mapping from the chase constants present in the chase configuration config$_i$ produced by the ith step of the algorithm to I which preserves all facts in config$_i$ within the original schema will be called a Sch config$_i$*-tuple of* I. As the notation implies, we consider such elements as tuples with attributes from the constants of config$_i$.

Let $[\![T_i]\!]_I$ be the instance of table T_i produced by PL$_i$ when run on an instance I of schema Sch. Although the notation omits the dependence on PL^i, the value of T_i in PL^j, whenever it is well-defined, is independent of j. We prove that the following "universality properties" hold for any instance I of Sch:

- For every Sch config_i-tuple of I, its projection onto the constants of config_i satisfying accessible is in $[\![T_i]\!]_I$.
- $[\![T_i]\!]_I$ is a subset of the tuples in $[\![\mathsf{InfAccQuery}(\mathsf{config}_i)]\!]_I$.

We explain why these two assertions together imply the first part of Theorem 4.1. First consider a tuple $\vec{t}$ returned by Q on a database instance I satisfying the Sch integrity constraints. I can be extended, just via duplicating its relations, to an instance I^* satisfying the accessible schema AcSch(Sch). Since $\vec{t}$ is returned by Q, there is a homomorphism h_1 of the canonical database of Q to $\vec{t}$. In I^*, we can mimic each rule firing that produced the facts of config_i, and thus for each j we can extend h_1 to a mapping h_i that preserves all facts of config_i. Restating in the terminology of this section, for each config_i we can extend $\vec{t}$ to a Sch config_i-tuple $\vec{t_i}$. Now by the first assertion above, the projection of $\vec{t_i}$ on the constants satisfying accessible in config_i is in $[\![T_i]\!]_I$. Thus, in particular, the projection on the constants corresponding to free variables, namely $\vec{t}$, is in $[\![T_k]\!]_I$, which is the final result of the top-level plan generated by the algorithm. Conversely, note that on the final configuration, $\mathsf{InfAccQuery}(\mathsf{config}_k)$ entails Q, as explained above. So by the second assertion above, any tuple in the projection of $[\![T_k]\!]_I$ must satisfy Q in I.

The two assertions above are proven by induction on i. We first deal with the basic version of the algorithm, ignoring repetition of variables and schema constants, and then discuss how to extend to incorporate the full version.

We consider the inductive step for both assertions corresponding to an application of an accessibility axiom. Fix a Sch config_i-tuple $\vec{s_i}$ and let $\vec{a_i}$ be its projection on the constants satisfying the relation accessible. By induction the projection of $\vec{s_i}$ on the accessible constants of config_{i-1} is in $[\![T_{i-1}]\!]_I$. In the absence of repetition of variables and constants, we know $[\![T_i]\!]_I$ is formed from $[\![T_{i-1}]\!]_I$ by "joining on the access": projecting tuples in $[\![T_{i-1}]\!]_I$ on the attributes corresponding to inputs to the access, performing the access, and joining the corresponding outputs to $[\![T_{i-1}]\!]_I$. We need to show that $\vec{s_i}$ extends some tuple returned by this join.

Assume that the accessibility axiom fired in the inductive step was associated with the exposure of some fact $R(c_1 \dots c_n)$, where $c_{j_1} \dots c_{j_m}$ satisfied accessible relations in the chase sequence up that point. Let input_i be the projection of $\vec{s_i}$ on these input attributes, and $\mathsf{allatts}_i$ be the projection on all the $c_1 \dots c_n$. We claim that $\mathsf{allatts}_i$ would be returned by an access on mt using input_i. This is clear, since for the corresponding accessibility axiom to fire, $R(c_1 \dots c_n)$ must hold in config_{i-1}, and thus the $c_1 \dots c_n$ attributes of a Sch config_i-tuple like $\vec{s_i}$ must satisfy R in I.

This completes the inductive argument for the first assertion in the case of the firing of an accessibility axiom, under the assumption of no repetition of variables and no schema constants. In the general case, we let input_i be formed from $\vec{s_i}$ as above, but incorporating selections and repetition of variables on the input positions corresponding to the fact being exposed. Let $\mathsf{allatts}_i$ be formed from a tuple in the accessed relation R consistent with input_i by applying further operations enforcing repetitions and constants in the output positions. We can see that $\mathsf{allatts}_i$ would be returned by the pre-processing, method access, and post-processing operations generated in the inductive step of the algorithm. This is because $\vec{s_i}$ is a Sch config_i-tuple and the corresponding fact added in config_i must have obeyed these selections in order for the corresponding accessibility axiom to fire.

We next verify the second assertion in the inductive case corresponding to the firing of an accessibility axiom. Let database instance I satisfy the constraints of the schema, and let $\vec{a}_i$ be a tuple of $[\![T_i]\!]_I$. We show that $\vec{a}_i$ is returned by the CQ $\mathsf{InfAccQuery}(\mathsf{config}_i)$. We first assume the basic version of the algorithm, with no repetition of variables or schema constants. In this case the axiom firing is of the form:

$$\mathsf{accessible}(c_{j_1}) \wedge \ldots \mathsf{accessible}(c_{j_m}) \wedge R(c_1 \ldots c_n) \rightarrow \mathsf{InfAcc}R(c_1 \ldots c_n) \wedge \bigwedge_j \mathsf{accessible}(c_j).$$

Recall that the access command produced by this rule firing would be

$$T_i' \Leftarrow \mathsf{mt} \Leftarrow \pi_{\{c_{j_1} \ldots c_{j_m}\}}(T_{i-1})$$

where mt is an access method on R with input positions $j_1 \ldots j_m$. To obtain $[\![T_i]\!]_I$, we joined T_i' with T_{i-1}.

By induction we know that $\vec{a}_{i-1}$, the projection of $\vec{a}_i$ on the accessible constants of config_{i-1}, satisfies $\mathsf{InfAccQuery}(\mathsf{config}_{i-1})$, since the construction shows that $\vec{a}_{i-1}$ must be in $[\![T_{i-1}]\!]_I$. We examine the new conjunct being added at this stage, corresponding to the fact produced by the firing of an accessibility axiom. Since $\vec{a}_i$ is in $[\![T_i]\!]_I$, its projection to $\{c_1 \ldots c_n\}$ must satisfy R. Therefore the atom corresponding to $R(c_1 \ldots c_n)$ in $\mathsf{InfAccQuery}(\mathsf{config}_i)$ is satisfied by $\vec{a}_i$.

The argument immediately above is easily generalized to the case with schema constants and repetitions of variables in the exposed facts. We argue that the pre- and post-processing operations guarantee that $\vec{a}_i$ must reflect the repetitions and schema constants present in the fact.

We move to the inductive cases corresponding to the firing of Sch or InfAccCopy rules. Note that the first assertion is preserved by these rules, since the set of Sch config_i-tuples can only become smaller or stay the same, as we are required to preserved more facts. For the second assertion, there is nothing to prove when a Sch constraint is fired. In an inductive step for an InfAccCopy constraint, conjuncts are added to $\mathsf{InfAccQuery}(\mathsf{config}_i)$. One can see that these conjuncts hold using the definition of $\mathsf{InfAccQuery}(\mathsf{config}_i)$ and the assumption that the instance I satisfies the integrity constraints of Sch.

This finishes the proof of the second assertion. It also completes the proof of Theorem 4.1.

From Theorem 4.1, we get the following corollary for the vocabulary-based case:

Corollary 4.2 *For any conjunctive query Q, basic schema* Sch *whose constraints are all TGDs, and subsignature $\mathcal{T}$ of the vocabulary of* Sch, *the following are equivalent:*

- *Q is monotonically-determined over $\mathcal{T}$ w.r.t.the constraints.*
- *Q has a $\exists^{+,\neq}$ reformulation over $\mathcal{T}$ w.r.t.the constraints.*

- *Q has a CQ reformulation over $\mathcal{T}$ w.r.t.the constraints.*

The "collapse" results will be strengthened later in Corollary 4.6.

4.4 RA-PLANS FOR SCHEMAS WITH TGDS

The proof-to-plan algorithm in the previous sections focused on access-monotonically-determined queries, which in the case of TGDs will generate not just positive existential formulas ($USPJ^{\neq}$-plans), but SPJ-plans. Even in the case of vocabulary-based constraints, one can show that there are conjunctive queries and TGD constraints for which there is a first-order reformulation but no positive existential one. In fact, it has been shown that even in the case of constraints that define conjunctive query views, there are conjunctive queries that have rewritings over the views, but the rewritings require the relational difference operator [Nash et al., 2010]. We will see a witness of this in Example 4.4 later in this chapter.

From this, it follows that there are access schemas with TGD constraints and conjunctive queries that have RA-plans but no SPJ-plans. From Theorem 3.9, we know that a boolean query Q has an RA-plan with respect to a schema Sch if and only if Q entails $\mathsf{InfAcc}Q$ with respect to $\mathsf{AcSch}^{\leftrightarrow}(\mathsf{Sch})$.

We explain how the more "concrete" approach to generating SPJ-plans for access schemas with TGDs, as given in Section 11, can be extended to give a simple algorithm for obtaining RA-plans whenever they exist, even for non-boolean conjunctive queries.

Throughout this section, Sch denotes a schema with access methods and TGD constraints. For convenience, we assume neither our queries nor our constraints contain schema constants or repeated variables—thus the chase proofs will not produce any configurations that contain such facts. The algorithm is generalized to the case with schema constants and repetition in the same way as the SPJ-plan algorithm, by introducing pre- and post-processing middleware query commands around access commands.

4.4.1 PROOF TO RA-PLAN ALGORITHM

The algorithm will proceed not by forward induction on proofs, as was the case with SPJ-plan generation, but by a *backward induction*.

The algorithm takes as input a suffix $\mathsf{config}_i \ldots \mathsf{config}_k$ of a full proof consisting of chase configurations $\mathsf{config}_1 \ldots \mathsf{config}_k$, and produces a nested plan PL_i, where nested plans are as defined in Section 3.3. The plan PL_i generated from suffix $\mathsf{config}_i \ldots \mathsf{config}_k$ will include a distinguished temporary table $T_{\vec{x}^i}$, with attributes $\vec{x}^i$ that are the *accessible chase constants* in config_i, denoted $\mathsf{accessible}(\mathsf{config}_i)$: those that satisfy the relation $\mathsf{accessible}$ in config_i. In the further inductive steps, PL_i will only be used in subplan calls with $T_{\vec{x}^i}$ being the table substituted. We thus write $\mathsf{PL}_i(\vec{x}^i)$ to indicate that PL_i is a nested plan with distinguished table $T_{\vec{x}^i}$, referring to $T_{\vec{x}^i}$ as the *parameter table* of the plan, and $\vec{x}^i$ as the *parameters*. The output of PL_i will be a table having attributes for chase constants that are either in $\mathsf{accessible}(\mathsf{config}_i)$ or which correspond to free variables of the query.

The algorithm proceeds by downward induction on i. If $i = k$, i.e., only one configuration in the proof suffix, the algorithm produces the single command Return $T_{\vec{x}^k}$. Note that in this case $\mathsf{accessible}(\mathsf{config}_k)$ must already contain the free variables of Q.

The pseudo-code for the inductive cases of the algorithm is listed in Figure 4.1. We can

- In the case where the suffix is $\mathsf{config}_i \ldots \mathsf{config}_k$ and the transition from config_i to config_{i+1} is a constraint of Sch or InfAccCopy the algorithm just returns PL_{i+1}. Note that $\mathsf{accessible}(\mathsf{config}_i) = \mathsf{accessible}(\mathsf{config}_{i+1})$ in this case.

- Let the suffix be $\mathsf{config}_i \ldots \mathsf{config}_k$ where the transition from config_i to config_{i+1} is formed by a forward accessibility axiom firing with access mt exposing fact $R(\vec{c})$. Then we generate the nested plan:

$$T_0^{i+1} \Leftarrow \mathsf{mt} \Leftarrow \pi_{c_{j_1} \ldots c_{j_m}}(T_{\vec{x}^i})$$
$$T_1^{i+1} := T_0^{i+1} \bowtie T_{\vec{x}^i}$$
$$T_{i+1} \Leftarrow \mathsf{PL}_{i+1}[T_{\vec{x}^{i+1}}] \Leftarrow T_1^{i+1}$$
$$\text{Return } \pi_{\mathsf{Free}(Q) \cup \mathsf{accessible}(\mathsf{config}_i)} T_{i+1}$$

- Let the suffix be $\mathsf{config}_i \ldots \mathsf{config}_k$ where the transition from config_i to config_{i+1} is formed via a backward accessibility axiom firing exposing fact $\mathsf{InfAcc}R(\vec{c})$. We generate a plan the differs from the plan in the forward case by replacing the last line by commands returning empty if T_0^{i+1} is empty, and otherwise returning:

$$\vec{u} \in \bigcap_{\vec{w} \in T_1^{i+1} \; \pi_{\vec{x}^i} \vec{w} = \vec{t}} \begin{array}{l} \{\vec{u} \in \pi_{\mathsf{Free}(Q) \cup \mathsf{accessible}(\mathsf{config}_i)}(T_{i+1}) \mid \exists \vec{t} \in T_{\vec{x}^i} \\ \pi_{\mathsf{Free}(Q) \cup \mathsf{accessible}(\mathsf{config}_i)}(\{\vec{z} \in T_{i+1} \mid \pi_{\mathsf{accessible}(\mathsf{config}_{i+1})} \vec{z} = \vec{w}\})\} \end{array}$$

  Although we have written the last expression in a mixture of relational algebra and logic, the generation of the last expression from T_{i+1} and T_1^{i+1} can be performed in relational algebra.

Figure 4.1: Inductive cases of RA-plan generation for schemas with TGDs.

verify that the plan generated by the algorithm indeed returns tuples with attributes for all $\mathsf{accessible}(\mathsf{config}_i) \cup \mathsf{Free}(Q)$-constants. Therefore the plan generated by a full proof will have output attributes corresponding to the free variables of the query Q. For a full proof the set of parameters $\vec{x}^1$ is empty, since no attributes in the initial configuration satisfy accessible. We take the top-level output of our plan-generation algorithm to be the result of substituting for the parameter table the singleton instance with only the empty tuple. We denote this instance by $\emptyset$ below. Thus the top-level algorithm takes a full proof as input, producing an ordinary relational algebra plan without reference to $T_{\vec{x}^1}$, and one whose output constants are exactly the free variables of Q.

We give some intuition for the steps above. In the case of a forward accessibility axiom, we generate a nested plan whose action, given an instance of the parameter table $T_{\vec{x}^i}$ consisting of a single tuple $\vec{t}$, is described as follows: it does an access to R using the projection of $\vec{t}$ to the chase constants $c_{j_1} \dots c_{j_m}$. For each result tuple $\vec{w}$ joining with $\vec{t}$, the plan calls $\mathsf{PL}_{i+1}(\vec{w} \bowtie \vec{t})$, where the join is on the common attributes (which will include $c_{j_1} \dots c_{j_m}$) and projects the results back to the constants $\vec{x}^i$ unioned with the free variables of Q. Finally, the plan returns the union of all of these projections.

In the step for the backward accessibility axiom, we generate a plan that is similar, but performing an intersection rather than a union. That is, our plan should behave as follows, given an instance of $T_{\vec{x}^i}$ consisting of a single tuple $\vec{t}$: it does an access to R using the projection of $\vec{t}$ to the chase constants $c_{j_1} \dots c_{j_m}$, then returns the intersection of the projections of the sets $\mathsf{PL}_{i+1}(\vec{w} \bowtie \vec{t})$ to the parameters $\vec{x}^i$ unioned with the free variables of Q, where $\vec{w}$ ranges over tuples in the result that join with t. We define the intersection to be empty if there are no such tuples.

We will first show that the algorithm returns nested plans that answer Q. By Corollary 3.5, we can "flatten" this to an ordinary RA-plan.

Example 4.4. We present a variant of an example due to [Afrati, 2011]. Our base signature consists of a binary relation R. We have views V_3 storing the set of pairs of nodes connected by a path of length 3, and V_4 storing the set of pairs connected by a path of length 4.

That is, we have constraints that are universal quantifications of the following rules, which give definitions for the view tables:

$$\begin{aligned} V_3(x,y) &\rightarrow \exists x_2\, \exists x_3\; R(x,x_2) \wedge R(x_2,x_3) \wedge R(x_3,y) \\ R(x,x_2) \wedge R(x_2,x_3) \wedge R(x_3,y) &\rightarrow V_3(x,y) \\ V_4(x,y) &\rightarrow \exists x_2\, \exists x_3\, \exists x_4\; R(x,x_2) \wedge R(x_2,x_3) \wedge R(x_3,x_4) \wedge R(x_4,y) \\ R(x,x_2) \wedge R(x_2,x_3) \wedge R(x_3,x_4) \wedge R(x_4,y) &\rightarrow V_4(x,y). \end{aligned}$$

Our query Q asks for all pairs x_1, x_6 such that x_1 reaches x_6 via a path of length 5. Afrati showed that Q can be rewritten over the views as:

$$\exists y_5\; [V_4(x_1,y_5) \wedge \forall y_2\; V_3(y_2,y_5) \rightarrow V_4(y_2,x_6)].$$

Afrati also argued that Q is not monotone in the views: we can have two instances such that for each view table the second instance has all the facts of the first instance, but the query result over the second instance does not contain the query result over the first. Hence there cannot be any $USPJ^{\neq}$-plan.

Let our access schema Sch have the constraints above, with the view relations having input-free access and the base tables have no access. We can derive an RA-plan equivalent to the above rewriting through our proof-based method.

The proof begins with the canonical database of query Q:

$$\mathsf{config}_1 = \{R(x_1, x_2), R(x_2, x_3), R(x_3, x_4), R(x_4, x_5), R(x_5, x_6)\}.$$

We then apply a chase step with the last constraint above, one part of the definition of V_4, obtaining configuration config_2 which adds the fact:

$$V_4(x_1, x_5).$$

We can apply a "forward accessibility axiom" to obtain a configuration config_3 with the additional fact:

$$\mathsf{InfAcc}V_4(x_1, x_5).$$

We can now apply the copy of the third constraint above, to obtain configuration config_4 adding additional facts:

$$\mathsf{InfAcc}R(x_1, z_2), \mathsf{InfAcc}R(z_2, z_3), \mathsf{InfAcc}R(z_3, z_4), \mathsf{InfAcc}R(z_4, x_5).$$

From this we can apply the copy of the second constraint, to obtain configuration config_5 adding fact:

$$\mathsf{InfAcc}V_3(z_2, x_5).$$

Applying a "backward accessibility axiom" we obtain configuration config_6 with the fact:

$$V_3(z_2, x_5).$$

And then applying a chase step with the first constraint above leads to configuration config_7 adding facts:

$$R(z_2, w_3), R(w_3, w_4), R(w_4, x_5).$$

We can then apply the last constraint to get to configuration config_8 adding fact:

$$V_4(z_2, x_6).$$

After this we can apply another "forward accessibility axiom" to obtain configuration config_9 adding fact:

$$\mathsf{InfAcc}V_4(z_2, x_6).$$

Finally, we apply a copy of the third constraint, reaching configuration config_{10} with additional facts:

$$\mathsf{InfAcc}R(z_2, q_3), \mathsf{InfAcc}R(q_3, q_4), \mathsf{InfAcc}R(q_4, q_5), \mathsf{InfAcc}R(q_5, x_6).$$

This configuration has a match for $\mathsf{InfAcc}Q$. Applying the algorithm discussed previously, we will find that it generates a nested RA-plan that corresponds to this rewriting. We give the interesting steps in the inductive construction, ignoring steps that only call the next inductively-defined program.

- From the final configuration config_{10}, we generate a plan P_{10} that takes as input a table with tuples having values for x_1, x_5, x_6, and z_2 and simply returns the table.
- From the suffix of the proof beginning at configuration config_8, we generate P_8, which takes a table T_{x_1,z_2,x_5}, and performs an access on V_4, naming the output results z_2, x_6 and joining them with T_{x_1,z_2,x_5}, returning a table with all joined tuples with attributes x_1, x_5, x_6, and z_2.
- From the suffix beginning with configuration config_5 we generate a plan P_5 that takes as input a table with tuples having attributes x_1 and x_5. P_5 performs an access on V_3 and selects all tuples (z_2, x_5) matching the input value for x_5, calls P_8 on each corresponding x_1, z_2, x_5, and intersects the projection of the results to x_1, x_5, x_6.
  Thus $P_5(x_1, x_5)$ outputs $\bigcap_{\{z_2 | V_3(z_2,x_5)\}} \{x_1, x_5, x_6 | V_4(z_2, x_6)\}$.
- From the suffix beginning with configuration config_2, we generate P_2 that has no input parameters. P_2 performs an access to V_4, calls P_5 on all the resulting tuples x_1, x_5, and then unions the projection of the results on to x_1, x_6.
  The plan P_1 returned as the top-level result of the algorithm will be equal to P_2.

◁

4.4.2 CORRECTNESS OF THE ALGORITHM

We give the argument that the RA-based algorithm is correct, completing the proof of Theorem 3.9:

Theorem 4.3 *For any conjunctive query Q that is access-determined with respect to schema* Sch*, Algorithm 4.1 produces an RA-plan that answers Q. Further, if Q is induced-subinstance-access-monotonically-determined, then the output of Algorithm 4.1 can be converted to an SPJ-plan.*

From the second statement combined with our earlier results, we conclude that for TGD constraints, a query is induced-subinstance-access-monotonically-determined if and only if it is access-monotonically-determined, and has a $USPJAD^{\neq}$-plan exactly when it has an SPJ-plan.

In the correctness proofs below, a Sch *fact* is a fact where the relation is in schema Sch. An InfAcc *fact* is a fact over a relation of the form $\mathsf{InfAcc}R$. We let $\mathsf{Sch}(\mathsf{config}_i)$ denote the set of constants that occur in a Sch fact of config_i.

The proof of correctness will consist of separate soundness and completeness claims, each of which is proven by induction on steps in the proof, as with the SPJ-plan algorithm. We require some definitions in order to give the inductive invariant on intermediate plans produced by the algorithm. The definitions assume a chase configuration config_i over the schema $\mathsf{AcSch}^{\leftrightarrow}(\mathsf{Sch})$ and an instance I for the relations in the original schema and the relations of the form $\mathsf{InfAcc}R$.

- A $\mathsf{Sch}(\mathsf{config}_i)$-tuple of I is a tuple $\vec{t}$ with attributes for each chase constant occurring in a Sch facts of config_i taking values in the domain of I, such that if a Sch fact $F(c_1 \dots c_n)$ holds in config_i then $F(\vec{t}.c_1 \dots \vec{t}.c_n)$ holds in I.

- An $\mathsf{InfAcc}(\mathsf{config}_i)$-tuple of I is as above, but replacing "Sch fact" with "InfAcc fact."

When I is clear from the context, we omit it from the notation. We also need the following observation:

Claim 5: At any configuration of a chase sequence starting from the canonical database of Q, and applying the rules of $\mathsf{AcSch}^{\leftrightarrow}$, the accessible constants are exactly the constants that occur in both a Sch fact and an InfAcc fact within a configuration. ■

This follows easily from the proof that entailment using $\mathsf{AcSch}^{\leftrightarrow}$ is equivalent to entailment using $\mathsf{AltAcSch}^{\leftrightarrow}$ (Proposition 3.13), which shows the accessible relations can be seen as "macros" capturing all values that are in both a Sch fact and an InfAcc fact. Recall that $\mathsf{accessible}(\mathsf{config}_i)$ denotes the set of constants satisfying accessible in a configuration config_i. In our correctness argument below, we make use of the equivalent definition of accessible constant given by the claim above.

We begin our analysis with the following lemma:

Lemma 4.4 *Let* $\mathsf{config}_1 \ldots \mathsf{config}_k$ *be a full proof witnessing that* Q *entails* $\mathsf{InfAcc}Q$ *w.r.t.* $\mathsf{AcSch}^{\leftrightarrow}(\mathsf{Sch})$, *and let* $\mathsf{config}_i \ldots \mathsf{config}_k$ *be a proof suffix. Let* I *be an instance for* $\mathsf{AcSch}^{\leftrightarrow}(\mathsf{Sch})$, *and* PL_i *be the nested plan generated from this suffix using the algorithm above. Let* $\vec{s}_i$ *be a* $\mathsf{Sch}(\mathsf{config}_i)$*-tuple of* I. *Then* $[\![\mathsf{PL}_i]\!]_{I,\pi_{\mathsf{accessible}(\mathsf{config}_i)}\vec{s}_i}$ *contains the tuple* $\pi_{\mathsf{accessible}(\mathsf{config}_i)\cup\mathsf{Free}(Q)}(\vec{s}_i)$.

Above $[\![\mathsf{PL}_i]\!]_{I,\vec{t}}$ represents the output of PL_i on instance I for Sch, where the unique free table of PL_i, $T_{\vec{x}_i}$, is interpreted by the single tuple $\vec{t}$.

Before proving the lemma, let us show that it implies that for a "full proof" (recall that this is a chase sequence witnessing $Q \models \mathsf{InfAcc}Q$ *w.r.t.* $\mathsf{AcSch}^{\leftrightarrow}(\mathsf{Sch})$) the plan produced by the algorithm returns a superset of the output of Q.

Assume we have a full proof that Q entails $\mathsf{InfAcc}Q$ with configurations $\mathsf{config}_1 \ldots \mathsf{config}_k$, and let PL_1 be the result of the algorithm applied to this proof, considered as a trivial suffix of itself. Fix an output tuple $\vec{o}$ for Q on a Sch-instance I_0. We can extend I_0 to an instance I for $\mathsf{AcSch}^{\leftrightarrow}(\mathsf{Sch})$ by setting the interpretation of each $\mathsf{InfAcc}R$ in I to be identical to R in I_0. Since $\vec{o}$ is in the output of Q, it is a $\mathsf{Sch}(\mathsf{config}_1)$-tuple. Its projection on $\mathsf{accessible}(\mathsf{config}_1)$ is the empty tuple $\emptyset$. Applying Lemma 4.4, we see that $[\![\mathsf{PL}_1]\!]_{I,\emptyset}$ will return $\pi_{\mathsf{Free}(Q)}(\vec{o}) = \vec{o}$.

***Proof of Lemma** 4.4.* Fix a full proof given by chase sequence $\mathsf{config}_1 \ldots \mathsf{config}_k$. We prove the statement by downward induction on i, that is, with base case $i = k$. The base case is clear, since PL_k just returns $T_{\vec{x}k}$.

We first deal with the inductive case where config_{i+1} is formed from config_i by firing a Sch constraint. $[\![\mathsf{PL}_i]\!]_{I,\vec{s}_i}$ is just $[\![\mathsf{PL}_{i+1}]\!]_{I,\vec{s}_i}$ in this case. Since I satisfies the constraints of $\mathsf{AcSch}^{\leftrightarrow}(\mathsf{Sch})$, there is an extension of $\vec{s}_i$ to a $\mathsf{Sch}(\mathsf{config}_{i+1})$-tuple $\vec{s}_{i+1}$. By induction, $[\![\mathsf{PL}_{i+1}]\!]_{I,\vec{s}_i}$ contains $\pi_{\mathsf{accessible}(\mathsf{config}_{i+1})\cup\mathsf{Free}(Q)}\vec{s}_{i+1}$. But $\mathsf{accessible}(\mathsf{config}_i) = \mathsf{accessible}(\mathsf{config}_{i+1})$ in this case, and hence we are done.

In the case where config_{i+1} is formed by firing an $\mathsf{InfAccCopy}$ constraint, we note that $\vec{s}_i$ is also a $\mathsf{Sch}(\mathsf{config}_{i+1})$-tuple, and thus the result follows again by induction.

We next look at the case where the transition from config_i to config_{i+1} involves the firing of a backward accessibility axiom exposing fact $\mathsf{InfAcc}R(c_1 \ldots c_n)$ using an access method on relation R with input positions $j_1 \ldots j_m$. Let $\vec{a}_i = \pi_{\mathsf{accessible}(\mathsf{config}_i)}\vec{s}_i$. We show that for every extension $\vec{a}_{i+1}$ of $\vec{a}_i$ on the accessible constants of config_{i+1} whose projection onto $c_1 \ldots c_n$ gives a tuple $\vec{r}$ in $[\![R]\!]_I$ agreeing with the values of $\vec{a}_i$ on the common attributes, $\pi_{\mathsf{Free}(Q)\cup\mathsf{accessible}(\mathsf{config}_i)}[\![\mathsf{PL}_{i+1}]\!]_{I,\vec{a}_{i+1}}$ returns $\pi_{\mathsf{accessible}(\mathsf{config}_i)\cup\mathsf{Free}(Q)}\vec{s}_i$. Recalling that the definition of PL_{i+1} for a backward accessibility axiom involves intersecting over all such extensions (whenever at least one such extension exists, which we will show further below), we see that this will imply the inductive step for such axioms. It is enough to show that there is some $\mathsf{Sch}(\mathsf{config}_{i+1})$-tuple $\vec{s}_{i+1}$ such that (i) $\vec{a}_{i+1}$ is the projection of $\vec{s}_{i+1}$ to the accessible constants of config_{i+1}, (ii) $\vec{s}_{i+1}$ projects on to $\vec{s}_i$. Assuming this, we get the conclusion we want by induction.

We observe that the constants in $\mathsf{Sch}(\mathsf{config}_i) - \mathsf{accessible}(\mathsf{config}_i)$ are disjoint from the constants in $\mathsf{domain}(\vec{r}) - \mathsf{accessible}(\mathsf{config}_i)$. This follows because, by Claim 5 mentioned above, the accessible constants are exactly those that occur in both Sch facts and InfAcc facts, and hence the constants in $\mathsf{Sch}(\mathsf{config}_i) - \mathsf{accessible}(\mathsf{config}_i)$ only appear in Sch facts of config_i, while those in $\mathsf{domain}(\vec{r}) - \mathsf{accessible}(\mathsf{config}_i)$ only appear in InfAcc facts of config_i. From the above we see that the domains of $\vec{s}_i$ and $\vec{r}$ overlap only in constants that are in $\mathsf{accessible}(\mathsf{config}_i)$, on which they are (by definition) compatible. Hence $\vec{s}_i$ and $\vec{r}$ have a join, which we denote as $\vec{s}_{i+1}$. We claim that $\vec{s}_{i+1}$ is the required tuple.

We first note that $\vec{s}_{i+1}$ is a tuple that projects onto $\vec{a}_{i+1}$. Each of the attributes of $\vec{s}_{i+1}$ is either an attribute of $\vec{r}$ or is an attribute of $\vec{s}_i$. $\vec{r}$ is a restriction of $\vec{a}_{i+1}$ by definition. For attributes in the domain of $\vec{s}_i$, if they are in the domain of $\vec{a}_{i+1}$ they must be in $\mathsf{accessible}(\mathsf{config}_i)$. For such attributes $\vec{a}_{i+1}$ is equal to $\vec{a}_i$, which is a restriction of $\vec{s}_i$, hence they must be compatible with $\vec{s}_{i+1}$. Recall that $\vec{s}_{i+1}$ is a mapping from attributes corresponding to constants in $\mathsf{Sch}(\mathsf{config}_{i+1})$ to I. We need to verify that $\vec{s}_{i+1}$ preserves every Sch fact F of config_{i+1}, not just those in config_i. If F is the newly added fact $R(c_1 \ldots c_n)$, then F will be preserved, since $\vec{s}_{i+1}$ restricted to these attributes is the same as $\vec{r}$, and by assumption $\vec{r}$ is returned by the access to R. Otherwise we can assume F was present in the prior configuration config_i. Since F is over the schema Sch, every constant c_i mentioned in it must be in the domain of $\vec{s}_i$. Then we are done because $\vec{s}_i$ is a $\mathsf{Sch}(\mathsf{config}_i)$-tuple.

We have shown that the algorithm's behavior for this inductive case is correct, assuming there is *some* extension $\vec{a}_{i+1}$ of $\vec{a}_i$ on the accessible constants of config_{i+1} that is "consistent with the access"—that is, which has an R fact whose values on positions corresponding to accessible constants of config_i match the values of $\vec{a}_i$. If there is no such extension, an access on the corresponding values of $\vec{a}_i$ will return empty, and recall that the algorithm gives empty output in this case. However the tuple $\vec{s}_i$ is itself an extension consistent with $\vec{a}_i$. Hence this case cannot occur.

We move to the firing of a forward accessibility axiom exposing fact $R(c_1 \ldots c_n)$ via an access method on R with input positions $j_1 \ldots j_m$. Letting $\vec{s}_i$ be as before, and $\vec{a}_i$ its projection to

$\mathsf{accessible}(\mathsf{config}_i)$. We need to show that for some extension $\vec{a}_{i+1}$ of $\vec{a}_i$ that is consistent with the access to R, the nested plan PL_{i+1} returns a tuple that projects on $\pi_{\mathsf{accessible}(\mathsf{config}_i)\cup\mathsf{Free}(Q)}\vec{s}_i$. Inductively, it suffices to show that $\vec{a}_i$ has an extension consistent with the access that is the projection of a Sch config_{i+1}-tuple to the accessible constants of config_{i+1}. Note that in this inductive case the Sch facts of config_{i+1} are the same as those of config_i. The restriction $\vec{a}_{i+1}$ of $\vec{s}_i$ to the accessible attributes of config_{i+1} can serve as the required extension. □

The corresponding "completeness" claim is as follows:

Lemma 4.5 *Let* $I, \mathsf{config}_i \ldots \mathsf{config}_k, \mathsf{PL}_i$ *be as in Lemma 4.4, and* $\overrightarrow{\mathsf{inf}}_i$ *be an* $\mathsf{InfAcc}(\mathsf{config}_i)$*-tuple of* I*. Let* $\vec{a}_i$ *be the projection of* $\overrightarrow{\mathsf{inf}}_i$ *on the accessible constants of* config_i*. Suppose* $[\![\mathsf{PL}_i]\!]_{I,\vec{a}_i}$ *returns the tuple* $\vec{o}$*. Then there is an* $\mathsf{InfAcc}(\mathsf{config}_k)$*-tuple* $\overrightarrow{\mathsf{inf}}_k$ *which projects onto* $\vec{o}$*.*

Recall that we use $\emptyset$ to denote the instance of a table with no attributes consisting only of the empty tuple. Reasoning as with Lemma 4.4, we now derive from this claim that:

> When PL_1 is the plan generated from a full proof that Q entails $\mathsf{InfAcc}Q$, then if PL_1 with parameter table set to $\emptyset$ returns a tuple $\vec{o}$ on an instance I_0 for the schema Sch, then Q evaluated on I_0 returns $\vec{o}$. That is, PL_1 returns a subset of the output of Q.

To prove this, extend I_0 to an instance I for $\mathsf{AcSch}^{\leftrightarrow}(\mathsf{Sch})$ by copying each relation R to $\mathsf{InfAcc}R$. The initial configuration config_1 has no InfAcc facts, and thus the empty tuple is an $\mathsf{InfAcc}(\mathsf{config}_1)$-tuple of I. Applying Lemma 4.5, we conclude that for any output tuple $\vec{o}$ of PL_1, there is an $\mathsf{InfAcc}(\mathsf{config}_k)$-tuple that projects onto it. But for a full proof, the projection of an $\mathsf{InfAcc}(\mathsf{config}_k)$-tuple onto constants for the free variables of Q will be an output of the query $\mathsf{InfAcc}Q$. Since the instance I is formed by "cloning" the instance I_0, we can conclude that the output of Q contains $\vec{o}$.

Proof of Lemma 4.5. We show this by downward induction on i. The base case is $i = k$. $[\![\mathsf{PL}_k]\!]_{I,\vec{a}_k}$ returns only $\vec{a}_k$, and $\vec{a}_k$ is the projection of an InfAcc config_k-tuple by assumption.

We turn to the inductive cases, starting with the case where a Sch constraint is applied. If $[\![\mathsf{PL}_i]\!]_{I,\vec{a}_i}$ returns $\vec{o}$, then $[\![\mathsf{PL}_{i+1}]\!]_{I,\vec{a}_i}$ returns $\vec{o}$ by definition. Then by induction, there is an $\mathsf{InfAcc}(\mathsf{config}_k)$-tuple $\overrightarrow{\mathsf{inf}}_k$ that projects onto $\vec{o}$, as required.

In the case where we apply an InfAcc constraint, we extend $\overrightarrow{\mathsf{inf}}_i$ to an InfAcc config_{i+1} tuple $\overrightarrow{\mathsf{inf}}_{i+1}$. By induction, there is an $\mathsf{InfAcc}(\mathsf{config}_k)$-tuple $\overrightarrow{\mathsf{inf}}_k$ that projects onto the output $\vec{o}$ of $[\![\mathsf{PL}_{i+1}]\!]_{I,\vec{a}_i}$ and since $\mathsf{PL}_i = \mathsf{PL}_{i+1}$ in this case, we are done.

Next consider the case where the next step is the firing of a backward accessibility axiom exposing fact $\mathsf{InfAcc}R(c_1 \ldots c_n)$ with an access method mt on R having input positions $j_1 \ldots j_m$. We know $\mathsf{InfAcc}R(c_1 \ldots c_n)$ must hold in config_i. Let $\overrightarrow{\mathsf{inf}}_{\mathsf{input}}$ be the restriction of $\overrightarrow{\mathsf{inf}}_i$ to the constants appearing in $\mathsf{InfAcc}R(c_1 \ldots c_n)$ within input positions of mt, and let $\vec{a}_{i+1}$ be the restriction of $\overrightarrow{\mathsf{inf}}_i$ to the accessible constants of config_{i+1}. Note that $\vec{a}_{i+1}$ extends $\vec{a}_i$. Since $[\![\mathsf{PL}_i]\!]_{I,\vec{a}_i}$ returns $\vec{o}$, we know that for every tuple $\vec{u}$ in I that extends $\vec{a}_i$ by joining on a tuple of R that extends $\overrightarrow{\mathsf{inf}}_{\mathsf{input}}$, $[\![\mathsf{PL}_{i+1}]\!]_{I,\vec{u}}$ returns a tuple that projects onto $\vec{o}$. We can see that $\vec{a}_{i+1}$ is such a tuple, and thus $[\![\mathsf{PL}_{i+1}]\!]_{I,\vec{a}_{i+1}}$ returns a tuple $\vec{o}_{i+1}$ that projects onto $\vec{o}$. By induction, there is an $\mathsf{InfAcc}(\mathsf{config}_k)$-tuple $\overrightarrow{\mathsf{inf}}_k$ that projects onto $\vec{o}_{i+1}$. But then $\overrightarrow{\mathsf{inf}}_k$ projects onto $\vec{o}$, which completes the proof in this case. Note that, as in Lemma 4.4, the inductive definition of PL_{i+1} in the case where the access to R returns no matching elements is irrelevant for the argument, since we are guaranteed that there always is at least one such extension, namely $\vec{a}_{i+1}$.

Finally, we argue the case where the next step is the firing of a forward accessibility axiom exposing fact $R(c_1 \dots c_n)$ via an access method on R with input positions $j_1 \dots j_m$. Then if $[\![\mathsf{PL}_i]\!]_{I,\vec{a}_i}$ returns $\vec{o}$ we know that for some extension $\vec{a}_{i+1}$ of $\vec{a}_i$ compatible with the access, $[\![\mathsf{PL}_{i+1}]\!]_{I,\vec{a}_{i+1}}$ returns some tuple $\vec{o}_{i+1}$ that projects onto $\vec{o}$. We argue that $\vec{a}_{i+1}$ must be the projection of an $\mathsf{InfAcc}(\mathsf{config}_{i+1})$-tuple. If we can prove this we are done, since by induction there would be an $\mathsf{InfAcc}(\mathsf{config}_k)$-tuple $\overrightarrow{\mathsf{inf}}_k$ that projects onto $\vec{o}_{i+1}$, and since $\vec{o}_{i+1}$ projects onto $\vec{o}$, $\overrightarrow{\mathsf{inf}}_k$ would also project onto $\vec{o}$.

The $\mathsf{InfAcc}(\mathsf{config}_i)$-tuple $\overrightarrow{\mathsf{inf}}_i$ and $\vec{a}_{i+1}$ are consistent on their common domain, and hence have a join $\overrightarrow{\mathsf{inf}}_{i+1}$. We claim $\overrightarrow{\mathsf{inf}}_{i+1}$ is the required $\mathsf{InfAcc}(\mathsf{config}_{i+1})$-tuple. Clearly $\overrightarrow{\mathsf{inf}}_{i+1}$ projects onto $\vec{a}_{i+1}$, so we need only show that $\overrightarrow{\mathsf{inf}}_{i+1}$ is an $\mathsf{InfAcc}(\mathsf{config}_{i+1})$-tuple. The newly added fact $\mathsf{InfAcc}R(c_1 \dots c_n)$ is preserved since the access producing $\vec{a}_{i+1}$ is compatible, while the config_i facts are preserved using the assumption on $\overrightarrow{\mathsf{inf}}_i$. □

Putting together the two lemmas, we have shown that whenever there is a full proof using $\mathsf{AcSch}^{\leftrightarrow}$, there is a plan that returns exactly the same output as Q, completing the proof of the first part of Theorem 4.3.

$\mathsf{AcSch}^{\neg}$ and $USPJAD^{\neq}$-plans. Recall the second part of Theorem 4.3:

> If Q is induced-subinstance-access-monotonically-determined, then using Algorithm 4.1, we can generate an SPJ-plan.

We argue here only that the output can be converted to an SPJ-plan. With more work, one can check that a direct conversion to SPJ-plans is obtained by combining Algorithm 4.1 with the conversion of nested plans to RA-plans presented in Corollary 3.5.

Recall the schema $\mathsf{AcSch}^{\neg}(\mathsf{Sch})$ which restricts the "backward accessibility axioms" to the case where every universally-quantified variable satisfies $\mathsf{accessible}$. In the inductive step of the RA-plan algorithm, these backward axioms will generate a command that takes a tuple $\vec{t}$ for the parameter table, checks whether a projection of $\vec{t}$ is in the relation R associated with the accessibility axiom, and if so, outputs $\mathsf{PL}_{i+1}(\vec{t})$ (otherwise, it returns empty). Thus the inductive step can be rephrased in terms of formulas as:

$$\varphi_{i+1}(\vec{x}) = R(x_{j_1} \dots x_{j_m}) \wedge \varphi_{i+1}(\vec{x})$$

while the forward axiom corresponds to the inductive rule:

$$\varphi_{i+1}(\vec{x}) = \exists \vec{y}\ R(x_{j_1} \ldots x_{j_m}, \vec{y}) \wedge \varphi_{i+1}(\vec{x}, \vec{y}).$$

By downward induction on i one can see that the formulas constructed by these two steps are executable CQs. Such CQs can be converted to SPJ-plans by Proposition 3.1.

This proves the second part of Theorem 4.3, which has a corollary for the vocabulary-based case:

Corollary 4.6 *For any conjunctive query Q, basic schema* Sch *whose constraints are all TGDs, and subsignature $\mathcal{T}$ of the vocabulary of* Sch, *the following are equivalent:*

- *Q is induced-subinstance-monotonically-determined over $\mathcal{T}$ w.r.t.the constraints.*
- *Q has an $\exists^{\neq}$ reformulation over $\mathcal{T}$ w.r.t.the constraints.*
- *Q has a CQ reformulation over $\mathcal{T}$ w.r.t.the constraints.*

4.5 CHASE-BASED AND INTERPOLATION-BASED PLAN-GENERATION

We have an inductive algorithm which creates temporary tables whose attributes are chase constants, whose inductive cases are given in Figure 4.1. In the boolean case, we also have an algorithm inherited from the general approach, based on tableau proofs, summarized in Figure 2.8. The outputs of these algorithms are both reformulations of the input query Q, so they must return the same results on any instance that satisfies the constraints. But we prove that they return the same output on *any* instance. In fact, our proof will show that the formulas produced by interpolation can be easily translated into the nested plans created by the RA-algorithm.

We have already explained in Section 1.3 that chase proofs can be seen as a special kind of tableau proof. For each chase configuration config_i, there is a corresponding tableau node $\mathsf{TabNode}_i$ containing the facts of config_i along with the TGDs and negation of the target conjunctive query. Now let us extend this correspondence between the chase and tableau proofs to interpolation and plan-generation.

We will show:

Proposition 4.7 *For any query Q and schema* Sch, *the formula generated by the interpolation-based reformulation algorithm returns the same output as the plan generated by the concrete algorithm for TGDs on any instance I.*

For simplicity we restrict to the case of a boolean query, where query and constraints do not use schema constants.

Recall that our proof goal is

$$Q \wedge \Sigma \wedge \mathsf{Ax}_{\mathsf{Back}} \models (\mathsf{Ax}_{\mathsf{For}} \wedge \Sigma') \rightarrow \mathsf{InfAcc}Q$$

where Σ are the Sch constraints, Σ' the InfAccCopy constraints, $\mathsf{Ax}_{\mathsf{For}}$ contains the forward accessibility axioms, and $\mathsf{Ax}_{\mathsf{Back}}$ the backward accessibility axioms. Thus, we are looking for a tableau rooted at

$$Q \wedge \Sigma \wedge \mathsf{Ax}_{\mathsf{Back}} \wedge \mathsf{Ax}_{\mathsf{For}} \wedge \Sigma' \wedge \neg\mathsf{InfAcc}Q.$$

In making this a labeled tableau proof, Q and Σ will be LEFT-annotated while the others will be RIGHT-annotated. We can convert a chase proof witnessing that Q is contained in $\mathsf{InfAcc}Q$ with respect to the TGDs in $\Sigma \cup \Sigma' \cup \mathsf{Ax}_{\mathsf{For}}$ into a tableau proof, using the correspondence outlined in Section 1.3. Our first observation about these tableaux is:

Claim 6: In any tableau node, the RIGHT-labeled facts that are generated will mention only InfAcc relations along with the relation accessible. The LEFT-labeled facts are exactly the facts over the original schema in the node. Thus the constants occurring in both a RIGHT-labeled and LEFT-labeled fact are those satisfying both an InfAcc and a Sch fact. ■

Proof. The proof is by induction on how the facts are generated. We begin with the inductive step for applying a $\mathsf{Ax}_{\mathsf{For}}$ constraint. The $\mathsf{Ax}_{\mathsf{For}}$ axioms are RIGHT-annotated, and when written out with relativized universal quantification there will be a sequence of quantifications, starting with a prefix of quantifications of the form $\forall x\ \mathsf{accessible}(x) \rightarrow \varphi$, ending with a quantification over the relation R associated with the fact being exposed. By induction, we can see that the first set of quantifications produce subformulas that are again RIGHT-annotated, since they will result from interaction of two RIGHT-annotated formulas. When the final quantifier is instantiated (via the relativized-quantifier universal rules of a tableau) it must be to a fact $R(\vec{c}, \vec{d})$, and by induction this fact must be LEFT-annotated. This means that when the annotation-propagation rules are applied, the generated fact $\mathsf{InfAcc}R(\vec{c}, \vec{d})$ will be RIGHT-annotated, which preserves the induction hypothesis.

In the inductive step for a $\mathsf{Ax}_{\mathsf{Back}}$ constraint, we are applying a LEFT-annotated universal assertion. Inductively we can show that the intermediate applications to $\mathsf{accessible}(x)$ produce LEFT-annotated subformulas, since the annotation resulting from instantiating a universally-quantified formula φ matches the annotation of φ. The final application of the universal quantifier rule is to a fact $\mathsf{InfAcc}R(\vec{c}, \vec{d})$, and by induction this fact must be RIGHT-annotated. Again, by the rules for annotation propagation, the resulting fact $R(\vec{c}, \vec{d})$ will be LEFT-annotated.

The other inductive steps are verified similarly. □

In addition, if a constant appears in both a LEFT- and a RIGHT-labeled formula within a node, then it must satisfy accessible within the node. This is argued as in Claim 5. Our assumptions ensure that we need consider only generated constants, not schema constants or constants generated from the free variables of the query. A generated constant with a LEFT-label can only move to a

RIGHT-labeled formula by the application of a forward axiom. In applying a forward axiom, in the conclusion all constants involved satisfy accessible. Similarly a generated constant with a RIGHT-label can only move to a LEFT-labeled formula through the application of a backward axiom. We conclude that:

> In any node, the constants that are in both LEFT- and RIGHT-labeled facts are the same as the constants satisfying accessible.

Now let us consider the interpolants γ_i produced at the tableau node corresponding to the ith chase node. The interpolants that are produced result from a downward induction on the number of axioms fired. Only application of the accessibility axioms will produce a non-trivial inductive step in the interpolation algorithm, since these are the only place where a LEFT- and RIGHT-labeled formula interact. Thus the interpolants can be written as $\chi_i; i = n \ldots 1$, where n is the number of applications of the accessibility axioms. We write out how the χ_i would be constructed inductively, using the interpolation rules from Figure 2.8.

The base case for χ_n is True. The inductive case for forward accessibility axioms is given by applying the interpolation rule for *relativized universal quantification on the right*, which in this case gives:

$$\exists x_{m_1} \ldots x_{m_k} \; (R(c_1^{i+1} \ldots c_n^{i+1}) \wedge \chi_{i+1})[c_{m_1}^{i+1} := x_{m_1} \ldots c_{m_k}^{i+1} := x_{m_k}]$$

where:

- The ith forward accessibility axiom corresponds to an access on R exposing fact $F = R(c_1^{i+1} \ldots c_n^{i+1})$ using an access method mt having input positions $j_1 \ldots j_m$
- The existential quantifiers are introduced for the constants $c_{m_1}^{i+1} \ldots c_{m_k}^{i+1}$ of χ_{i+1} which occur in $R(c_1^{i+1} \ldots c_n^{i+1}) \wedge \chi_{i+1}$ and which do not satisfy accessible in configuration i. We can further impose that the existentially quantified constants occur in output positions of $R(c_1^{i+1} \ldots c_n^{i+1})$, since all constants occurring in χ_{i+1} which do not appear in output positions of R must be accessible constants of i.

The inductive case for backward accessibility axioms is given by applying the interpolation rule for *relativized universal quantification on the left*, which specializes here to:

$$\forall x_{m_1} \ldots x_{m_k} \; (R(c_1^{i+1} \ldots c_n^{i+1}) \rightarrow \chi_{i+1})[c_{m_1}^{i+1} := x_{m_1} \ldots c_{m_k}^{i+1} := x_{m_k}]$$

where $c_{m_1}^{i+1} \ldots c_{m_k}^{i+1}$ are as above.

Above we have devised a simplified recursive definition for the formulas produced by our interpolation-based reformulation algorithm. Let $\mathsf{PL}_n \ldots \mathsf{PL}_1$ be the plans produced by the RA-algorithm. The theorem below completes the proof of Proposition 4.7:

Theorem 4.8 *For each i γ_i corresponds to PL_i, in that for any tuple $\vec{c}^i$ and instance I, $[\![\mathsf{PL}_i]\!]_{I,\vec{c}^i}$ returns $\vec{c}_i$ if and only if $I, \vec{c}_i \models \gamma_i$. That is, the plans PL_i filter the input parameter to check that it satisfies γ_i.*

Proof. We proceed by downward induction on i. In the base case, the query always holds and the plan always returns $\vec{c}_i$, so the invariant holds.

We give the induction for forward accessibility axioms. There the formula χ_{i+1} requires a tuple that

1. agrees with the tuple of free variables on variables corresponding to accessible constants
2. has a projection on the variables corresponding to constants in F which is in the relation R
3. satisfies χ_{i+1}.

This is the same as saying that we have a tuple which joins with the input tuple, is consistent with the access on R, and satisfies χ_{i+1}. By induction and the definition of PL_{i+1}, this holds exactly when $[\![\mathsf{PL}_i]\!]_{I,\vec{c}^i}$ is true. This completes the induction step for applying a $\mathsf{Ax}_{\mathsf{For}}$ axiom.

We turn to the induction step for backward accessibility axiom. The proof of Theorem 4.3 shows that in the inductive step for a backward accessibility axiom in the TGD-based RA-plan algorithm, the policy of returning empty in the plan when the access returns no matching tuples can be replaced by any other policy that respects the type of the output. This includes the policy of returning True, which represents the usual semantics of relativized universal quantification. With this substitution, the equivalence is argued as with the forward accessibility axioms. □

In summary, we have shown that the "chase-based" reformulation algorithms are just special cases of the interpolation-based algorithm. Nevertheless it will often be more convenient to deal directly with the chase-based algorithms in order to see additional properties of the reformulations they produce.

4.6 SUMMARY

In this chapter we have provided specialized proof-to-plan algorithms for TGDs. These algorithms are special cases of interpolation, and thus fit into the general meta-algorithm that we have been exploring in the prior chapters. But they allow us to generate a plan directly, without going through a logical formula. This direct correspondence between proofs and physical plans will be explored further in Chapter 5.

4.7 BIBLIOGRAPHIC REMARKS

The SPJ-reformulation algorithm for TGDs in the case of vocabulary-based restrictions can be seen as a variant of the Chase and Backchase method originating in the work of Tannen, Deutsch, and Popa [Deutsch et al., 1999]. An explanation of this method and its relation with the TGD algorithms is deferred to the bibliographic remarks of Chapter 5.

The presentation here expands on the conference paper [Benedikt et al., 2014b]. But several of the algorithms are similar to those given for the case of views in Nash, Segoufin, and

Vianu's [Nash et al., 2010]. For example, the reader should compare the RA-plan generation algorithm with the rewriting algorithm on page 21:20 of [Nash et al., 2010].

As mentioned in the bibliographic remarks of Chapter 3, the interaction of access methods and constraints was first explored by [Deutsch et al., 2007] in the case of TGDs with terminating chase. The problem of querying with constraints and access restrictions was studied for a number of constraint classes, including inclusion dependencies, in the later work [Bárány et al., 2013]: there the goal is not to get an operational plan using the access methods, but a rewriting that makes use of the accessible data. The plan language used in this chapter is formalized in [Benedikt et al., 2014b], with an accompanying system demonstration in [Benedikt et al., 2014a].

An observation that is new in this presentation is that the chase-based approach should not be seen as an *alternative* to interpolation, but as a *special case* of interpolation. As Section 4.5 explains, the chase-based algorithms for reformulation—including those in [Benedikt et al., 2014b, Deutsch et al., 2007, Nash et al., 2010]—are what one obtains when restricting interpolation algorithms to restricted constraints and target languages.

CHAPTER 5

Low-cost Plans Via Proof Search

In the previous chapters, we have seen that proofs of an entailment can lead us to *some* reformulation to our target query Q, respecting the restrictions (e.g., access methods), whenever such a reformulation exists. We now look at finding efficient reformulations. We focus on the setting where the interface is given by access methods, the goal is to generate an SPJ-plan equivalent to a CQ Q, and where the constraints in our schema consist of TGDs. In Chapter 4 we have presented a direct proof-to-plan algorithm for converting proofs witnessing that $Q \models \mathsf{InfAcc}Q$ *w.r.t.* $\mathsf{AcSch}(\mathsf{Sch})$ to SPJ-plans, Algorithm 1. We build on that algorithm in this chapter. Therefore in this chapter there is no need to refer directly to interpolation.

After explaining our cost model, we will look at an example of a query where there are multiple reformulations with different costs. The example motivates us to study whether the lowest-cost plan that answers a query can always be taken to be a proof-based plan. We show that for restricted cost functions the answer is "yes." Intuitively, for these cost functions all of the "essential cost optimizations" can be captured by exploring different proofs, rather than having to post-process the plans to tune the cost. We then present algorithms that find proof-based plans with optimal cost. We end the chapter with a discussion of how less restrictive proof systems can lead to exploration of a larger and more efficient class of plans.

5.1 COST FUNCTIONS ON PLANS

We start with a very general definition of plan cost. A *plan cost function* is any function associating each plan with a non-negative integer-valued cost. The *minimal cost problem* for an access schema, query, and cost function is the problem of finding a plan answering the query with minimal value of the cost function. The algorithms we present will "make sense" for a cost function in this broad sense, but our completeness results will require stronger assumptions. We explain our main assumption on cost, capturing the intuition that the cost depends only on the access commands being used in the plan.

Given a plan PL whose access commands, ordered by appearance, are $\mathsf{Command}_1 \ldots \mathsf{Command}_j$, its *method sequence* denoted $\mathsf{Methods}(\mathsf{PL})$ is the sequence of $\mathsf{mt}_1 \ldots \mathsf{mt}_j$, where mt_i is the method used in $\mathsf{Command}_i$. We say that PL *uses no more methods than* PL', denoted

$\mathsf{PL} \preceq_{\mathsf{mt}} \mathsf{PL}'$, if the method sequence of PL is a subsequence (not necessarily contiguous) of the method sequence of PL'. A cost function Cost is *simple* if $\mathsf{PL} \preceq_{\mathsf{mt}} \mathsf{PL}'$ implies $\mathsf{Cost}(\mathsf{PL}) \leq \mathsf{Cost}(\mathsf{PL}')$.

Example 5.1. Consider a cost function Cost_1 that assigns a cost to plan PL equal to the number of access commands in PL. If the method sequence of plan PL is a subsequence of that in PL', then $\mathsf{Cost}_1(\mathsf{PL}) \leq \mathsf{Cost}_1(\mathsf{PL}')$, so Cost_1 is simple. Similarly, if Cost_2 is a cost function that takes a weighted sum of the access commands in PL, where each method mt is assigned a non-negative integer weight w_{mt}, then Cost_2 is simple.

In the two examples above the cost only depended on the number of times each access method occurred in the plan, not the order. But our definition allows some order-dependent examples as well.

Let w_{mt} be a non-negative integer weight assigned to each method mt. Consider a cost function Cost_3 that assigns to plan PL the cost $\Sigma_i\, i \cdot w_i$, where w_i is w_{mt} for the method mt used in the ith access command. Thus Cost_3 gives higher weight to later commands in a plan. If the method sequence of plan PL is a subsequence of that in PL', $\mathsf{Cost}_3(\mathsf{PL}) \leq \mathsf{Cost}_3(\mathsf{PL}')$, so Cost_3 is again a simple cost function. ◁

All of the optimality guarantees we state are for simple cost functions. The following example will motivate the basic idea behind the cost-based variations of our proof-to-plan algorithms.

Example 5.2. We return to the variant of Example 1.3 mentioned in the introduction to see what impact cost considerations might have on a search for good plans using proofs.

Suppose we have a $\mathsf{Profinfo}(\mathsf{eid}, \mathsf{onum}, \mathsf{lname})$ datasource with one access method $\mathsf{mt}_{\mathsf{Profinfo}}$ requiring an eid as an input. There are also tables $\mathsf{Udirectory}_1(\mathsf{eid}, \mathsf{lname})$ with input-free access method mt_1 and $\mathsf{Udirectory}_2(\mathsf{eid}, \mathsf{lname})$ with input-free access method mt_2. The constraints include two inclusion dependencies:

$$\forall \mathsf{eid}\ \forall \mathsf{onum}\ \forall \mathsf{lname}\ \mathsf{Profinfo}(\mathsf{eid}, \mathsf{onum}, \mathsf{lname}) \rightarrow \mathsf{Udirectory}_i(\mathsf{eid}, \mathsf{lname})$$

for $i = 1, 2$. Our goal is to generate an SPJ-plan for query $Q = \mathsf{Profinfo}(\mathsf{eid}, \mathsf{onum}, \text{“Smith”})$.

The corresponding auxiliary schema will add tables $\mathsf{InfAccUdirectory}_1$, $\mathsf{InfAccUdirectory}_2$, and $\mathsf{InfAccProfinfo}$. The axioms will include the Sch constraints, $\mathsf{InfAccCopy}$ constraints, and “accessibility axioms” that include the following constraints, labeled (UA_i), for $i = 1, 2$:

$$\begin{aligned} &\forall \mathsf{eid}\ \forall \mathsf{lname}\ \mathsf{Udirectory}_i(\mathsf{eid}, \mathsf{lname}) \rightarrow \\ &\mathsf{InfAccUdirectory}_i(\mathsf{eid}, \mathsf{lname}) \wedge \mathsf{accessible}(\mathsf{eid}) \wedge \mathsf{accessible}(\mathsf{lname}). \end{aligned}$$

There will also be an accessibility axiom (PA)

$$\begin{aligned} &\forall \mathsf{eid}\ \forall \mathsf{onum}\ \forall \mathsf{lname}\ \mathsf{accessible}(\mathsf{eid}) \wedge \mathsf{Profinfo}(\mathsf{eid}, \mathsf{onum}, \mathsf{lname}) \rightarrow \\ &\mathsf{InfAccProfinfo}(\mathsf{eid}, \mathsf{onum}, \mathsf{lname}) \wedge \mathsf{accessible}(\mathsf{onum}) \wedge \mathsf{accessible}(\mathsf{lname}) \end{aligned}$$

and a ground accessibility axiom:

$$\text{accessible}(\text{“Smith”})$$

A chase proof will begin with the canonical database of Q, namely:

$$\text{Profinfo}(\text{eid}_0, \text{onum}_0, \text{“Smith”}).$$

Recall from Chapter 3 that it is convenient to restrict to eager proofs, in which we must look for any non-accessibility axiom to apply first. In such a proof, we should now apply the two original inclusion dependencies to add facts:

$$\text{Udirectory}_1(\text{eid}_0, \text{“Smith”}), \text{Udirectory}_2(\text{eid}_0, \text{“Smith”}).$$

We should also fire the axiom generating fact accessible(“Smith”), representing the fact that “Smith” is a known constant. If we model this accessibility axiom as corresponding to a special kind of “access method” it would clearly be a method with no cost. Continuing from this are several possible proofs. One proof will apply a chase step with the rule (UA_1) to add facts

$$\text{InfAccUdirectory}_1(\text{eid}_0, \text{“Smith”}), \text{accessible}(\text{eid}_0)$$

followed by a chase step with (PA) to add fact

$$\text{InfAccProfinfo}(\text{eid}_0, \text{onum}_1, \text{“Smith”}), \text{accessible}(\text{onum}_1).$$

At this point we have a match for InfAcc$Q$, and hence a complete chase proof. Instantiating the TGD-based plan-generation algorithm (Algorithm 1, modified as in the previous chapter to account for constants) we will generate the plan:

$$\begin{aligned}
&T_1 \Leftarrow \text{mt}_1 \Leftarrow \emptyset\\
&T_2 := \sigma_{\text{lname}=\text{“Smith”}} T_1\\
&T_3 \Leftarrow \text{mt}_{\text{Profinfo}} \Leftarrow \pi_{\text{eid}}(T_2)\\
&T_4 := T_3 \bowtie T_2\\
&\text{Return } \pi_{\text{onum}}(T_4).
\end{aligned}$$

A second proof would be similar, but using (UA_2) rather than (UA_1). This would generate a plan that corresponded to an access to Udirectory_2 rather than Udirectory_1. A third proof would first fire (UA_1) and then (UA_2), followed by (PA). Applying the TGD-based algorithm would automatically generate the plan:

$$
\begin{aligned}
&T_1 \Leftarrow \mathsf{mt}_1 \Leftarrow \emptyset \\
&T_2 := \sigma_{\mathsf{lname}=\text{``Smith''}} T_1 \\
&T_3 \Leftarrow \mathsf{mt}_2 \Leftarrow \emptyset \\
&T_4 := \sigma_{\mathsf{lname}=\text{``Smith''}} T_3 \\
&T_5 := T_2 \bowtie T_4 \\
&T_6 \Leftarrow \mathsf{mt}_{\mathsf{Profinfo}} \Leftarrow \pi_{\mathsf{eid}}(T_5) \\
&T_7 := T_6 \bowtie T_5 \\
&\text{Return } \pi_{\mathsf{onum}}(T_7).
\end{aligned}
$$

What we see is that each "interesting plan" is captured by a distinct proof. Which of these plans has the lowest cost will depend on, e.g., the relative efficiency of the access methods mt_1 and mt_2, along with the amount of tuples each returns. We cannot make a decision on which plan is most efficient simply by looking at the proof. What we can do is explore this space of proofs while measuring the efficiency of the corresponding plans. ◁

Example 5.2 shows that many interesting plans can be captured by distinct proofs of the entailment. Put another way, in many cases better plans could be found by just exploring more proofs, rather than by post-processing the first correct plan found. We next investigate to what extent we can validate the idea that proof-based plans are "as good as general plans."

5.2 HOW GOOD ARE PROOF-BASED PLANS?

We will compare proof-based plans and general plans under various notions of plan quality.

5.2.1 OPTIMALITY IN TERMS OF METHODS USED

We first look at a cost comparison between the plans generated from proofs and executable conjunctive queries. Recall from Section 3.3 that a conjunctive query Q with atoms $A_1 \dots A_n$ is *executable* relative to a schema with access methods if there is an annotation of each atom $A_i = R_i(\vec{x}_i)$ with an access method mt_i on R such that for each variable x of Q, for the first A_i containing x, x occurs only in an output position of mt_i. Recall also from Proposition 3.1 that every executable query Q can be converted naïvely to an SPJ-plan $\mathsf{PlanOf}(Q)$ such that the number of atoms in Q is exactly the number of access commands in the plan. Conversely, each of the plans PL produced by the SPJ proof-to-plan algorithm can be converted into an executable query $\mathsf{CQOf}(\mathsf{PL})$, where the number of atoms equals the number of accesses.

The following proposition shows that proof-based plans perform as well as executable CQs if one converts the plan to a query and takes the cost as the number of atoms. It also shows that proof-based plans perform as well as executable CQs for any simple cost function.

Proposition 5.1 *For every CQ Q, schema* Sch, *and executable query Q' equivalent to Q there is a proof v such that if PL^v is the SPJ-plan produced by the proof-to-plan algorithm, then $\mathsf{CQOf}(\mathsf{PL}^v)$ has at most the number of atoms as Q', and PL^v uses no more methods than $\mathsf{PlanOf}(Q')$.*

In particular the cost of PL^v *will be no more than that of* $\mathsf{PlanOf}(Q')$ *under any simple cost function.*

Proof. Let Q' be an executable query as above, with atoms $A_1 \dots A_n$, $A_i = R_i(\vec{x}_i)$, and let Q'_i be the subquery conjoining atoms $A_1 \dots A_i$. Let config_∞ be a (possibly infinite) instance resulting from chasing the canonical database of Q with the constraints of Sch. Q has a match on config_∞: that is, a mapping to the elements corresponding to free variables of Q. Since Q' is equivalent to Q on instances satisfying the constraints, Q' must have a match on config_∞ too.

There is thus a finite subinstance config_0 of config_∞ on which Q' returns a tuple of elements corresponding to the free variables. Although Q' consisted of n atoms, when evaluating them on config_0, we may have accessed many more than n facts. However, we can choose a single fact F_i matching atom A_i so that there is a match of Q' using only $F_1 \dots F_n$.

We will use config_0 and $F_1 \dots F_n$ to build a chase proof whose corresponding plan competes with Q. We begin our proof by rule firings that build config_0 and then fire the accessibility axioms that correspond to exposing each F_i. Using the fact that Q' was executable, we can see that after exposing $F_1 \dots F_{i-1}$, the values in F_i occurring in the input positions of method mt_i will satisfy $\mathsf{accessible}$, so we do have a sequence of firings that exposes each F_i in sequence.[1] Let config_n be the chase configuration achieved at the end of this process.

So far we have a chase sequence which we will complete to get a proof. Consider the instance consisting of $F_1 \dots F_n$, with each relation R renamed to $\mathsf{InfAcc}R$, and let config'_∞ result from chasing this instance with the $\mathsf{InfAccCopy}$ rules. It is clear that config'_∞ satisfies all the InfAcc constraints. Since $F_1 \dots F_n$ led to a match for Q', the query $\mathsf{InfAcc}Q'$ has a match on config'_∞. Further, as Q and Q' are equivalent on instances satisfying the Sch constraints, $\mathsf{InfAcc}Q'$ and $\mathsf{InfAcc}Q$ are equivalent on instances satisfying the $\mathsf{InfAccCopy}$ constraints. Therefore there is a finite subinstance config'_0 of config'_∞ containing a match for $\mathsf{InfAcc}Q$. We complete our chase sequence into a proof by firing $\mathsf{InfAccCopy}$ rules starting with config_n to generate config'_0. The resulting chase sequence v consists of Sch integrity constraint rules, accessibility axioms, and $\mathsf{InfAccCopy}$ constraints, beginning with the canonical database of Q and leading to a configuration with a match for $\mathsf{InfAcc}Q$. Hence v represents a chase proof of our entailment. Therefore the corresponding plan PL^v is equivalent to Q. The access commands in PL^v correspond to the accessibility axioms needed to expose $F_1 \dots F_n$, which will in turn correspond to methods used in $\mathsf{PlanOf}(Q')$. □

A similar argument shows that any plan that has a "left-deep" structure, joining a temporary table to the result of one access in each step, there is a proof-based plan that uses no more methods than it. However, this may not hold for general plans. The following example shows a case where proof-based plans are not as efficient as general ones.

Example 5.3. Let the query Q be:

$$\exists xyz\ S(x) \wedge S(y) \wedge R(x,w) \wedge R(y,z) \wedge U(w) \wedge V(z)$$

[1] Note that the facts $F_1 \dots F_n$ may not be distinct, in which case it will be unnecessary to fire n accessibility axioms to expose $F_1 \dots F_n$.

and in our schema

- there is an input-free access mt_S on S,
- there is an access method mt_R accessing R on the first position,
- there are access methods mt_U and mt_V requiring input on the sole positions of U and V, respectively.

This is an executable CQ with six atoms. However, one can obtain the following plan PL to answer Q which uses only four access commands:

$$
\begin{array}{ll}
T_1(x) & \Leftarrow \mathsf{mt}_S \Leftarrow \emptyset \\
T_2(y) & := \rho(T_1) \\
T_3(x,w) & \Leftarrow \mathsf{mt}_R \Leftarrow T_2 \\
T_4(y,z) & := \rho(T_3) \\
T_5(2) & \Leftarrow \mathsf{mt}_U \Leftarrow \pi_w(T_3) \\
T_6(z) & \Leftarrow \mathsf{mt}_V \Leftarrow \pi_z(T_4) \\
\text{Return} & T_1 \bowtie T_2 \bowtie T_3 \bowtie T_4 \bowtie T_5 \bowtie T_6.
\end{array}
$$

Above, the renaming operations (with arguments omitted) and the placing of attributes in parentheses in table names on the left are syntactic sugar to make the variables clearer. The plan first accesses S to get possible values of x and y, then uses the resulting values in R. The output is then put in U and in V, and then the results are stitched together using a join. The plan answers Q.

Note that this plan does not have the "left-deep" shape produced by either proof-based plans or the naïve translation of executable queries. And indeed there is no proof-based plan that generates a plan with this number of access commands.

Let the initial configuration of the chase contain

$$\{S(x_0), S(y_0), R(x_0, w_0), R(y_0, z_0), U(w_0), V(z_0)\}.$$

A chase-based proof along the lines above would proceed via the following rule firings:

$$
\begin{array}{rl}
S(x_0) & \rightarrow \mathsf{InfAcc}S(x_0) \wedge \mathsf{accessible}(x_0) \\
S(y_0) & \rightarrow \mathsf{InfAcc}S(y_0) \wedge \mathsf{accessible}(y_0) \\
R(x_0, w_0) \wedge \mathsf{accessible}(x_0) & \rightarrow \mathsf{InfAcc}R(x_0, w_0) \wedge \mathsf{accessible}(w_0) \\
R(y_0, z_0) \wedge \mathsf{accessible}(x_0) & \rightarrow \mathsf{InfAcc}R(y_0, z_0) \wedge \mathsf{accessible}(z_0) \\
U(w_0) \wedge \mathsf{accessible}(w_0) & \rightarrow \mathsf{InfAcc}U(w_0) \\
V(z_0) \wedge \mathsf{accessible}(z_0) & \rightarrow \mathsf{InfAcc}V(z_0).
\end{array}
$$

These rules generate inferred accessible facts that match $\mathsf{InfAcc}Q$. We see that there are two rule firings on relation S and also two firings on R.

If we put the proof sequence above into our plan-generation algorithm, we get a plan with six access commands, one for each firing. In particular, the plan PL' will still generate two calls to access method R, unlike the one above. These calls will use the same inputs, and in an intelligent wrapper that caches the results of prior accesses made, the second call will require no tuples. Related observations about the superiority of "bushy-plans" to left-deep plans in the presence of access restrictions have been known for some time; see Example 3.2 of [Florescu et al., 1999].

One can see that the two plans generate exactly the same concrete accesses. But the number of "bulk method calls" is larger in PL', so a cost function that counts the number of calls will give a higher cost to PL' than to PL. ◁

5.2.2 OPTIMALITY OF PROOF-BASED PLANS IN RUNTIME ACCESSES

We compare proof-based plans and general plans (not necessarily left-deep, as in the previous comparison) in terms of the set of accesses made at runtime. An SPJ-plan PL *uses at most as many runtime accesses* SPJ-plan PL', denoted $\mathsf{PL} \preceq_{\mathsf{RT}} \mathsf{PL}'$ if for every pair consisting of a method mt and method input $\vec{t}$ that is executed in running PL on instance I of the schema, the same pair is also executed in running PL' on I.

We show that proof-based plans are optimal with respect to arbitrary plans with respect to runtime-domination:

Theorem 5.2 *For conjunctive query Q and schema with TGD constraints Σ and access restrictions, for every SPJ-plan PL that answers Q, there is a chase sequence v proving $\mathsf{InfAcc}Q$, such that PL^v, the SPJ-plan generated from v via the proof-to-plan algorithm, uses at most as many runtime accesses as* PL.

Note that this theorem does not imply anything about the cost of proof-based plans vs. arbitrary plans according to particular cost functions, since cost functions look at plans statically, and are thus not necessarily monotone in the set of (method, input) pairs produced at runtime. Furthermore realistic cost functions take into account the cost of transforming data in temporary tables, not just the cost of accessing data. In particular, the proof-based plans produced by Algorithm 3 are left-deep, and there may be "bushy plans" that perform better. A more general notion of proof-based plan that addresses this issue is discussed in Section 5.4.

We turn to the proof of Theorem 5.2.

Normal form for plans. We start by showing that the shape of plans can be restricted. First, we can assume that a plan performs no middleware query command, with all the middleware query commands being pushed into the expressions that are inputs to the access commands or into the Return command. This "inlining" can blow up the size of the expressions, since the use of middleware queries gives the ability to iteratively create views, which may require exponential space to flatten back to a conjunctive query. But it will not impact the accesses performed, which is all that matters for this theorem. We can also assume that every temporary table is the output table of at most one access command. This can be achieved by renaming tables. We refer to these as *normalized plans* below.

Construction. Given an arbitrary normalized plan $\mathsf{PL} = \mathsf{Command}_1 \ldots \mathsf{Command}_j$, equivalent to some conjunctive query Q, we consider the behavior of PL on the configuration config_∞—any database (possibly infinite) generated from the canonical database of Q by repeatedly firing all Sch constraints. For $i \leq j$, we let $\mathsf{PL}_i = \mathsf{Command}_1 \ldots \mathsf{Command}_i$, the ith prefix of PL. Q has a match on the elements in config_∞ corresponding to free variables of Q, and since PL is equivalent to Q on instances satisfying the constraints, PL must have such a match on config_∞ as well. There is thus a finite subinstance config_0 of config_∞ on which PL returns the elements corresponding to the free variables of Q.

We construct a chase proof v which begins with config_0, proceeds by firing accessibility axioms only, and which includes distinguished intermediate configurations $\mathsf{config}_1 \ldots \mathsf{config}_j$. We will ensure that v is *chase-faithful to* PL, meaning (informally) that the accesses made by PL_i on config_0 are those predicted by "accessible facts" in config_i—those facts that are generated by an accessibility axiom. Formally, we will construct the proof so that if $\mathsf{Command}_i$ resulted in an access being made on config_0 using access method mt that returned $R(\vec{c})$ then fact $\mathsf{InfAcc}R(\vec{c})$ will be generated by an accessibility axiom corresponding to method mt associated with relation R in one of the rule firings linking config_{i-1} to config_i.

We construct the proof v, and thus the corresponding proof-based plan PL^v, by induction on i. In the inductive step, we have a prefix of PL, PL_i of the form $\mathsf{PL}_{i-1} \cdot \mathsf{Command}_i$, where $\mathsf{Command}_i$ is an access command $R \Leftarrow \mathsf{mt} \Leftarrow E$. Let $j_1 \ldots j_m$ be the input positions of mt.

By the induction hypothesis, for every fact $R(\vec{c})$ returned by an access of PL_{i-1} on config_0, $\mathsf{InfAcc}R(\vec{c})$ was generated by an accessibility axiom in the proof leading up to config_{i-1}. Since the temporary tables produced by PL_{i-1} all use values that come from these accesses, we can conclude that all values returned by E on config_0 must be members of the relation $\mathsf{accessible}$ in config_{i-1}. Hence for any fact F returned by the access command $R \Leftarrow \mathsf{mt} \Leftarrow E$, we can fire an accessibility axiom in config_{i-1} to expose F. Iterating this, we arrive at an extension of the proof that exposes every such fact. This completes the induction.

We claim that we can complete the proof to get a match for $\mathsf{InfAcc}Q$. Consider the facts generated by PL's accesses, and let config'_∞ be the result of chasing this set of facts with the Sch constraints. It is clear that config'_∞ satisfies the constraints, and its accessible part contains the accessible part of config_0. Since Q has an SPJ-plan it is access-monotonically-determined, and hence config'_∞ has a match for Q. Thus renaming the facts generated by accesses of PL to use InfAcc-relations and taking the $\mathsf{InfAccCopy}$ version of the rules fired to get a match for Q, we get an extension of the chase sequence with a set of firings of $\mathsf{InfAccCopy}$ rules leading to a configuration with a match for $\mathsf{InfAcc}Q$. The extended chase sequence began with the finite instance config_0, rather than with the canonical database of Q, as required of a full proof that Q entails $\mathsf{InfAcc}Q$. But we can generate config_0 by a finite sequence of firings of the Sch constraints, which we can add as a prefix to get a full proof.

Correctness of the construction. Above we have constructed a valid proof v of $\mathsf{InfAcc}Q$ from Q using AcSch, and hence the corresponding proof-based plan PL^v will answer Q. Further, PL^v performs no more accesses than PL when run on the database config_0. We know also that PL^v will make the same accesses on config_∞ as it does on config_0, and PL will make at least as many accesses on config_∞ as on config_0. Hence PL^v performs no more accesses than PL on config_∞. We argue that on an arbitrary instance I satisfying the constraints of Sch, accesses made by PL^v must also be made by PL.

Consider an access $(\mathsf{mt}, \mathsf{AccBind})$ made by PL^v on such an I. There is an access command such that the access is generated by an access command $\mathsf{Command}'_i$ of the form $T' \Leftarrow \mathsf{mt} \Leftarrow E'$, for method mt on relation R having input positions $j_1 \dots j_m$, with a tuple $\vec{t}$ being returned by expression E' on I. Let config_i be the chase configuration at which the accessibility axiom corresponding to $\mathsf{Command}'_i$ was fired.

The proof of Theorem 4.1 shows that E' is a projection of a temporary table T_{i-1} storing all tuples with a homomorphism from the facts exposed by accessibility axioms in the corresponding chase configuration. It follows that there is some tuple $\vec{c_{\vec{t}}}$ in the interpretation of R in config_∞, and a homomorphism h preserving the facts generated by an accessibility axiom fired prior to config_i which maps $\vec{c_{\vec{t}}}$ to $\vec{t}$. Let $\mathsf{AccFacts}(\mathsf{config}_{i-1})$ denote the set of facts generated by an accessibility axiom fired prior to config_i.

From the construction and the argument above it follows that if an access command of PL^v generated an access to method mt using some tuple $\vec{c_{\vec{t}}}$ on config_∞, then some prefix PL_j of PL also generated an access to mt using the tuple $\vec{c_{\vec{t}}}$ as input when run on config_∞, via executing some command $\mathsf{Command}_j$ of form $T_j \Leftarrow \mathsf{mt} \Leftarrow E_j$. Additionally, $j \leq i$, since each access command of PL generates at least one access command in PL^v. It suffices to show that when E_j is evaluated on the temporary tables produced by PL_{j-1} on I, t is in the result. This will guarantee that the access $(\mathsf{mt}, \mathsf{AccBind})$ is performed by PL on I. The expression E_j produces $\vec{c}_t$ when evaluated on the temporary tables produced by PL_{j-1} on config_∞. Therefore the tuple $\vec{c_{\vec{t}}}$ is produced by an SPJ-expression applied to facts in $\mathsf{AccFacts}(\mathsf{config}_{j-1})$. But h preserves all such facts, and hence preserves SPJ queries over the facts. Since h maps $\vec{c_{\vec{t}}}$ to $\vec{t}$, we can conclude that $\vec{t}$ is in the result of E_j evaluated on the temporary tables produced by PL_{j-1} on I, as required.

This completes the proof of Theorem 5.2.

□

Summarizing, if we are interested only in the number of accesses generated at runtime, it suffices to look at proof-based plans. In addition, if we measure cost via some function of the set of access commands (ignoring middleware cost), then proof-based plans are as good as arbitrary "left-deep" plans. Although most realistic cost functions would not be based solely on the set of commands, we take this as a rough justification for restricting to proof-based plans.

5.3 SIMULTANEOUS PROOF AND PLAN SEARCH

We turn to algorithms that search for a low-cost proof-based plan. Recall that in the algorithm that generated SPJ-plans from proofs, Algorithm 2, the plans were generated inductively on the number of steps in a prefix of the proof. Consequently, we can associate a partial plan to a partial proof. This allows us to measure the cost of the corresponding partial plan during proof exploration. These two observations underline the main theme of this section: *we can find low-cost plans by exploring the space of proofs.*

Our search will maintain a *partial proof tree*—a tree consisting of chase sequences, ordered by extension. We refer to the configuration of the final element in the chase sequence associated with a node v as $\mathsf{config}(v)$. The plan associated with v is the one generated by the proof-to-plan algorithm given previously. By the cost of v, we mean the cost of the associated plan. We will describe an algorithm for extending the tree to find new proofs.

Consider a node v such that there is a fact $R(c_1 \ldots c_m)$ in $\mathsf{config}(v)$ with $\mathsf{InfAcc}R(c_1 \ldots c_m)$ not yet in $\mathsf{config}(v)$ and there is an access method mt on R with input positions $j_1 \ldots j_m$ such that $\mathsf{accessible}(c_{j_1}) \ldots \mathsf{accessible}(c_{j_m})$ all hold in $\mathsf{config}(v)$. We call $R(c_1 \ldots c_m)$ a *candidate for exposure* at v, and mt an *exposing method for* $R(c_1 \ldots c_m)$. If a fact is a candidate for exposure, then firing an accessibility axiom will add that fact to the associated chase sequence.

When we explore the impact of making an access, we want to include all relevant consequences that do not involve further accesses, thus producing an eager proof (as defined in Section 4.2). This corresponds to the following requirements on the configurations in a partial proof tree:

Original Schema Reasoning First. The configuration of the root node (henceforward "initial configuration") corresponds to the canonical database of Q plus the result of firing Sch integrity constraints until a termination condition is reached—the termination condition will be explained further below.

Fire Inferred Accessible Rules Immediately. For a non-root node v, there is a candidate fact for exposure $R(c_1 \ldots c_m)$ in its parent with exposing method mt such that $\mathsf{config}(v)$ is obtained from the parent by

- adding the *fact induced by firing* mt *with* $c_{j_1} \ldots c_{j_m}$, namely $\mathsf{InfAcc}R(d_1 \ldots d_m)$.
- firing $\mathsf{InfAccCopy}$ on the result until a termination condition is reached that guarantees that firing more rules will not assist in finding a proof. This termination check is explained below.

Thus the successive configurations are connected by firing a rule associated with an accessibility axiom and exploring the cost-free consequences. This means we can also characterize a node v by the sequence of rule firings of accessibility axioms leading to it. We label a node as *successful* if $\mathsf{InfAcc}Q$ holds in the corresponding configuration (preserving free variables in the non-boolean case), corresponding to a full proof. We explore downward from a node v of a partial proof tree by choosing a *candidate fact for exposure* at $\mathsf{config}(v)$ along with the methods that expose the fact. A node is *terminal* if it has no candidate facts. The basic search structure is outlined in Algorithm 3.

At each iteration of the while loop at line 5 we have a partial proof/plan tree satisfying the properties above. We look for a node v corresponding to a partial proof that is not yet successful, and for which the firings of accessibility axioms can add new facts. We non-deterministically choose such a node and such a rule (lines 6–7), and calculate the new configuration that comes from firing the rule, along with the commands that will be added to the corresponding plan (line 8). We update the candidate list (line 9), marking v as terminal if it has no more candidate (line 10). Finally, we determine whether the new path is successful (line 11), recording whether this gives the new lowest-cost plan (lines 12–14).

Algorithm 3: Generic search

Input: query Q, schema Sch
Output: plan BestPlan

1 ProofTree := an initial node v_1 labeled with the configuration obtained by firing a sufficient number of Sch constraints.
2 Set Candidates(v_1) = all pairs $(R(c_1 \dots c_n), \mathsf{mt})$ with $R(c_1 \dots c_n)$ a fact in the configuration of v_1 and mt a method on R.
3 BestPlan := $\bot$
4 BestCost := ∞
5 **while** $\exists v \in$ ProofTree *that is neither terminal nor successful* **do**
6   Choose such a node v.
7   Choose a candidate fact and method $(R(c_1 \dots c_n), \mathsf{mt}) \in$ Candidates(v) with accessible$(c_{j_1}) \dots$ accessible$(c_{j_m}) \in$ config(v) and mt having inputs $j_1 \dots j_m$.
8   Add a new node v' as a child of v with configuration formed by adding InfAcc$R(c_1 \dots c_n)$ and then closing under a sufficient number of firings of InfAccCopy rules.
9   Remove $(R(c_1 \dots c_n), \mathsf{mt})$ from Candidates(v);
10   Mark v as terminal if it has no more candidates;
11   Determine if v' is successful by checking if InfAcc$Q$ holds.
12   **if** v' *is successful and* Cost(Plan(v')) < BestCost **then**
13   BestPlan := Plan(v');
14   BestCost := Cost(BestPlan) ;
15 **return** BestPlan;

Search order. Algorithm 3 leaves a few issues open. The first is how the non-terminal node is chosen on line 6. A number of policies can be utilized here—e.g., depth-first, breadth-first. Similarly one needs a policy that tells which candidate fact to choose when there is more than one at a node, and which exposure method mt to choose for candidates that can be exposed by more than one method. For the latter, some ordering could be chosen based on expected cost.

Termination. In Algorithm 3, there are several points where we limit the search to achieve termination. Formally, we need: (i) A chase sequence v_1 formed by closing the query Q under firings of Sch rules. We use v_1 in the step of chasing with Sch constraints in line 1. Given v_1, we have a bound on termination of the while loop of line 5, since we only expose facts from v_1. (ii) For each chase sequence w, an extension $v_2(w)$ of w by firing InfAccCopy constraints, used within every step of the while loop on line 8. We say that v_1 and $v_2(w)$ are *sufficient sets* for the algorithm. We explain how such sets are defined for a set of constraints with terminating chase. There we can set v_1 to be any set of firings of Sch rules such that there are no active triggers of Sch constraints. We let $v_2(w)$ be any extension of w by InfAccCopy constraints with no active triggers among InfAccCopy constraints.

Example 5.4. We return to the setting of Example 1.3, assuming we have three directory sources $\mathsf{Udirectory}_1, \mathsf{Udirectory}_2, \mathsf{Udirectory}_3$. The integrity constraints contain:

$$\mathsf{Profinfo(eid, onum, lname)} \rightarrow \mathsf{Udirectory}_i\mathsf{(eid, lname)}$$

for $i = 1,2,3$, with Profinfo having an access method that requires the first arguments to be given and each $\mathsf{Udirectory}_i$ having unrestricted access. Let our query Q be $\exists\mathsf{eid\ onum\ lname\ Profinfo(eid, onum, lname)}$.

The behavior of our exploration is illustrated in Figure 5.1. The canonical database of Q consists of the fact $\mathsf{Profinfo(eid_0, onum_0, lname_0)}$. The configuration of the initial node n_0 will then add $\mathsf{Udirectory}_i\mathsf{(eid_0, lname_0)}$ for $i = 1,2,3$. There are thus three candidates facts to expose, $\mathsf{Udirectory}_i\mathsf{(eid_0, lname_0)} : i = 1,2,3$ in the initial node.

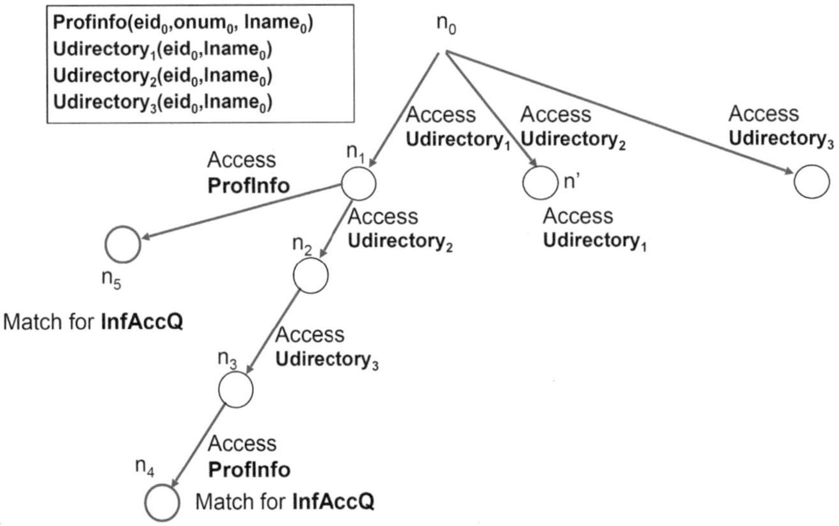

Figure 5.1: Exploration in the running example.

We might choose $\mathsf{Udirectory}_1(\mathsf{eid}_0, \mathsf{lname}_0)$ to expose first. This creates a child n_1 with transition from parent to child associated with an access on $\mathsf{Udirectory}_1$, putting the output into a table T_1 with attributes $\{\mathsf{eid}_0, \mathsf{lname}_0\}$. The configuration for n_1 adds the fact $\mathsf{InfAccUdirectory}_1(\mathsf{eid}_0, \mathsf{lname}_0)$, $\mathsf{accessible}(\mathsf{eid}_0)$, and $\mathsf{accessible}(\mathsf{lname}_0)$.

In n_1 there are three candidates to expose: $\mathsf{Udirectory}_2(\mathsf{eid}_0, \mathsf{lname}_0)$, $\mathsf{Udirectory}_3(\mathsf{eid}_0, \mathsf{lname}_0)$, and now also $\mathsf{Profinfo}(\mathsf{eid}_0, \mathsf{onum}_0, \mathsf{lname}_0)$, since there is an accessibility axiom that would expose this last fact now. We might choose $\mathsf{Udirectory}_2(\mathsf{eid}_0, \mathsf{lname}_0)$ to expose, and a child n_2 will be generated (again including the exposed fact $\mathsf{InfAccUdirectory}_2(\mathsf{eid}_0, \mathsf{lname}_0)$). The transition to n_2 will be associated with an access command on $\mathsf{Udirectory}_2$ and a command joining the results with the previous table.

The node n_2 will have two candidates to expose, $\mathsf{Udirectory}_3(\mathsf{eid}_0, \mathsf{lname}_0)$ and $\mathsf{Profinfo}(\mathsf{eid}_0, \mathsf{onum}_0, \mathsf{lname}_0)$. We choose to expose $\mathsf{Udirectory}_3(\mathsf{eid}_0, \mathsf{lname}_0)$ next, and we will generate a child n_3, whose configuration adds the exposed fact.

The node n_3 will have only one candidate fact, corresponding to $\mathsf{Profinfo}(\mathsf{eid}_0, \mathsf{onum}_0, \mathsf{lname}_0)$. Selecting this fact, a child n_4 will be generated. The query $\mathsf{InfAcc}Q$ matches the configuration of n_4, so it is designated a success node, hence is a leaf in the search.

$$
\begin{aligned}
&T_1 \Leftarrow \mathsf{mt}_1 \Leftarrow \emptyset \\
&T_2' \Leftarrow \mathsf{mt}_2 \Leftarrow \emptyset \\
&T_2 := T_2' \bowtie T_1 \\
&T_3' \Leftarrow \mathsf{mt}_3 \Leftarrow \emptyset \\
&T_3 := T_3' \bowtie T_2 \\
&T_4 \Leftarrow \mathsf{mt}_{\mathsf{Profinfo}} \Leftarrow \pi_{\mathsf{eid}}(T_3) \\
&\text{Return } \pi(T_4 \bowtie T_3).
\end{aligned}
$$

Moving back up the search tree, we might consider exposing the fact $\mathsf{Profinfo}(\mathsf{eid}_0, \mathsf{onum}_0, \mathsf{lname}_0)$ from n_1, creating node n_5. This configuration is also successful, one can see that its plan has lower cost than that of n_1, making strictly less access than the one previously found. Thus n_5's plan will replace n_4's as the best configuration so far.

□

◁

Correctness of the search algorithm. We can show that this approach will solve the low-cost plan problem for proof-based plans.

Theorem 5.3 *Let* Cost *be a simple cost function, schema* Sch *consist of access restrictions and TGDs with terminating chase, and Q be a conjunctive query. Then Algorithm 3, instantiated with the sufficient sets described for terminating chase and the cost function* Cost, *will always return a plan with the* *lowest cost among all those proof-based plans that completely answer* Q *w.r.t.* Sch, *or return* $\perp$ *if there is no plan (proof-based or otherwise) that answers* Q.

Proof. Note that our prior results already guarantee that there is a plan exactly when there is a proof-based plan.

Fix a chase proof v' witnessing that Q entails $\mathsf{InfAcc}Q$. Such a v' can be extended so that there are no active triggers among Sch or InfAccCopy constraints, without changing the resulting plan. Let $\mathsf{PL}^{v'}$ be the plan and $\mathsf{mt}_1 \ldots \mathsf{mt}_n$ the sequence of access methods within the access commands of $\mathsf{PL}^{v'}$. Let v_1 be the chase sequence produced at the beginning of Algorithm 3 when run with Q, and config_1 be the last chase configuration in the sequence. When $\mathsf{PL}^{v'}$ is run on config_1, it will execute access commands $\mathsf{Command}'_1 \ldots \mathsf{Command}'_n$ with inputs $I_1 \ldots I_n$, and outputs $O_1 \ldots O_n$. As in the proof of Proposition 5.1, we can find facts $F_1 \ldots F_n$ with corresponding tuples $\vec{t}_1 \in O_1 \ldots \vec{t}_n \in O_n$ accessed by $\mathsf{PL}^{v'}$ such that these outputs suffice to return the tuple corresponding to the free variables of Q. Let v_2 be the chase sequence corresponding to firings of accessibility axioms exposing $F_1 \ldots F_n$ within config_1. Arguing as in the proof of Proposition 5.1, we can see that this represents a valid sequence of firings, since the values of $\vec{t}_i$ within input positions of mt_i will satisfy accessible. Arguing as in Proposition 5.1 again, we see that $v_1 \cdot v_2$ can be extended by the firing of some collection of InfAccCopy constraints v_3, giving a proof of the entailment of $\mathsf{InfAcc}Q$ from Q. Letting $v = v_1 \cdot v_2 \cdot v_3$, we claim that v will be discovered by the algorithm, and so the corresponding plan PL^{v} will be considered. Since PL^{v} uses no more methods than $\mathsf{PL}^{v'}$, and our cost function is simple, the cost of PL^{v} will be no higher than that of $\mathsf{PL}^{v'}$. Thus if PL^{v} is discovered by the algorithm we have proven optimality.

Consider the chase sequence v^* formed from $v_1 \cdot v_2 \cdot v_3$ by removing v_3 and inserting after each prefix p_3 of $v_1 \cdot v_2$ a chase sequence formed from firing InfAccCopy constraints that are applicable after that prefix, until there are no InfAccCopy constraints that can apply. The plans PL^{v^*} and PL^{v} are the same, since the accessibility axiom firings in both sequences are identical. We can also see that v^* will have a match for $\mathsf{InfAcc}Q$. This holds because both v^* and v extend the sequence $v_1 \cdot v_2$ by firing InfAccCopy constraints until there are no active triggers by InfAccCopy constraints, hence they both satisfy exactly the CQs that are implied by the final configuration of $v_1 \cdot v_2$ and the InfAccCopy constraints.

We argue that in every iteration of the while loop, (i) if v^* has not been discovered then the while loop at line 5 will not yet terminate, (ii) v^* will always have a prefix in ProofTree with a non-empty set of candidates. Since we remove candidates in each iteration of the loop, eventually such an ancestor prefix will be chosen to be expanded, and thus v^* will be discovered. □

In fact, Algorithm 3 considers "all" proof-based plans, except for superficial differences due to ordering of firings in the chase.

Example 5.5. Let our access schema have binary relations A and B, where A has no access and B has an input-free access. Suppose we have the following integrity constraints:

$$A(x, y) \rightarrow B(y, y)$$
$$A(x, y) \rightarrow \exists z\ B(y, z)$$
$$B(x, y) \rightarrow \exists u\ w\ A(u, w).$$

We look at how the algorithm behaves with query $Q = \exists x\ y\ A(x, y)$. We start with the canonical database of Q, $\{A(x_0, y_0)\}$, and chase using the Sch constraints in an arbitrary order until no active trigger is present. Thus we might choose an ordering that avoids using the (logically redundant) second constraint above, resulting in a chase sequence v_1 with final configuration $\mathsf{config}_1 = \{A(x_0, y_0), B(y_0, y_0)\}$.

In the search stage of the algorithm, there is only one candidate fact for exposure to examine, corresponding to application of a forward accessibility axiom on $B(y_0, y_0)$. This application produces $\mathsf{InfAcc}B(y_0, y_0)$, and then the InfAccCopy constraints would add $\mathsf{InfAcc}A(u_0, w_0)$, yielding a match of $\mathsf{InfAcc}Q$ and thus a successful configuration. We call this proof v, and the corresponding plan PL^v found by our algorithm is:

$$T_1 \Leftarrow B \Leftarrow \emptyset$$
$$T_2 \Leftarrow \sigma_{\#2=\#1}(T_1)$$
$$\text{Return } \pi_{\emptyset}(T_2).$$

Another proof v' would begin with the canonical database of Q, and then apply the second constraint to obtain configuration

$$\{A(x_0, y_0), B(y_0, z_0)\}.$$

It would then apply the accessibility axiom to get $\mathsf{InfAcc}B(y_0, z_0)$, followed by application of the InfAccCopy constraints to obtain $\mathsf{InfAcc}A(y_0, z_0)$. Since $\mathsf{InfAcc}Q$ has a match on the resulting configuration, this is a full proof.

The corresponding plan $\mathsf{PL}^{v'}$ is similar to PL^v, but slightly different:

$$T_1 \Leftarrow B \Leftarrow \emptyset$$
$$\text{Return } \pi_{\emptyset}(T_1).$$

Recall the optimality proof that shows that Algorithm 3 finds a plan at least as good as $\mathsf{PL}^{v'}$. We begin by considering a run of $\mathsf{PL}^{v'}$ on the chase configuration config_1. $\mathsf{PL}^{v'}$ will access only the fact $B(y_0, y_0)$, and we thus generate a proof that exposes fact $B(y_0, y_0)$, and then fires InfAccCopy rules. This proof is exactly v. ◁

Since Theorem 5.3 applies to any set of TGDs with terminating chase, it shows that Algorithm 3 will return a proof-based plan with minimal cost when applied to constraints generated from view definitions. In particular, the algorithm can find reformulations over views that have minimal size.

The requirement of terminating chase in Theorem 5.3 is a strong one. But for some classes without terminating chase, such as GTGDs, there are alternative "sufficient sets" which can be used as termination conditions in Algorithm 3. Instead of firing the rules until termination, it is enough to fire them a sufficient number of times.

We explain in more detail how Algorithm 3 can be instantiated with termination conditions to make the analog of Theorem 5.3 hold. For a chase sequence $v = \mathsf{config}_1 \ldots \mathsf{config}_j$ let $\mathsf{RulesOf}(v)$ be the sequence $\tau_1 \ldots \tau_{j-1}$ where, for $i \leq j-1$, τ_i is the TGD fired in going from config_i to config_{i+1}. We will make use of the following fact, proved in [Lukasiewicz et al., 2012]:

For any queries Q and Q' and finite collection of GTGDs Σ, there is a number k at most doubly exponential in $|Q'|$ and $|\Sigma|$ such that: for any chase sequence v starting at the canonical database of Q and ending in a match of Q', there is another sequence v' of size at most k, starting at the canonical database of Q, ending in a configuration with a match of Q', with $\mathsf{RulesOf}(v')$ a subsequence of $\mathsf{RulesOf}(v)$.

This is shown in the proof of Lemma 4 of [Lukasiewicz et al., 2012], with the bound $|Q'| \cdot |\Sigma| \cdot (2w)^w \cdot 2^{|\Sigma| \cdot (2w)^w}$, where w is the maximal arity of any relation in the schema. It is shown that when the final configuration of a chase sequence of length longer than this is arranged in a forest reflecting the relationship of guard atoms to the generated children, then there are two nodes h and h' with h an ancestor of h' in the forest, such that the path between them can be "collapsed" without losing a match of Q'. Collapsing here means having the parent of h generate h' instead of h. Clearly this collapsing operation does not increase the number of firings of any rule. This can also be proven by using a tree automaton or pushdown automaton representation of the chase for GTGDs (mentioned in Chapter 3), since it is well-known that an arbitrary accepting run of a pushdown automaton or tree automaton can be trimmed to a small accepting run by collapsing subtrees.

Setting k as in the fact from [Lukasiewicz et al., 2012] above, with Q' being $\mathsf{InfAcc}Q$, we let v_1 be the result of k rounds of chase steps starting with the canonical database of Q, where in each round we fire all triggers for Sch constraints, active or not. We let $v_2(w)$ be the same number of rounds of chasing of w. We claim that the algorithm instantiated with these sufficient conditions returns the optimal proof-based plan:

Theorem 5.4 *Let* Cost *be a simple cost function,* Sch *be a schema consisting of access restrictions and GTGD constraints, and Q be conjunctive query. Then Algorithm 3, instantiated with the sufficient sets above and the cost function* Cost, *will always return a plan with the lowest cost among all those proof-based plans that completely answer Q w.r.t.*Sch, *or return $\perp$ if there is no plan that answers Q.*

Proof. Assume that we have a chase proof v' witnessing that Q entails $\mathsf{InfAcc}Q$, with $\mathsf{PL}^{v'}$ the resulting plan and $\mathsf{mt}_1 \ldots \mathsf{mt}_j$ the sequence of methods used in access commands. By the fact above, there is another proof v of size k such that the sequence of accessibility axioms fired in v will be a subsequence of the sequence in v'. In particular, the plan for v, PL^v, will use no more methods than the plan for v', and hence the cost will be no more than v' under a simple cost function. Further, PL^v will use at most k accessibility axioms. We can move all the firings of Sch constraints in v to the beginning, where they will be embedded in k rounds of chasing with the Sch constraints. Similarly, blocks of InfAccCopy firings in v can be distributed so that they are performed as soon as they are applicable. Let v^* be the resulting proof.

We argue again that in every iteration of the while loop, if v^* has not been discovered then the while loop at line 5 will not terminate, and at each iteration v^* will have a prefix in ProofTree with a non-empty set of candidates. Since candidates are removed in each iteration of the while loop, eventually such an ancestor prefix will be chosen to be expanded. At that point the algorithm will return v^*. □

In practice we do not need to use such conservative termination conditions. For example, since cost will increase with the number of accesses, we can safely cap the number of accessibility axioms fired at some threshold for cost.

Optimizations. Nodes in our search space are associated with both a cost and a collection of facts associated with the last configuration of the chase sequence (the *output facts* below). In determining the potential of further exploring below a node, one must take into account both its cost and its output facts. We briefly mention cases where we can discard a node for search purposes based on one or both of these dimensions.

- For any monotone cost function, we can discard any node such that corresponding partial plan has a cost already worse than that of the best plan so far. This is a standard "branch and bound" optimization.
- Several chase sequences can produce the same configuration. If v and v' have identical output facts, then the search spaces beneath them are identical. In particular, if the cost function is simple, then we need only keep one representative of each equivalence class, tracking the cost of the representative with lowest cost. The same is true, again assuming simple cost functions, if there is an isomorphism mapping the facts of v to those of v'.
- For simple cost functions, we can abort the exploration of certain partial paths without considering the best plan found so far, using an asymmetric variant of state equivalence. Suppose we have discovered a node v in the search space and have a candidate fact c at v and method mt for exposing c such that when we generate a new node v' from c, we find that there is a node v'' already in PlanTree such that
  - the final configuration of v'' has all the facts in the final configuration of v'
  - the cost of the plan for v'' is lower than the cost of the plan for v'

In this case there is no need to generate v'. The intuition here is that if a sequence of accesses added on to the actions of v' generates a plan answering Q, the same sequence can be added on to the actions of v'', generating a plan with no higher cost. Note that for general cost functions, this might not be valid, since v' might produce some temporary relations that are smaller than those of v'', and the size of these relations may diminish the cost of later accesses.

5.4 BEYOND PREFIX PROOFS AND LEFT-DEEP PLANS

The previous algorithms implement a search for proofs that $Q \models \mathsf{InfAcc}Q$ with respect to the auxiliary schema $\mathsf{AcSch}(\mathsf{Sch})$, with each proof corresponding to a plan. But the search was restricted to very specialized proofs, and this limited the corresponding query plans. By changing the proof search or the proof system being used, we can change the class of plans that are being considered.

For example, in Algorithm 3 every proof that was explored during the search was a potential *prefix* of a full proof, a chase sequence starting with the canonical database of Q. And larger proofs were built by adding on the firing of a single accessibility axiom and closing under $\mathsf{InfAccCopy}$ rules. This is analogous to searching for a path from a source to a sink in a graph by starting at the source and moving forward a single step at a time. The restriction to "prefix proofs" guarantees that each subplan being considered is closed—that is, has no free tables, as defined in Section 3.1. The second restriction ensures that plans are "left-deep": built up by joining on the result of one access command at a time. However, in the presence of access restrictions, limiting the search to left-deep plans can be problematic, forcing the creation of cross products. We will see this phenomenon later in Example 5.6.

An alternative to starting with the canonical database would be to build up proofs that are sequences starting with an arbitrary set of facts over the auxiliary schema. These proofs are potential *infixes* of a complete proof. Rather than extending sequences by firing one accessibility axiom at a time, we would allow proofs to be combined by concatenating the chase sequences. The corresponding plans need not be either closed or left-deep.

To demonstrate the idea that different proof search algorithms or different proof systems correspond to different kinds of plans, we discuss a special case of the approach above, explored in more detail in [Benedikt et al., 2015]. In this special case, we do not look at all chase sequences but ones that have compact representations. From each representation, we will be able to quickly read off the initial and final configurations of the sequence, and will be able to combine sequences.

Let v_1 be obtained by chasing the canonical database of the query Q with Sch constraints until some termination condition (as in Section 5.3) is satisfied. We will restrict to chase sequences whose configurations include the facts of v_1 and are closed under sufficiently many firings of the Sch constraints. An *atomic chase sequence representation*, denoted $\mathsf{AtomicProof}(\mathsf{Ax}_{\mathsf{For}}, F)$, is associated with some firing of an accessibility axiom using a method mt on R with input positions $j_1 \ldots j_m$, exposing a fact $F = R(c_1 \ldots c_n)$ from v_1. This corresponds to a chase sequence that goes from an extension v_1 with $\mathsf{accessible}(c_{j_1}) \ldots \mathsf{accessible}(c_{j_m})$ to a v_1' in which the fact $\mathsf{InfAcc}R(\vec{c})$ is added, and then the resulting configuration is closed under sufficiently many firings of the InfAccCopy rules.

Chase sequence representations are built up by the *sequence composition operator*, denoted $\mathsf{CompProof}(\mathsf{ChaseSeqRep}_a, \mathsf{ChaseSeqRep}_b)$, which we explain now. Let $\mathsf{ChaseSeqRep}_a$ represent the chase sequence $\mathsf{config}_1 \ldots \mathsf{config}_m$ and $\mathsf{ChaseSeqRep}_b$ represent the chase sequence $\mathsf{config}_{m+1} \ldots \mathsf{config}_n$. First suppose that $\mathsf{ChaseSeqRep}_a$ produces all the facts required for the initial configuration of $\mathsf{ChaseSeqRep}_b$. This means that the final configuration of $\mathsf{ChaseSeqRep}_a$, config_m, contains all facts in the initial configuration config_{m+1} of $\mathsf{ChaseSeqRep}_b$. Then $\mathsf{CompProof}(\mathsf{ChaseSeqRep}_a, \mathsf{ChaseSeqRep}_b)$ represents the chase sequence that begins with

$$\mathsf{config}_1 \ldots \mathsf{config}_m, (\mathsf{config}_m \cup \mathsf{config}_{m+2}) \ldots (\mathsf{config}_m \cup \mathsf{config}_n)$$

and then closes $\mathsf{config}_m \cup \mathsf{config}_n$ under sufficiently many firings of the InfAccCopy constraints. So we concatenate the corresponding proofs, identifying config_m and config_{m+1}, and then add at the end any InfAccCopy consequences that can be derived from combining the final configurations of both sequences.

We allow CompProof to be defined for any $\mathsf{ChaseSeqRep}_a$ and $\mathsf{ChaseSeqRep}_b$, even when $\mathsf{ChaseSeqRep}_a$ does not provide all the hypotheses needed for $\mathsf{ChaseSeqRep}_b$. In the general case, the composed sequence begins from a configuration having all the assumptions needed for $\mathsf{ChaseSeqRep}_a$, as well as all those needed for $\mathsf{ChaseSeqRep}_b$ that are not provided by $\mathsf{ChaseSeqRep}_a$. Formally, if $\mathsf{ChaseSeqRep}_a$ and $\mathsf{ChaseSeqRep}_b$ represent sequences as above, $\mathsf{CompProof}(\mathsf{ChaseSeqRep}_a, \mathsf{ChaseSeqRep}_b)$ represents the chase sequence beginning with

$$\mathsf{config}^*_1 \ldots \mathsf{config}^*_m, \mathsf{config}^*_{m+2} \ldots \mathsf{config}^*_n$$

and then closing under sufficiently many firings of the InfAccCopy constraints, where

- for $i \leq m$, config^*_i is formed from config_i by adding any facts in config_{m+1} that are not present in config_m. Thus config^*_m will be the same as config_{m+1}.
- for $m + 2 \leq i \leq n$, config^*_i is $\mathsf{config}_i \cup \mathsf{config}_m$

That is, we start out with all the initial facts of the first sequence, plus all the facts that are needed by the second sequence and not produced by the first. We then fire every rule that is in either sequence. We thus obtain a final configuration that will expose every fact exposed in either sequence, and we close this under the InfAccCopy rules.

Example 5.6. We present a variant of an example in [Florescu et al., 1999]. We have an access schema with unary relations $A(x), B(u), F(x)$, and binary relations $C(x, y), D(u, v), E(y, v)$. We have input-free access to A and B, access to C on the first position, access to D on the first position, and access to E requiring both arguments. We have no access to F. The integrity constraints are:

$$F(x) \rightarrow A(x)$$
$$A(x) \rightarrow F(x).$$

Let our query Q be:

$$F(x) \wedge C(x,y) \wedge B(u) \wedge D(u,v) \wedge E(y,v).$$

One can see that there is a plan answering Q. Intuitively, we can replace $F(x)$ by $A(x)$ in the query, and then perform accesses corresponding to each atom moving from left to right. There are other plans that interleave access to B and D with access to F and C in a different way. But any left-deep plan answering the query—and in particular, any proof-based plan produced by the previous algorithms—will include building up the cross-product of A and B.

Building a large intermediate result such as a cross-product is extremely costly, and avoiding them whenever possible is a basic rule in query optimization. We will see that our more general approach will be able to generate a plan that avoids cross products. For the moment we look at the proof representations that would be generated in this example.

The initial chase configuration v_1 in this case is formed via the canonical database of Q, consisting of facts $\{A(x_0), F(x_0), C(x_0, y_0), B(u_0), D(u_0, v_0), E(y_0, v_0)\}$, where $A(x_0)$ is generated from $F(x_0)$ using the constraint above. We look at the proofs we can build up via chase sequence representations.

- There is an atomic chase sequence representation $\mathsf{ChaseSeqRep}_A$ corresponding to exposing fact $A(x_0)$. It represents a chase sequence starting with v_1 itself, then firing a rule which adds the facts $\mathsf{InfAcc}A(x_0)$ and $\mathsf{accessible}(x_0)$. Computing the closure under the InfAccCopy rules, we add on the additional fact $\mathsf{InfAcc}F(x_0)$. Similarly, there is an atomic chase sequence representation $\mathsf{ChaseSeqRep}_B$ corresponding to exposing fact $B(u_0)$.
- There is an atomic chase sequence representation $\mathsf{ChaseSeqRep}_C$ corresponding to an accessibility axiom firing and exposing $C(x_0, y_0)$. This represents a chase sequence that starts at a configuration extending v_1 with $\mathsf{accessible}(x_0)$ and proceeding to a configuration that adds $\mathsf{InfAcc}C(x_0, y_0)$ as well as $\mathsf{accessible}(y_0)$. Likewise there is an atomic chase sequence representation $\mathsf{ChaseSeqRep}_D$ corresponding to exposing fact $D(u_0, v_0)$. There is an atomic chase sequence representation $\mathsf{ChaseSeqRep}_E$ corresponding to exposing fact $E(y_0, v_0)$. It represents a chase sequence that starts with a configuration extending v_1 with $\mathsf{accessible}(y_0)$ and $\mathsf{accessible}(v_0)$, proceeding by adding fact $E(y_0, v_0)$.
- There is a compound chase sequence representation

  $$\mathsf{ChaseSeqRep}_{AC} = \mathsf{CompProof}(\mathsf{ChaseSeqRep}_A, \mathsf{ChaseSeqRep}_C)$$

  which corresponds to a chase sequence starting from v_1 and then arriving at a configuration containing facts

  $$\{\mathsf{InfAcc}A(x_0), \mathsf{InfAcc}F(x_0), \mathsf{InfAcc}C(x_0, y_0), \mathsf{accessible}(x_0), \mathsf{accessible}(y_0)\}$$

- $\mathsf{ChaseSeqRep}_{BD} = \mathsf{CompProof}(\mathsf{ChaseSeqRep}_B, \mathsf{ChaseSeqRep}_D)$ corresponds to a sequence starting from v_1 and arriving at a configuration containing

  $$\{\mathsf{InfAcc}B(u_0), \mathsf{InfAcc}D(u_0, v_0), \mathsf{accessible}(u_0), \mathsf{accessible}(v_0)\}$$

- $\mathsf{ChaseSeqRep}_{ACBD} = \mathsf{CompProof}(\mathsf{ChaseSeqRep}_{AC}, \mathsf{ChaseSeqRep}_{BD})$ represents a chase sequence which begins at v_1 and arrives at a configuration containing

$$\{\mathsf{InfAcc}A(x_0), \mathsf{InfAcc}F(x_0), \mathsf{InfAcc}B(u_0), \mathsf{InfAcc}C(x_0, y_0), \mathsf{InfAcc}D(u_0, v_0), \\ \mathsf{accessible}(x_0), \mathsf{accessible}(y_0), \mathsf{accessible}(u_0), \mathsf{accessible}(v_0)\}\}$$

- $\mathsf{ChaseSeqRep}_{ACBDE} = \mathsf{CompProof}(\mathsf{ChaseSeqRep}_{ACBD}, \mathsf{ChaseSeqRep}_{E})$ corresponds to a sequence beginning at v_1 and arriving at a configuration containing all of the output facts listed above for $\mathsf{ChaseSeqRep}_{ACBD}$ and also the fact $\mathsf{InfAcc}E(y_0, v_0)$. Since this sequence begins with v_1, which can be generated from the canonical database, and ends with a match of $\mathsf{InfAcc}Q$, it represents a full proof.

◁

Representations could be transformed into plans by first compiling them into the chase sequences they represent, and then applying a modification of the SPJ proof-to-plan algorithm in the previous chapter (the modification consists in handling proofs with hypothesis about accessibility).

However, the representations can also be converted to plans directly in a compositional manner. An atomic representation gives rise to an atomic plan, i.e., an access command given by the access method associated with $\mathsf{Ax}_{\mathsf{For}}$. The plan for $\mathsf{CompProof}(\mathsf{ChaseSeqRep}_a, \mathsf{ChaseSeqRep}_b)$ is the composition of the plans obtained for $\mathsf{ChaseSeqRep}_a$ and $\mathsf{ChaseSeqRep}_b$.

Example 5.7. Consider the subplans built up from the proof representations in Example 5.6.

- $\mathsf{ChaseSeqRep}_A$ generates a plan PL_A consisting of

$$T_A \Leftarrow \mathsf{mt}_A \Leftarrow \emptyset \\ \mathsf{Return}\ T_A$$

  where T_A is a table with attribute x_0.

  Similarly $\mathsf{ChaseSeqRep}_B$ generates a plan PL_B returning the result of the access command $T_B \Leftarrow \mathsf{mt}_B \Leftarrow \emptyset$, where T_B is a table with attribute u_0.

- $\mathsf{ChaseSeqRep}_C$ generates plan PL_C returning the result of the access command:

$$T_C \Leftarrow \mathsf{mt}_C \Leftarrow T_{x_0}$$

  where T_C has attributes x_0 and y_0. Notice that this is an "open" plan, in that it makes use of the free table T_{x_0}.

  In the same way, $\mathsf{ChaseSeqRep}_D$ generates an open plan accessing D and returning a table with attributes u_0 and v_0, while $\mathsf{ChaseSeqRep}_E$ generates an open plan requiring an input table having attributes y_0 and v_0, with output table also having attributes y_0, v_0.

- The composed proof $\mathsf{ChaseSeqRep}_{AC}$ generates plan PL_{AC} formed by composing PL_A with PL_C. This plan is closed, since PL_A required no free table as input, while the inputs to PL_C were supplied as the output from PL_A. This plan returns a table with attributes $\{x_0, y_0\}$.

  Similarly, the composed proof $\mathsf{ChaseSeqRep}_{BD}$ generates plan PL_{BD} formed via composing PL_B and PL_D, whose output has attributes $\{u_0, v_0\}$.

- The composed proof $\mathsf{ChaseSeqRep}_{ACBD}$ yields plan PL_{ACBD} formed by composing PL_{AC} with PL_{BD}. This is a closed plan whose output is a table with attributes $\{x_0, y_0, u_0, v_0\}$.

- The composed proof $\mathsf{ChaseSeqRep}_{ACBDE}$ yields plan PL_{ACBDE} formed by composing PL_{ACBD} with PL_E. By composing here, we mean that the output of PL_{ACBD} is projected onto the input attributes of PL_E, namely $\{x_0, y_0\}$, PL_E is run on each resulting tuple, and the results are joined up with the inputs. Since the proof $\mathsf{ChaseSeqRep}_{ACBDE}$ was successful, we know that this plan answers the query.

◁

We see that the search space includes compositions of open plans, which were not taken into account in the previous algorithm. We can modify the previous search algorithm to build up these plans, as shown in Algorithm 4.

We begin by initializing the search (lines 1–10) by first chasing the canonical database of Q with sufficiently many firings of the Sch constraints, forming the configuration v_1, and then adding to the plan space all atomic chase sequence representations. We then iteratively compose to form new representations (lines 11–20), generating the plan for each representation and measuring its cost. We assume each representation object contains the facts in its initial and final configurations. In forming the new representation $\mathsf{CompProof}(\mathsf{ChaseSeqRep}_1, \mathsf{ChaseSeqRep}_2)$, we need to combine the output facts of $\mathsf{ChaseSeqRep}_1$ and $\mathsf{ChaseSeqRep}_2$ and then chase under sufficiently many firings of the $\mathsf{InfAccCopy}$ constraints.

Our search algorithm builds up larger and larger proofs "in bulk," and at the same time building up sets of plans with larger and larger number of accesses. In addition to being able to explore more general plans, this approach produces a search algorithm that is more similar to the approaches taken in traditional cost-based optimization of database queries, which searches the plan-space for larger and larger subqueries, starting at single-atom subqueries [Ramakrishnan and Gehrke, 2003]. Thus many optimizations used in classical search, such as dynamic programming, can be applied.

5.5 SUMMARY

The previous chapters presented algorithms for generating query plans from "proofs of the answerability of a query." These reduced the question of existence of a plan to the question of existence of a certain kind of proof. In this chapter, we have shown that the relationship between proofs

Algorithm 4: Bushy plan search

Input: query Q, access schema Sch
Output: plan BestPlan

Let PlanSpace $:= \emptyset$;
Let BestPlan $:= \bot$;
Let BestCost $:= \infty$;
Initialize the set v_1 obtained by chasing InfAcc$Q$ with Sch constraints;
foreach $(\mathsf{Ax}_R^{mt}, \vec{b})$ **do**
    /* where Ax_R^{mt} is an accessibility axiom corresponding to access method mt of relation R and $\vec{b}$ is a match from v_1 to the inputs of mt */
    Add the corresponding AtomicProof$(\mathsf{Ax}_R^{mt}, \vec{b})$ to PlanSpace;
    Let PL := ToPlan(AtomicProof$(\mathsf{Ax}_R^{mt}, \vec{b})$);
    if AtomicProof$(\mathsf{Ax}_R^{mt}, \vec{b})$ *is a proof and* Cost(PL) $<$ BestCost **then**
        BestPlan := PL;
        BestCost := Cost(BestPlan)

$r := 0$;
while PlanSpace *has changed from previous* r **do**
    Select (ChaseSeqRep$_1$, ChaseSeqRep$_2$) from PlanSpace with CompProof(ChaseSeqRep$_1$, ChaseSeqRep$_2$) $\notin$ PlanSpace;
    Let ChaseSeqRep := CompProof(ChaseSeqRep$_1$, ChaseSeqRep$_2$);
    Let PL := ToPlan(ChaseSeqRep);
    Add ChaseSeqRep to PlanSpace;
    if ChaseSeqRep *is a full proof and* Cost(PL) $<$ BestCost **then**
        BestPlan := PL ;
        BestCost := Cost(BestPlan)
    $r := r + 1$;
return BestPlan;

and plans is much closer than just a reduction between existence problems. Different proofs can represent different plans, and many common optimizations in plan-generation can be captured by looking at distinct proofs. We gave evidence (e.g., Proposition 5.1 and Theorem 5.2) that considering plans generated from proofs does not force one to miss optimal plans, for some simple notions of optimality. We also outlined how a cost-based search of the space of proof-based plans might be performed. In the process we produced algorithms guaranteed to find optimal proof-based plans, albeit for restricted classes of constraints and with high complexity.

Our optimality results concerning proof-based plans applied only to very crude cost functions. These restrictions partially reflect the simplicity of the proofs system we have applied—more flexible proof systems will allow one to consider a wider range of plans: we presented one example of a more general proof system in Section 5.4. They also underscore the fact that many additional considerations in query optimization must be integrated with proof-based query planning. We have briefly discussed how the idea of proof-based search might be used in conjunction with some of the existing search methods in query optimization, such as dynamic programming.

5.6 BIBLIOGRAPHIC REMARKS

This chapter looks at algorithms for getting the lowest-cost plan that is built on a given set of access methods, and which answers a query relative to a set of integrity constraints. The impact of access restrictions on cost-based optimization has been considered before. Florescu et al. [1999] look at integrating access restrictions into a cost-based optimizer, following up on earlier cost-agnostic work on querying with access methods [Li, 2003, Li and Chang, 2001]. In the absence of integrity constraints, querying with access methods amounts to a limitation on the search space, restricting the ordering of atoms within a query plan. In contrast, schemas with integrity constraints and access methods can simultaneously restrict the search space (via access restrictions) and extend it (via integrity constraints, which allow relations outside of the query to become relevant).

Comparison with the Chase and BackChase. The Chase and Backchase (C&B) is a common technique for reformulating a conjunctive query Q. It originated in [Deutsch et al., 1999, 2006, Popa, 2000]. It exists in various forms, but a frequently cited version of it matches the case of reformulating a source conjunctive query Q as a CQ over a restricted set of relations, matching our vocabulary-based setting from Section 2.3. In terms of the constraints considered in the C&B, there are versions for mixtures of TGDs and equality-generating dependencies (EGDs). The main assumption on constraints that the technique relies on is that we have a notion of the chase which terminates. In the presence of EGDs, the requirements for termination of the chase are very strong [Onet, 2013]. For simplicity, we assume constraints contain only TGDs in the description below.

The idea behind the C&B is to first produce a "universal plan" by chasing the canonical instance of query Q with the constraints to get a collection of facts U: this is the "chasing phase." Then we search for a smaller plan that uses only the distinguished relations from $\mathcal{T}$. We do this by selecting a set S of such facts within the chase, re-chasing it by tracing out the closure of S in U under the dependencies. If this closure has a match of the query Q (that is, a homomorphism mapping the free variables of Q to the corresponding constant) then we know that the set of atoms S, when converted to a query Q_S, is in fact equivalent to Q under the constraints. This is the "back-chasing" phase. Ideally, it will select a set S that is minimal with respect to having a chase-closure with a match for Q, thus producing a Q_S that is a minimal reformulation [Ileana et al., 2014]. By maintaining auxiliary information about the way in which the atoms in U are generated in the chase, the back-chasing phase can be made more efficient. For example, in [Ileana et al., 2014], provenance information is maintained to speed up the back-chasing phase.

In this work, we have approached the reformulation problem from the general standpoint of first-order constraints, and our methodology—auxiliary schemas, two copies of the relations, etc.—may seem very distinct from the C&B. But we will explain here that in the case of terminating chase, the approach here is a variation of the C&B.

Recall that in Algorithm 3 we first form an initial chase using the original integrity constraints Σ, and then apply steps consisting of firing an accessibility axiom followed by "follow-up rules"—the application of copies of the constraints. Instead of firing an accessibility axiom to explicitly generate a fact of the form $\mathsf{InfAcc}R(\vec{c})$, we could simply decorate the fact $R(\vec{c})$ by a special relation B (for "back-chased") and then propagate B through the initial chase. Thus choosing a path of accessibility axioms corresponds exactly to choosing a sequence of distinct atoms $s_1 \dots s_n$. The result of our reformulation algorithm is a physical plan implementing the conjunctive query corresponding to the underlying set of atoms $\{s_1 \dots s_n\}$. If we take as a cost metric the number of atoms in the corresponding query, then our cost-based method will automatically minimize this, giving a minimal reformulation.

We can see that from a high-level the C&B method is a special case of interpolation: the chasing phase corresponds to applying Sch constraints, choosing a set of atoms corresponds to applying forward accessibility axioms, and the back-chasing phase can be seen as applying InfAccCopy constraints.

The comparison exposes some distinctions between Algorithm 3 and the C&B:

- Algorithm 3 explores multiple chase *sequences*, and in doing so explores different orderings of accesses. The C&B takes an unordered view on the chase, producing just a set of atoms that is turned into a query. For binding pattern based access-restrictions, the ordering is critical to making the plan executable. For vocabulary-based restrictions, Algorithm 3 is dealing with join ordering issues while C&B is not.

- Algorithm 3 is cost-based, while at least the classic C&B algorithm deals only with getting minimal reformulations. However, cost-based extensions are considered in [Popa, 2000].

- By considering the back-chasing phase as a re-tracing of the original chase graph, the C&B can speed up the process of checking equivalence of S. This viewpoint is critical to the optimizations performed in C&B papers, such as [Meier, 2014] and [Ileana et al., 2014]. This optimization is presented in the setting of terminating chase, although it may be possible to adapt it to the setting of broader classes (e.g., GTGDs) for which the chase does not terminate. While the C&B couples a "proof-to-reformulation" algorithm with a particular algorithmic strategy of forming the full universal chase first, these two could also be decoupled, as our algorithms are presented here. For instance, one could interleave chasing the canonical database and "back-chasing" (choosing some atoms and seeing their consequences); this might be particularly advantageous when the full chase is infinite.

Both the C&B and Algorithm 3 are specific to the setting of conjunctive reformulation. We have seen that the interpolation-based method works also for RQFO reformulation, and in principle one should be able to extend our algorithm transforming proofs to RA-plans in Section 4.4 to a cost-aware search algorithm, along the lines of Algorithm 3.

The work of Toman and Weddell. Chapter 5 of the book [Toman and Weddell, 2011] outlines an approach to reformulating queries with respect to a physical schema that is based on proofs. They discuss proofs using the chase algorithm, as well as an extended proof system connected to Craig Interpolation. As in the C&B, Toman and Weddell divide a schema up into physical and logical subschema, with the target being a query over the physical subschema, which is given a canonical implementation. Their approach also considers finer-grained access restrictions and safety issues, but this is done via post-processing. Initially, a first-order reformulation of the query under the constraints is produced, which may not obey access restrictions and may not be safe. Secondly, rules are applied to transform the query into a safe and executable form. The book also discusses a number of important practical issues, such as dealing with built-in functions and the impact of datatypes.

CHAPTER 6

Conclusion

The main goal of this work is to study a general recipe for translating queries in a source language into a target language, in the presence of integrity constraints:

- formulate a semantic property the query needs to have in order to have a translation,
- capture the property as a logical entailment,
- come up with a proof system that is complete for the class of entailments of interest,
- create an algorithm that translates proofs of the entailment into an object in the target query language.

We have shown that the last step can be done in the setting of general relational algebra or first-order logic integrity constraints via algorithms for solving a fundamental problem in logic, interpolation. We have also shown that for special kinds of integrity constraints (e.g., TGDs as in Chapter 4), we can develop custom algorithms for this last step, which do not refer explicitly to interpolation. We have exhibited the recipe for a number of different target languages, looking at restrictions related to the kind of primitive data access the target has (relations vs. access methods) and restrictions related to the kinds of manipulations that can be performed on acquired data (e.g., transforming it via relational algebra, or SPJ queries).

We looked at this recipe from the point of view of existence results, then moving to decidability results, and finally to concrete algorithms. The final algorithmic approach gives a means for generating query plans from "proofs of the answerability of a query." Finally, we showed that by exploring many proofs, one can guide the search for good query plans by the structure of proofs.

We now consider the possible significance of this technique, looking in turn at the three target audiences for this book mentioned in the abstract of the book.

For theoretical computer scientists, particularly those working in finite model theory and database theory, a main advantage of the approach is as a unified way of looking at problems related to reformulating or translating logical formulas in one language within another language. It allows one to examine the existence of reformulations independently of complexity or decidability considerations. It also gives a uniform way of proving effective reformulation results. We have shown that it yields a way to see some "classic results" in the database theory literature, e.g., [Levy et al., 1995], and that it can also provide new decidability and complexity results.

For mathematical logicians, it gives a different perspective on the significance of fundamental results in logic, such as the Craig Interpolation Theorem, the Beth Definability theorem, and preservation theorems such as the Łoś-Tarski preservation theorem. We hope that by connecting these results to algorithmic issues, we can see new links between classical logic and computer science.

We have not dealt with any practical concerns in query reformulation or data integration in this text, but we also hope that the technique will be of interest to applied researchers in database systems.

The first strength of the approach is its wide applicability. It applies to reformulation problems in the presence of rich relational integrity constraints, far beyond those that can be exploited by query planners in current database management systems. In fact, the applicability may be wider than that, since the steps mentioned above make sense for any data model and query language for sources and targets. In this work we have considered only relational databases as the database model, while our query and constraint languages have been variants of first-order logic. But one can investigate what happens when one varies the data model to, e.g., nested data, or when one varies the query language to allow fixpoints. One can also vary the proof system, moving away from the tableau-based proof systems we have focused on here.

Secondly, it provides a modular approach to reformulation, which may be attractive from the point of view of separation of concerns at a more practical level. It allows one to factor reformulation into a number of orthogonal components: proof systems for specific sets of integrity constraints, interpolation/proof-to-plan algorithms, and search algorithms. In outlining the foundation here, we are hopeful that this can be a step toward developing a reformulation system that can accommodate a number of constraint languages, query languages, and target implementation languages.

Bibliography

Abiteboul, S., Hull, R., and Vianu, V. (1995). *Foundations of Databases*. Addison-Wesley. 7, 9, 13, 14, 15, 17, 18, 24, 29, 59

Afrati, F. N. (2011). Determinacy and query rewriting for conjunctive queries and views. *Theoretical Computer Science*, 412(11):1005–1021. DOI: 10.1016/j.tcs.2010.12.031. 76, 132

Areces, C., Blackburn, P., and Marx, M. (2001). Hybrid logic: Characterization, interpolation and complexity. *Journal of Symbolic Logic*, 66(3):977–1010. DOI: 10.2307/2695090. 120

Bárány, V., Benedikt, M., and Bourhis, P. (2013). Access restrictions and integrity constraints revisited. In *ICDT*. DOI: 10.1145/2448496.2448522. 77, 115, 119, 120, 143

Bárány, V., Benedikt, M., and ten Cate, B. (2013). Rewriting guarded negation queries. In *MFCS*. DOI: 10.1007/978-3-642-40313-2_11. 77

Bárány, V., Gottlob, G., and Otto, M. (2010). Querying the guarded fragment. In *LICS*. DOI: 10.1109/lics.2010.26. 71, 72

Bárány, V., ten Cate, B., and Segoufin, L. (2011). Guarded negation. In *ICALP*. DOI: 10.1007/978-3-642-22012-8_28. 62, 63, 64, 72

Ben-Ari, M. (2012). *Mathematical Logic for Computer Science*. Springer. DOI: 10.1007/978-1-4471-0335-6. 29

Benedikt, M., Leblay, J., and Tsamoura, E. (2014a). PDQ: Proof-driven query answering over web-based data. In *VLDB*. DOI: 10.14778/2733004.2733028. 143

Benedikt, M., Leblay, J., and Tsamoura, E. (2015). Querying with access patterns and integrity constraints. *PVLDB*, 8(6):690–701. DOI: 10.14778/2735703.2735708. 162

Benedikt, M., ten Cate, B., and Tsamoura, E. (2014b). Generating low-cost plans from proofs. In *PODS*. DOI: 10.1145/2594538.2594550. 76, 77, 119, 142, 143

Benedikt, M., ten Cate, B., and Vanden Boom, M. (2014c). Effective interpolation and preservation in guarded logics. In *CSL-LICS*. DOI: 10.1145/2603088.2603108. 64

Beth, E. W. (1953). On Padoa's method in the theory of definitions. *Indagationes Mathematicae*, 15:330 – 339. DOI: 10.1016/s1385-7258(53)50042-3. 51, 74, 75

Blackburn, P. and Marx, M. (2003). Constructive interpolation in hybrid logic. *Journal of Symbolic Logic*, 68(2):463–480. DOI: 10.2178/jsl/1052669059. 120

Borgida, A., de Bruijn, J., Franconi, E., Seylan, I., Straccia, U., Toman, D., and Weddell, G. E. (2010). On finding query rewritings under expressive constraints. In *SEBD*. 76

Calì, A., Gottlob, G., and Kifer, M. (2008). Taming the infinite chase: Query answering under expressive relational constraints. In *KR*. 120

Casanova, M. A., Fagin, R., and Papadimitriou, C. H. (1984). Inclusion dependencies and their interaction with functional dependencies. *Journal of Computer and Systems Science*, 28(1):29–59. DOI: 10.1016/0022-0000(84)90075-8. 65

Chandra, A. K. and Merlin, P. M. (1977). Optimal implementation of conjunctive queries in relational data bases. In *STOC*. DOI: 10.1145/800105.803397. 68

Chang, C. C. and Keisler, H. J. (1990). *Model Theory*. North-Holland. 6, 42, 76, 113

Craig, W. (1957a). Linear reasoning. a new form of the Herbrand-Gentzen theorem. *The Journal of Symbolic Logic*, 22(03):250–268. DOI: 10.2307/2963593. 34, 76

Craig, W. (1957b). Three uses of the Herbrand-Gentzen theorem in relating model theory and proof theory. *Journal of Symbolic Logic*, 22(3):269–285. DOI: 10.2307/2963594. 34, 51, 74, 75

Deutsch, A., Ludäscher, B., and Nash, A. (2007). Rewriting queries using views with access patterns under integrity constraints. *Theoretical Computer Science*, 371(3):200–226. DOI: 10.1016/j.tcs.2006.11.008. 93, 94, 97, 119, 120, 143

Deutsch, A. and Nash, A. (2009). Chase. In *Encyclopedia of Database Systems*, pages 323–327. DOI: 10.1007/springerreference_64165. 29

Deutsch, A., Nash, A., and Remmel, J. (2008). The chase revisited. In *PODS*, pages 149–158. DOI: 10.1145/1376916.1376938. 29

Deutsch, A., Popa, L., and Tannen, V. (1999). Physical data independence, constraints, and optimization with universal plans. In *VLDB*. 142, 168

Deutsch, A., Popa, L., and Tannen, V. (2006). Query reformulation with constraints. *SIGMOD Record*, 35(1):65–73. DOI: 10.1145/1121995.1122010. 168

Duschka, O., Genesereth, M., and Levy, A. (2000). Recursive query plans for data integration. *The Journal of Logic Programming*, 43(1):49 – 73. DOI: 10.1016/s0743-1066(99)00025-4. 97

Ebbinghaus, H.-D. and Flum, J. (1999). *Finite Model Theory*. Springer-Verlag. Second edition. DOI: 10.1007/3-540-28788-4. 71

Fagin, R., Kolaitis, P. G., Miller, R. J., and Popa, L. (2005). Data exchange: Semantics and query answering. *Theoretical Computer Science*, 336(1):89–124. DOI: 10.1016/j.tcs.2004.10.033. 25, 29, 68, 69

Feferman, S. (1968). Persistent and invariant formulas for outer extensions. *Composito Mathematica*, 20(29-52). 120

Feferman, S. (2008). Harmonious logic: Craig's interpolation theorem and its descendants. *Synthese*, 164(3):341–357. DOI: 10.1007/s11229-008-9354-2. 76

Fitting, M. (1996). *First-order Logic and Automated Theorem Proving*. Springer. DOI: 10.1007/978-1-4684-0357-2. 19, 29

Florescu, D., Levy, A. Y., Manolescu, I., and Suciu, D. (1999). Query optimization in the presence of limited access patterns. In *SIGMOD*. DOI: 10.1145/304181.304210. 119, 151, 163, 168

Franconi, E., Kerhet, V., and Ngo, N. (2013). Exact query reformulation over databases with first-order and description logics ontologies. *Journal of Artifical Intelligence Research*, 48:885–922. 76, 77

Gogacz, T. and Marcinkowski, J. (2015). The hunt for a red spider: Conjunctive query determinacy is undecidable. In *LICS*. DOI: 10.1109/lics.2015.35. 68, 75, 76, 118

Haas, L. M., Hernández, M. A., Ho, H., Popa, L., and Roth, M. (2005). Clio grows up: From research prototype to industrial tool. In *SIGMOD*. DOI: 10.1145/1066157.1066252. 29

Hirsch, C. and Tobies, S. (2000). A tableau algorithm for the clique guarded fragment. In *Advances in Modal Logic*. DOI: 10.1142/9789812776471_0014. 64

Ileana, I., Cautis, B., Deutsch, A., and Katsis, Y. (2014). Complete yet practical search for minimal query reformulations under constraints. In *SIGMOD*. DOI: 10.1145/2588555.2593683. 168, 169

Johnson, D. S. and Klug, A. C. (1984). Testing Containment of Conjunctive Queries under Functional and Inclusion Dependencies. *Journal of Computer and Systems Science*, 28(1):167–189. DOI: 10.1016/0022-0000(84)90081-3. 65

Knoblock, C. A., Minton, S., Ambite, J. L., Ashish, N., Modi, P. J., Muslea, I., Philpot, A., and Tejada, S. (1998). Modeling web sources for information integration. In *AAAI*. 118

Lenzerini, M. (2002). Data integration: A theoretical perspective. In *PODS*. DOI: 10.1145/543613.543644. 5

Levy, A. Y., Mendelzon, A. O., Sagiv, Y., and Srivastava, D. (1995). Answering queries using views. In *PODS*. DOI: 10.1145/212433.220198. 68, 77, 171

Levy, A. Y., Rajaraman, A., and Ordille, J. J. (1996). Query-answering algorithms for information agents. In *AAI*. 77

Li, C. (2003). Computing complete answers to queries in the presence of limited access patterns. *VLDB Journal*, 12(3):211–227. DOI: 10.1007/s00778-002-0085-6. 118, 168

Li, C. and Chang, E. (2000). Query planning with limited source capabilities. In *ICDE*. DOI: 10.1109/icde.2000.839440. 85

Li, C. and Chang, E. (2001). Answering queries with useful bindings. *ACM Transactions on Database Systems*, 26(3):313–343. DOI: 10.1145/502030.502032. 118, 168

Lopez-Escobar, E. G. K. (1965). An interpolation theorem for infinitary long formulas. *Fundamenta Mathematicae*, 57(3):253–257. 76

Lukasiewicz, T., Calì, A., and Gottlob, G. (2012). A general datalog-based framework for tractable query answering over ontologies. *Journal of Web Semantics*, 14(0):57–83. DOI: 10.1016/j.websem.2012.03.001. 120, 160

Lutz, C. (2007). Inverse roles make conjunctive queries hard. In *Description Logics*. 65

Lutz, C. (2008). The complexity of conjunctive query answering in expressive description logics. In *IJCAR*. DOI: 10.1007/978-3-540-71070-7_16. 65

Lyndon, R. C. (1959). An interpolation theorem in the predicate calculus. *Pacific Journal of Mathemantics*, 9:129–142. DOI: 10.2140/pjm.1959.9.129. 53

Maier, D., Mendelzon, A. O., and Sagiv, Y. (1979). Testing implications of data dependencies. *ACM Trans. Database Syst.*, 4(4):455–469. DOI: 10.1145/320107.320115. 24, 25, 29

Marx, M. (2007). Queries determined by views: Pack your views. In *PODS*. DOI: 10.1145/1265530.1265534. 77

McMillan, K. (2005). Applications of craig interpolants in model checking. In Halbwachs, N. and Zuck, L., editors, *Tools and Algorithms for the Construction and Analysis of Systems*. DOI: 10.1007/b107194. 76

Meier, M. (2014). The backchase revisited. *VLDB Journal*, 23(3):495–516. DOI: 10.1007/s00778-013-0333-y. 169

Nash, A. and Ludäscher, B. (2004a). Processing first-order queries under limited access patterns. In *PODS*. DOI: 10.1145/1055558.1055601. 86, 118

Nash, A. and Ludäscher, B. (2004b). Processing union of conjunctive queries with negation under limited access patterns. In *EDBT*. DOI: 10.1007/978-3-540-24741-8_25. 118

Nash, A., Segoufin, L., and Vianu, V. (2010). Views and queries: Determinacy and rewriting. *ACM Transactions on Database Systems*, 35(3). DOI: 10.1145/1806907.1806913. 31, 51, 68, 70, 72, 76, 77, 130, 143

Onet, A. (2013). The chase procedure and its applications in data exchange. In *Data Exchange Intregation and Streams*. 3, 29, 66, 168

Otto, M. (2000). An interpolation theorem. *Bulletin of Symbolic Logic*, 6(4):447–462. DOI: 10.2307/420966. 6, 47, 76, 120

Papadimitriou, C. M. (1994). *Computational complexity*. Addison-Wesley. 29

Pasailă, D. (2011). Conjunctive queries determinacy and rewriting. In *ICDT*. DOI: 10.1145/1938551.1938580. 76

Popa, L. (2000). *Object/Relational Query Optimization with Chase and Backchase*. PhD thesis, U. Penn. 168, 169

Pottinger, R. and Halevy, A. Y. (2001). Minicon: A scalable algorithm for answering queries using views. *VLDB J.*, 10(2-3):182–198. 77

Rajaraman, A., Sagiv, Y., and Ullman, J. D. (1995). Answering queries using templates with binding patterns. In *PODS*. DOI: 10.1145/212433.220199. 118

Ramakrishnan, R. and Gehrke, J. (2003). *Database Management Systems*. McGraw-Hill, Inc., 3 edition. 166

Reiter, R. (1984). Towards a logical reconstruction of relational database theory. In *On Conceptual Modelling*, pages 191–238. DOI: 10.1007/978-1-4612-5196-5_8. 10

Segoufin, L. and Vianu, V. (2005). Views and queries: determinacy and rewriting. In *PODS*. DOI: 10.1145/1065167.1065174. 6, 31, 33, 76

Toman, D. and Weddell, G. (2011). *Fundamentals of Physical Design and Query Compilation*. Morgan Claypool. DOI: 10.2200/s00363ed1v01y201105dtm018. xviii, 26, 29, 61, 76, 170

Ullman, J. D. (1989). *Principles of Database and Knowledge-Base Systems, V2*. Comp. Sci. Press. DOI: 10.5860/choice.26-5107. 118

Authors' Biographies

MICHAEL BENEDIKT

Michael Benedikt is Professor of Computer Science at Oxford University and a fellow of University College Oxford. He came to Oxford after a decade in U.S. industrial research laboratories, including positions as Distinguished Member of Technical Staff at Bell Laboratories and visiting researcher at Yahoo! Labs. He has worked extensively in mathematical logic, finite model theory, verification, database theory, and database systems, and has served as chair of the ACM's main database theory conference, Principles of Database Systems. The current focus of his research is Web data management, with recent projects including querying of the deep Web, querying and integration of annotated data, and querying of web services.

JULIEN LEBLAY

Julien Leblay is a Research Scientist at the National Institute of Advanced Industrial Science and Technology (AIST) in Tokyo, Japan. As part of the Artificial Intelligence Research Center, his research interests encompass data management and query processing in general, with a particular focus on applications to Web data, i.e., data typical found on web services and Open Data repositories. From October 2013 to February 2015, Julien was a postdoctoral research assistant at the University of Oxford under the supervision of Michael Benedikt. During this period, his work covered query optimization under constraints and access restrictions. Julien obtained his Ph.D. in Computer Science from the Université Paris-Sud and Inria, France, under the supervision of François Goasdoué and Ioana Manolescu. Prior to his academic career, he worked in industry for several years as a software engineer and consultant on topics ranging from machine translation to data integration.

BALDER TEN CATE

Balder ten Cate is a software engineeer at Google. He is also an Associate Adjunct Professor at UC Santa Cruz, where he is a member of the database research group and is currently advising two graduate students. Previously, he was a computer scientist at LogicBlox Inc, contributing to the development of a smart database system that combines transactions, analytics, planning, and business logic, powering a new class of smart enterprise applications. He was also a visiting researcher at INRIA, ENS de Cachan, and IBM Research – Almaden. Balder ten Cate received his Ph.D. from the University of Amsterdam for a thesis on the model theory of extended modal languages. His research interests are in data management and applications of logic in computer science.

EFTHYMIA TSAMOURA

Efthymia Tsamoura received her B.Sc. in 2007 and her Ph.D. in 2013 both from the computer science department of Aristotle University of Thessaloniki, Greece. Since 2013, Efthymia is a postdoctoral researcher in the computer science department of Oxford University. Her research interests lie in the fields of distributed query optimization, multi-objective query optimization, data integration, and query answering under constraints. Efthymia received several awards during both her undergraduate and postgraduate studies.

Index

Printed in the United States
by Baker & Taylor Publisher Services